# Neural Networks Demystified: A Deep Learning Guide

**Gilbert Gutiérrez**

Unlock the Secrets of Neural Networks and Master Deep Learning from the Ground Up Artificial intelligence has revolutionized the world, and at the heart of its transformation lies one of the most powerful concepts—neural networks. Whether you're an aspiring AI practitioner, a software engineer looking to upskill, or a researcher diving into deep learning, Neural Networks Demystified: A Deep Learning Guide is your ultimate step-by-step resource.

This book is the seventh installment in the AI from Scratch: Step-by-Step Guide to Mastering Artificial Intelligence series, providing an intuitive yet in-depth exploration of how neural networks function, how they learn, and how they can be implemented in real-world applications. Written in an accessible manner, this guide balances theory, mathematical intuition, and hands-on coding to help readers build their own deep learning models from scratch.

## Who Is This Book For?

- **Beginners & Enthusiasts** – If you're curious about how neural networks work but feel overwhelmed by complex math and jargon, this book will break everything down step by step.
- **Software Engineers & Data Scientists** – If you want to master deep learning concepts and implement them efficiently, this book provides practical guidance with Python, TensorFlow, and PyTorch.
- **Researchers & AI Professionals** – If you seek a strong theoretical foundation to explore cutting-edge research in deep learning, this book offers insights into modern architectures, optimization techniques, and real-world applications.

## What You'll Learn

This book is divided into four comprehensive parts, each building upon the previous one to create a structured learning experience.

## Part 1: Foundations of Neural Networks

Neural networks may seem like magic, but at their core, they are a mathematical system designed to mimic the way the human brain processes information. In this section, you will:

- Discover the history of neural networks and their role in AI.
- Understand the mathematics behind neural networks, including linear algebra, calculus, and probability.

- Learn how the perceptron, the first artificial neuron, led to the modern deep learning revolution.
- Dive into the mechanics of multilayer perceptrons (MLPs) and how backpropagation enables them to learn.

## Part 2: Building Neural Networks from Scratch

Before using powerful frameworks like TensorFlow and PyTorch, it's crucial to understand the inner workings of neural networks. This section teaches you:

- The different types of activation functions and their impact on learning.
- Optimization algorithms, including gradient descent, Adam, and RMSprop, to improve network training.
- How to implement a fully functional neural network from scratch using Python and NumPy.
- Regularization techniques like dropout, batch normalization, and weight decay to prevent overfitting.

By the end of this section, you'll be able to build and train a neural network using only fundamental programming techniques, giving you a deep understanding of the entire process.

## Part 3: Deep Learning Architectures

Once you grasp the basics, it's time to explore advanced neural network architectures that power today's AI applications:

- **Convolutional Neural Networks (CNNs)** – Learn how CNNs process image data, extract features, and classify objects with remarkable accuracy.
- **Recurrent Neural Networks (RNNs) & LSTMs** – Understand how RNNs and Long Short-Term Memory (LSTM) networks handle sequential data such as text and speech.
- **Transformers & Attention Mechanisms** – Delve into the models behind state-of-the-art natural language processing, including the Transformer architecture that powers GPT and BERT.
- **Autoencoders & Generative Models** – Explore the fascinating world of generative deep learning, from autoencoders to GANs (Generative Adversarial Networks).

This section includes hands-on projects that guide you through building your own CNN for image classification, an LSTM for time-series forecasting, and a GAN for image generation.

## Part 4: Advanced Topics & Real-World Applications

A strong understanding of neural networks is just the beginning. To apply deep learning in real-world scenarios, you'll need to master additional techniques:

- **Hyperparameter Tuning & Model Selection** – Learn how to optimize neural networks with techniques like grid search, Bayesian optimization, and transfer learning.
- **Deploying Neural Networks in Production** – Discover best practices for deploying AI models, including model compression, inference optimization, and cloud integration.
- **Ethical Considerations in Deep Learning** – Understand the challenges of bias in AI, interpretability of neural networks, and the energy cost of large-scale models.
- **The Future of Neural Networks** – Explore upcoming trends, including neuromorphic computing, edge AI, and self-supervised learning.

By the end of this book, you'll be equipped with both the theoretical knowledge and practical skills to develop, optimize, and deploy neural networks for real-world AI applications.

## Why This Book?

Unlike other deep learning books that assume prior knowledge of AI, Neural Networks Demystified follows a structured, beginner-friendly approach while also covering advanced topics for experienced practitioners. Key highlights include:

- **Clear Explanations with Visual Aids** – Intuitive diagrams and real-world analogies make complex concepts easy to understand.
- **Step-by-Step Coding Implementations** – Hands-on coding tutorials using Python, NumPy, TensorFlow, and PyTorch.
- **Practical Case Studies & Projects** – Build deep learning models for image recognition, NLP, and generative AI.
- **Industry Best Practices** – Learn how neural networks are applied in healthcare, finance, robotics, and more.

Whether you want to build a career in AI, enhance your machine learning skills, or simply satisfy your curiosity about how neural networks work, this book provides a solid foundation for your deep learning journey.

**Final Thoughts**

Artificial intelligence is reshaping industries, and neural networks are at the core of this transformation. Whether you're looking to start your AI journey or take your deep learning expertise to the next level, Neural Networks Demystified: A Deep Learning Guide is the perfect resource to guide you through every step.

From understanding the basics to implementing advanced architectures, this book provides a complete roadmap for mastering neural networks. Are you ready to dive into the world of deep learning? Let's demystify neural networks together!

*Get Your Copy Today and Start Your Deep Learning Journey!* 🚀

# 1. Introduction to Neural Networks

Neural networks have revolutionized artificial intelligence, enabling machines to recognize patterns, process natural language, and even generate human-like content. But what exactly are neural networks, and how do they work? This chapter explores the fundamental concepts behind these powerful models, tracing their origins from early perceptrons to modern deep learning architectures. You'll discover how neural networks are inspired by the human brain, understand their role in AI advancements, and get a glimpse of the key components that make them function. By the end of this chapter, you'll have a solid foundation for diving deeper into the mechanics of neural networks and their real-world applications.

## 1.1. What Are Neural Networks?

Neural networks are a class of machine learning models designed to recognize patterns and make predictions based on data. Inspired by the human brain, neural networks consist of layers of interconnected "neurons," which work together to process input data, detect patterns, and generate outputs. These models have become the foundation of modern artificial intelligence (AI), powering applications ranging from image and speech recognition to self-driving cars and natural language processing.

To understand neural networks, let's first break down their components, how they work, and what makes them so powerful.

### The Biological Inspiration

The concept of neural networks is rooted in neuroscience. In the human brain, neurons are the fundamental building blocks of cognitive processes. Each neuron receives signals from other neurons through synapses, processes them, and then sends the processed information to other neurons. This process allows the brain to learn, adapt, and make decisions based on the input it receives.

Artificial neural networks (ANNs) mimic this structure in a simplified, mathematical form. Instead of biological neurons, ANNs consist of nodes (or artificial neurons) that receive, process, and transmit data through weighted connections. Although ANNs are inspired by the brain, they do not replicate its complexity. However, they are incredibly powerful at learning from data and solving complex problems, which has made them a cornerstone of AI.

## The Structure of Neural Networks

A neural network consists of three primary layers:

**Input Layer**: This is where the network receives its data. The input layer consists of nodes that represent the features or characteristics of the data. For example, in image recognition, each pixel of an image could be treated as a feature, with the input layer nodes representing each pixel.

**Hidden Layers**: Between the input and output layers lie one or more hidden layers. These layers perform most of the computations in a neural network, transforming the input data through a series of mathematical operations. Each node in a hidden layer is connected to nodes in the previous and subsequent layers through weighted connections. The hidden layers allow the network to learn complex patterns by adjusting these weights during training.

**Output Layer**: The output layer produces the final result or prediction. The number of nodes in the output layer corresponds to the number of classes or possible outcomes in a given problem. For example, in a binary classification task (such as distinguishing between spam and non-spam emails), the output layer would consist of two nodes. In a multi-class classification task (like recognizing different types of animals in an image), the output layer would contain multiple nodes, each corresponding to a different class.

## How Do Neural Networks Work?

Neural networks work by processing input data through layers of neurons, adjusting the weights of the connections between neurons to improve accuracy over time. The basic operation of a neural network can be broken down into the following steps:

**Forward Propagation**: The first step in the process is forward propagation, where input data is passed through the network layer by layer. Each node in a layer receives input from the previous layer, performs a weighted sum of the inputs, and passes the result through an activation function. The activation function introduces non-linearity into the model, enabling it to learn more complex patterns in the data. The transformed data is then passed to the next layer, and this process continues until the output layer is reached.

**Activation Functions**: An activation function determines whether a neuron should be activated or not based on the input it receives. Common activation functions include Sigmoid, Tanh, and ReLU (Rectified Linear Unit). Each of these functions introduces a different kind of non-linearity into the model, enabling it to handle more complex relationships between the input and output.

- **Sigmoid**: Outputs values between 0 and 1, making it useful for binary classification.
- **Tanh**: Outputs values between -1 and 1, often used for hidden layers in RNNs and LSTMs.
- **ReLU**: Outputs the input value if it's positive, and zero otherwise. It's widely used in modern neural networks due to its simplicity and efficiency.

**Loss Function**: Once the network has made a prediction, it's compared to the actual result using a loss function. The loss function calculates the error (or loss) between the predicted output and the true value. Common loss functions include Mean Squared Error (MSE) for regression tasks and Cross-Entropy for classification tasks. The goal of training a neural network is to minimize this error by adjusting the weights.

**Backpropagation**: The key to improving a neural network's accuracy is backpropagation. After calculating the loss, the network uses a process called backpropagation to adjust the weights in the network. Backpropagation is an optimization technique that propagates the error backward through the network, starting from the output layer and working backward through each hidden layer. During this process, the weights are adjusted using Gradient Descent or other optimization algorithms to minimize the loss function.

**Training**: The network is trained using a dataset, and the weights are updated through multiple iterations (called epochs). Each time the network processes a batch of data, it makes a prediction, calculates the error, and updates the weights accordingly. As training progresses, the network becomes better at recognizing patterns and making more accurate predictions.

### Why Are Neural Networks So Powerful?

Neural networks are highly flexible and can be applied to a wide range of problems. Here are some key reasons why they are so powerful:

**Non-Linearity**: The use of activation functions in neural networks allows them to model non-linear relationships in the data. This is a critical feature, as many real-world problems involve complex, non-linear patterns that simple linear models cannot capture.

**Feature Learning**: Neural networks are capable of learning relevant features automatically, without needing explicit feature engineering. This is particularly useful in domains like image and speech recognition, where the raw input data (such as pixels or sound waves) can be transformed into meaningful representations by the network during training.

**Scalability**: Neural networks can scale to handle large amounts of data and complex problems. With the advent of deep learning and powerful hardware like GPUs, neural networks are now able to process vast amounts of data and learn from it effectively.

**Adaptability**: Neural networks can be adapted to a wide range of tasks, from supervised learning problems (such as classification and regression) to unsupervised learning tasks (like clustering and anomaly detection). With the right architecture and training, neural networks can be fine-tuned to solve a variety of complex problems.

## Applications of Neural Networks

Neural networks are used in a wide variety of fields and industries, including:

- **Image Recognition**: CNNs (Convolutional Neural Networks) are commonly used for image classification and object detection tasks, from facial recognition to self-driving cars.
- **Speech Recognition**: RNNs and LSTMs are used to process and transcribe spoken language, powering voice assistants like Siri and Alexa.
- **Natural Language Processing (NLP):** Neural networks, particularly transformers, are used in language models like GPT and BERT to process and generate human-like text.
- **Game AI**: Neural networks are employed to train agents to play video games or board games, achieving superhuman performance in games like Go and chess.
- **Medical Diagnosis**: Neural networks are used in healthcare to analyze medical images, predict diseases, and assist in decision-making.

Neural networks are a transformative technology at the heart of modern AI. Inspired by the brain, they can automatically learn from data, adapt to new information, and make predictions with remarkable accuracy. Whether you're analyzing images, recognizing speech, or processing language, neural networks have proven to be invaluable tools across a wide range of applications. By understanding their structure, function, and underlying principles, you're stepping into the exciting world of AI, where neural networks power some of the most innovative advancements of our time.

## 1.2. Evolution of Neural Networks: From Perceptrons to Transformers

The journey of neural networks has been nothing short of revolutionary. From the early days of simple mathematical models to the sophisticated deep learning architectures we use today, neural networks have undergone remarkable growth and transformation. This evolution has been driven by advances in both theoretical understanding and computational power, allowing neural networks to solve increasingly complex problems. In this section, we will explore the history and evolution of neural networks, beginning with the foundational perceptron and moving through to modern architectures like transformers that are powering state-of-the-art AI applications today.

### The Birth of Neural Networks: The Perceptron (1950s-1960s)

The story of neural networks began in the 1950s with the development of the perceptron, a simple algorithm invented by Frank Rosenblatt. The perceptron was the first artificial neural network model and laid the groundwork for future developments in machine learning and AI. It was inspired by the way biological neurons process information in the human brain.

A perceptron is essentially a single-layer neural network consisting of an input layer and an output layer. Each input node receives a value, which is multiplied by a weight. The weighted inputs are then summed up, and the result is passed through an activation function. The perceptron made decisions by outputting one of two possible states, typically "yes" or "no," which made it suitable for binary classification tasks.

Though simple, the perceptron was groundbreaking for its time. It demonstrated that artificial intelligence could be trained to make decisions based on data, much like a human brain. However, the perceptron's limitations were quickly recognized. The model could only solve linearly separable problems, meaning that it struggled with more complex tasks where the decision boundary between classes wasn't a straight line (e.g., XOR problems). This limitation led to a period of reduced interest in neural networks, as the perceived capability of the perceptron seemed too limited.

### The Neural Network Winter: The Challenges of the 1970s-1980s

After the initial excitement surrounding the perceptron, neural networks faced a significant setback. In the late 1960s and 1970s, prominent figures like Marvin Minsky and Seymour Papert published critiques that highlighted the perceptron's inability to solve non-linearly separable problems. Their work, particularly the book Perceptrons (1969), led to a decline in research funding and interest in neural networks, resulting in what is now referred to as the "AI winter."

However, the story of neural networks didn't end there. In the 1980s, researchers like Geoffrey Hinton, David Rumelhart, and Ronald Williams rekindled interest in neural networks by introducing backpropagation, an algorithm that allowed multi-layer networks to be trained effectively. This breakthrough enabled neural networks to overcome the limitations of the perceptron and tackle non-linear problems by adjusting the weights of the network through the process of gradient descent.

Backpropagation worked by calculating the error at the output layer and propagating it back through the hidden layers, adjusting the weights in the process. This innovation made it possible to train networks with multiple layers, which are now called multilayer perceptrons (MLPs) or feedforward neural networks. The use of backpropagation allowed neural networks to become much more powerful and flexible, capable of solving complex tasks like image recognition, speech processing, and more.

Despite these advances, the 1980s and 1990s still presented challenges in training deep networks. Limited computational power and data availability kept neural networks from reaching their full potential, while other machine learning techniques, such as decision trees and support vector machines, gained prominence.

## The Rise of Deep Learning: The 2000s and 2010s

The major breakthrough for neural networks came in the 2000s, with the rise of deep learning. Deep learning refers to the use of deep neural networks with many hidden layers, often referred to as deep neural networks (DNNs). The combination of large-scale datasets, more powerful GPUs, and improved training algorithms enabled neural networks to be scaled up and trained on massive amounts of data, resulting in dramatic improvements in performance.

One of the key developments during this time was the use of Convolutional Neural Networks (CNNs), which revolutionized image recognition tasks. CNNs were designed to automatically learn hierarchical features from data, allowing them to recognize patterns like edges, textures, and shapes in images. This made CNNs highly effective for computer vision tasks such as object detection, facial recognition, and image classification.

In 2012, a landmark moment occurred with the introduction of AlexNet, a deep CNN that won the ImageNet Large Scale Visual Recognition Challenge by a significant margin.

AlexNet's success demonstrated the power of deep learning and CNNs in tackling large-scale image recognition tasks. This victory sparked a wave of interest in deep learning and led to rapid advancements in neural networks across various fields, from natural language processing (NLP) to reinforcement learning.

During the same period, Recurrent Neural Networks (RNNs) and their more advanced variant, Long Short-Term Memory (LSTM) networks, emerged as powerful models for sequential data. RNNs excel at tasks like speech recognition, machine translation, and time-series forecasting by processing input sequences in a manner that takes into account temporal dependencies between data points. LSTMs helped solve the problem of vanishing gradients in traditional RNNs, enabling them to capture long-term dependencies in sequences.

**Transformers: A New Era in NLP and Beyond (2017-Present)**

In 2017, a new architecture called the Transformer was introduced by Vaswani et al. in the paper Attention Is All You Need. The Transformer represented a paradigm shift in neural network design, particularly for tasks involving sequential data, such as natural language processing. Unlike RNNs and LSTMs, which process sequences step-by-step, transformers process entire sequences simultaneously, using a mechanism called self-attention.

Self-attention allows transformers to focus on different parts of the input sequence when making predictions, regardless of the position of the elements in the sequence. This makes transformers highly parallelizable and more efficient than previous architectures, allowing them to handle longer sequences of data and learn complex dependencies across long ranges of input.

Transformers have become the backbone of many state-of-the-art models in NLP, including BERT (Bidirectional Encoder Representations from Transformers), GPT (Generative Pre-trained Transformer), and T5 (Text-to-Text Transfer Transformer). These models have achieved remarkable success in tasks such as machine translation, question answering, and text generation.

The introduction of transformers also led to the development of pretrained models, where large-scale models are first trained on massive amounts of text data and then fine-tuned for specific tasks. This has significantly reduced the computational cost of training models from scratch and democratized access to powerful AI systems.

Beyond NLP, transformers have been adapted for other domains such as computer vision, where models like Vision Transformers (ViT) apply self-attention mechanisms to image data and achieve performance comparable to CNNs. Similarly, transformers are being explored for tasks in audio processing, reinforcement learning, and even bioinformatics.

**The Future of Neural Networks**

The evolution of neural networks is ongoing, with new models and techniques emerging rapidly. Innovations like transformer-based architectures, generative adversarial networks (GANs), and neural architecture search are pushing the boundaries of what neural networks can achieve. As computational power continues to increase and more data becomes available, neural networks will likely become even more capable, efficient, and versatile.

We are also seeing the development of multi-modal models, which combine different types of data (such as text, images, and video) to create more robust and versatile AI systems. Ethics, interpretability, and sustainability will play a critical role in shaping the future of neural networks, ensuring that these technologies are used responsibly and in ways that benefit society.

From the early days of the perceptron to the cutting-edge transformers of today, neural networks have evolved dramatically, enabling breakthroughs in AI that were once thought impossible. This evolution has been driven by advancements in theory, computational power, and data availability, and neural networks continue to be at the forefront of AI innovation. Understanding this evolution not only gives us insight into the capabilities of neural networks but also lays the foundation for the exciting future of artificial intelligence.

# 1.3. Real-World Applications of Neural Networks

Neural networks have rapidly evolved from theoretical models to practical tools that drive some of the most innovative and transformative technologies in our daily lives. Their ability to learn patterns from data and make predictions or decisions has enabled them to solve a wide variety of complex problems across different industries. In this section, we will explore several real-world applications where neural networks have made a significant impact, demonstrating their versatility and power in tackling challenges ranging from image recognition to healthcare and autonomous systems.

**1. Image Recognition and Computer Vision**

One of the most widely known applications of neural networks is image recognition, a task that has been revolutionized by Convolutional Neural Networks (CNNs). CNNs are specialized neural networks designed to process grid-like data, such as images, by automatically learning to detect patterns such as edges, textures, and shapes at different levels of abstraction. This has enabled machines to perform complex visual tasks with impressive accuracy.

In image classification, neural networks are used to categorize images into predefined classes. For example, in medical imaging, CNNs can be trained to distinguish between healthy and diseased tissue in X-rays, MRIs, or CT scans. In the consumer tech space, image recognition is used in face recognition systems (such as those in smartphones and security cameras) and object detection (used in apps that identify products or landmarks from images).

Self-driving cars heavily rely on neural networks for computer vision tasks, such as identifying pedestrians, other vehicles, road signs, and lane boundaries in real time. By processing the data from cameras, LiDAR, and radar sensors, self-driving vehicles can navigate complex environments safely.

## 2. Natural Language Processing (NLP)

Neural networks have also transformed the field of Natural Language Processing (NLP), enabling machines to understand, interpret, and generate human language. NLP is a crucial component in technologies such as speech recognition, machine translation, and chatbots.

One of the most important advancements in NLP is the Transformer architecture, which powers many state-of-the-art language models like BERT and GPT. These models have revolutionized tasks such as text generation, summarization, and question answering.

**Text Generation and Conversational AI**: GPT models, such as OpenAI's GPT-3, have demonstrated an incredible ability to generate human-like text, making them useful for applications like writing assistance, content creation, and even conversational AI. Chatbots powered by neural networks are becoming increasingly sophisticated and are now used in customer service, virtual assistants, and even therapy bots.

**Machine Translation**: Neural networks have significantly improved machine translation systems, enabling the translation of text or speech between languages with greater accuracy. Popular platforms like Google Translate use neural networks to provide high-quality translations that were previously impossible with rule-based systems.

**Speech Recognition**: Deep neural networks have powered advancements in speech-to-text systems, enabling devices like smartphones and smart speakers to understand spoken commands. Neural networks help transcribe speech accurately even in noisy environments, powering systems like Siri, Alexa, and Google Assistant.

### 3. Healthcare and Medical Diagnosis

Neural networks are also making a significant impact in healthcare, particularly in medical imaging and diagnosis. With their ability to learn patterns in large datasets, neural networks can assist doctors in identifying diseases earlier and with greater precision.

**Medical Imaging**: Neural networks, particularly CNNs, have been widely adopted for tasks such as tumor detection, organ segmentation, and disease classification in medical images like X-rays, MRIs, and CT scans. For example, neural networks are used to detect conditions such as lung cancer, breast cancer, and diabetic retinopathy by analyzing medical images and spotting abnormalities that may be difficult for human doctors to identify.

**Predictive Modeling**: Neural networks can be used to predict disease outcomes and personalize treatment plans based on patient data. For example, neural networks can analyze electronic health records (EHRs) to predict which patients are at risk of developing chronic conditions like heart disease or diabetes, enabling early interventions and more effective treatments.

**Drug Discovery**: Neural networks are also being used in the field of drug discovery to predict the efficacy of potential new drugs by analyzing molecular structures and biological data. By processing vast amounts of data, neural networks can help accelerate the development of new therapies and treatments, leading to breakthroughs in personalized medicine.

### 4. Finance and Fraud Detection

In the finance industry, neural networks are employed for a wide range of applications, including fraud detection, credit scoring, and algorithmic trading. With the ability to analyze large volumes of financial data and identify complex patterns, neural networks are revolutionizing the way financial institutions operate.

**Fraud Detection**: Neural networks are commonly used to detect fraudulent activities in banking transactions, credit card payments, and insurance claims. By analyzing historical transaction data, neural networks can recognize patterns of normal behavior and flag anomalies that may indicate fraudulent activity. This helps financial institutions prevent fraud and minimize financial losses.

**Algorithmic Trading**: Neural networks are used in algorithmic trading to predict market trends and make buy or sell decisions based on historical market data. By analyzing patterns in stock prices, trading volumes, and other financial indicators, neural networks can generate trading strategies that maximize returns or minimize risks.

**Credit Scoring**: Neural networks are also employed in assessing credit risk and generating credit scores. By analyzing various factors such as income, employment history, and spending behavior, neural networks can more accurately predict an individual's ability to repay a loan, allowing financial institutions to make better lending decisions.

## 5. Autonomous Vehicles and Robotics

Autonomous vehicles and robotics represent one of the most exciting and high-impact applications of neural networks. Neural networks power systems that allow robots and self-driving cars to perceive their environment, make decisions, and navigate in complex and dynamic situations.

**Self-Driving Cars**: Neural networks are the backbone of autonomous driving technology, enabling cars to perceive their surroundings, make real-time decisions, and safely navigate the road. Through the use of sensors, cameras, and LiDAR, neural networks help autonomous vehicles understand their environment, identify obstacles, follow traffic rules, and drive safely.

**Robotics**: In robotics, neural networks are used to enable robots to perform complex tasks such as object manipulation, navigation, and interaction with humans. Robots powered by neural networks can learn new tasks through reinforcement learning, enabling them to adapt to different environments and improve their performance over time.

## 6. Gaming and Entertainment

Neural networks have also found applications in the gaming and entertainment industries, where they are used for everything from creating realistic game environments to generating new forms of digital art and media.

**Game AI**: Neural networks are used in video games to control the behavior of non-playable characters (NPCs), making them appear more intelligent and responsive. Additionally, neural networks are used in game design to generate dynamic, evolving content such as levels, quests, and storylines based on player behavior and preferences.

**Generative Art and Music**: Neural networks, especially Generative Adversarial Networks (GANs), have been used to create original art, music, and even video content. GANs can generate realistic images, animations, and sounds based on training data, making them useful for creative industries like animation, graphic design, and music production.

## 7. Marketing and Customer Insights

In the marketing world, neural networks are used to analyze customer data and optimize marketing strategies. By learning patterns in customer behavior, neural networks can help businesses improve targeting, increase customer engagement, and boost sales.

**Customer Segmentation**: Neural networks can analyze customer data, including purchase history, browsing behavior, and demographics, to segment customers into different groups. This helps businesses tailor their marketing strategies and product recommendations to specific customer needs.

**Personalized Recommendations**: Neural networks are the driving force behind recommendation systems used by platforms like Amazon, Netflix, and Spotify. By analyzing user preferences and behaviors, neural networks can predict which products, movies, or songs a user is most likely to enjoy, improving the overall customer experience.

Neural networks are transforming industries and enabling breakthroughs in fields ranging from healthcare and finance to autonomous systems and entertainment. By learning from vast amounts of data, they can identify patterns, make predictions, and automate complex tasks with impressive accuracy. As neural networks continue to evolve, their applications will only grow, driving further innovation and creating new opportunities for businesses and individuals alike. Whether improving medical diagnoses, enabling self-driving cars, or personalizing marketing strategies, neural networks are at the heart of many of the most exciting advancements in technology today.

# 1.4. How Neural Networks Differ from Traditional Algorithms

Neural networks and traditional algorithms are both powerful tools used to solve problems in machine learning and artificial intelligence. However, they operate based on fundamentally different principles, leading to significant differences in how they process data, make decisions, and learn from experience. Understanding these differences is essential to recognizing the strengths and weaknesses of each approach, as well as knowing when to use one over the other. In this section, we will explore how neural networks differ from traditional algorithms in several key areas, including data processing, learning methodologies, adaptability, interpretability, and scalability.

## 1. Data Processing: Feature Engineering vs. Learning Features

One of the most significant differences between neural networks and traditional algorithms is how they handle data and features. Traditional algorithms often require manual feature engineering—a process where domain experts extract and select relevant features from raw data before passing it to the algorithm. These features might be things like customer demographics for a marketing algorithm or pixel values for an image classification task.

For example, in a traditional machine learning approach, an algorithm like logistic regression or decision trees needs well-structured data with pre-defined features to make predictions. This means that a large part of the algorithm's success is dependent on how well these features are chosen, and experts need to have a deep understanding of the problem domain to identify the right features.

In contrast, neural networks can automatically learn relevant features directly from raw data. For instance, in image recognition tasks, neural networks—especially Convolutional Neural Networks (CNNs)—are capable of identifying key features like edges, shapes, and textures without human intervention. As the network processes more data, it automatically learns increasingly abstract features at different layers. This ability to learn relevant features from data itself is one of the key advantages of neural networks over traditional algorithms, making them highly effective for tasks like image classification, speech recognition, and natural language processing.

## 2. Learning Process: Supervised vs. Unsupervised Learning

The learning processes of neural networks and traditional algorithms are often based on different principles, particularly when it comes to how they learn from data.

**Traditional Algorithms (Supervised and Unsupervised Learning):** In traditional machine learning algorithms like decision trees, k-nearest neighbors (KNN), and support vector machines (SVMs), learning is typically based on supervised or unsupervised learning methods. In supervised learning, the algorithm learns from labeled data (i.e., each training example has an associated output or target), whereas unsupervised learning algorithms try to find hidden patterns in data without explicit labels. These traditional algorithms generally use predefined mathematical models to adjust weights or parameters in response to the data they process.

**Neural Networks (Deep Learning):** Neural networks, particularly deep learning models, are designed to learn complex patterns from data through a process called backpropagation. Backpropagation adjusts the weights of the network's neurons based on the error between the predicted output and the actual target, allowing the network to minimize this error over time. This learning process is typically supervised, but neural networks can also be used in unsupervised learning tasks, such as generative modeling with autoencoders or clustering with deep models. Unlike traditional algorithms that rely on predefined rules and simpler models, neural networks can adjust their internal structure (weights and connections) to better capture the complexities of the data.

### 3. Adaptability: Flexibility to Handle Complex Data

Another key difference lies in how neural networks and traditional algorithms handle data complexity and adaptability.

**Traditional Algorithms:** Most traditional algorithms perform well on structured data (e.g., tabular data with clear columns and rows, such as sales figures, customer demographics, etc.). However, when it comes to handling unstructured or complex data, such as images, audio, or text, traditional algorithms often struggle. Traditional algorithms require significant preprocessing, feature extraction, and sometimes manual tuning to deal with these types of data effectively.

**Neural Networks:** Neural networks, especially deep learning models, are inherently more adaptable to complex data types. Recurrent Neural Networks (RNNs) and Long Short-Term Memory (LSTM) networks excel at handling sequential data, such as time series or text, by processing input data in order. Convolutional Neural Networks (CNNs) are specialized for spatial data, such as images or videos, by learning hierarchical features that capture patterns across different levels of abstraction. Neural networks can automatically handle and learn from raw, unstructured data, making them far more flexible and scalable when it comes to complex data.

## 4. Interpretability: Black Box vs. Transparency

While neural networks have revolutionized machine learning, they have introduced new challenges in terms of interpretability—understanding how a model makes its predictions. Traditional algorithms, on the other hand, tend to be more transparent in their decision-making process.

**Traditional Algorithms (Transparent Models):** Many traditional algorithms, such as linear regression, decision trees, and logistic regression, are considered more interpretable. In these models, you can usually trace the relationship between inputs and outputs easily, and the model's decisions are based on clear rules or mathematical formulas. For instance, in a decision tree, each branch represents a decision rule, and the leaf nodes correspond to predicted outcomes, making it easy to understand why a decision was made.

**Neural Networks (Black Box Models):** Neural networks, particularly deep neural networks, are often described as "black box" models. This is because it's difficult to understand exactly how a neural network arrives at a particular decision, especially with large, deep architectures involving millions of parameters. While the network learns to map inputs to outputs through complex transformations, tracing the individual contributions of each weight or neuron to a specific output is challenging. This lack of transparency can be a concern in critical applications such as healthcare, finance, and autonomous driving, where understanding the reasoning behind decisions is crucial.

Efforts to improve the interpretability of neural networks include techniques like Layer-wise Relevance Propagation (LRP), SHAP (SHapley Additive exPlanations), and Grad-CAM (Gradient-weighted Class Activation Mapping), which attempt to explain how neural networks make predictions by highlighting the most important features contributing to a decision. However, compared to traditional algorithms, neural networks still face challenges in terms of transparency.

## 5. Scalability: Handling Large Datasets

The scalability of a model refers to its ability to handle large and increasing amounts of data efficiently.

**Traditional Algorithms:** Traditional machine learning algorithms often perform well with smaller datasets. However, they may struggle to scale effectively when the size of the data increases significantly. For example, algorithms like decision trees or k-nearest neighbors can become computationally expensive or less accurate as data grows in size and complexity. Additionally, traditional algorithms may require more extensive feature engineering to maintain performance as the dataset becomes larger or more complex.

**Neural Networks**: One of the defining features of neural networks is their ability to scale to large datasets, especially with the advancements in deep learning. Deep neural networks can process vast amounts of data, learning more nuanced and complex patterns as the dataset grows. This scalability is one of the reasons neural networks have been so successful in domains like computer vision, natural language processing, and speech recognition, where the amount of data required to train effective models is enormous. With advancements in hardware (like GPUs) and parallel computing, neural networks are able to process large datasets much faster than traditional algorithms, enabling them to take advantage of the growing availability of big data.

## 6. Performance: Accuracy and Precision

Finally, the most noticeable difference between neural networks and traditional algorithms is in performance, particularly in tasks that involve large, high-dimensional datasets.

**Traditional Algorithms**: While traditional algorithms are efficient and accurate in many domains, they tend to perform poorly when dealing with large-scale, complex data. For example, traditional algorithms can struggle with tasks like image recognition or speech-to-text, where the data is high-dimensional and non-linear relationships exist between inputs and outputs.

**Neural Networks**: Neural networks, particularly deep learning models, have shown remarkable success in areas where traditional algorithms struggle. For example, CNNs have achieved state-of-the-art performance in image recognition tasks, and transformers have revolutionized natural language processing. Neural networks have a unique ability to generalize patterns and produce more accurate results when dealing with large and complex datasets. While they require significant computational resources and large datasets, the accuracy of neural networks in many applications, such as self-driving cars or medical diagnostics, has far exceeded that of traditional machine learning methods.

In summary, while both neural networks and traditional algorithms are valuable tools in the machine learning toolkit, they differ fundamentally in how they process data, learn from it, and adapt to complex problems. Neural networks excel in handling unstructured, complex data and can automatically learn features, making them particularly effective in fields such as computer vision, natural language processing, and autonomous systems. However, they also come with challenges, such as lower interpretability and the need for large datasets and computational resources. Traditional algorithms, on the other hand, tend to be more interpretable, efficient with smaller datasets, and easier to implement for less complex tasks. Understanding these differences can help you choose the right approach for specific tasks and applications.

# 2. Mathematics Behind Neural Networks

At the core of every neural network lies a foundation of mathematics that enables it to learn and make predictions. This chapter breaks down the essential mathematical concepts behind neural networks, including linear algebra, calculus, and probability. You'll explore how vectors and matrices represent data, how activation functions introduce non-linearity, and how derivatives drive learning through backpropagation. With step-by-step explanations and intuitive examples, this chapter equips you with the mathematical tools needed to understand and build deep learning models with confidence.

## 2.1. Linear Algebra Essentials (Vectors, Matrices, and Tensors)

Linear algebra forms the mathematical foundation for neural networks and deep learning, providing the tools to represent and manipulate data in ways that machine learning models can process and learn from. Whether you are dealing with high-dimensional data, performing optimization, or implementing backpropagation, a strong understanding of linear algebra is essential. In this section, we will focus on the three fundamental concepts of linear algebra that are critical for understanding neural networks: vectors, matrices, and tensors. We will explore what they are, how they are represented, and their role in the inner workings of neural networks.

### 1. Vectors: The Building Blocks of Data Representation

A vector is a one-dimensional array of numbers, often representing a point in space or a set of features. Vectors are used to represent various kinds of data in machine learning, such as individual data points, input features, and parameters (weights) in a neural network.

- **Definition:** A vector is an ordered collection of numbers that can be written as $\mathbf{v} = [v_1, v_2, ..., v_n]$, where each $v_i$ is a scalar value, and $n$ is the dimension of the vector. The dimension tells us how many values or components the vector has.

- **Geometric Interpretation:** Vectors can be interpreted geometrically as points or directed line segments in space. For example, in a two-dimensional space, a vector could represent a point $(x, y)$, and in three-dimensional space, it could represent a point $(x, y, z)$.

- **Operations with Vectors:** Several important operations are performed with vectors, including:

  - **Addition:** Two vectors can be added component-wise. If $\mathbf{v} = [v_1, v_2]$ and $\mathbf{w} = [w_1, w_2]$, then $\mathbf{v} + \mathbf{w} = [v_1 + w_1, v_2 + w_2]$.

  - **Scalar Multiplication:** A vector can be multiplied by a scalar, scaling each component of the vector. For example, if $\mathbf{v} = [v_1, v_2]$ and $\alpha$ is a scalar, then $\alpha \cdot \mathbf{v} = [\alpha \cdot v_1, \alpha \cdot v_2]$.

  - **Dot Product:** The dot product between two vectors $\mathbf{v} = [v_1, v_2]$ and $\mathbf{w} = [w_1, w_2]$ is $\mathbf{v} \cdot \mathbf{w} = v_1 w_1 + v_2 w_2$. This operation is key for calculating the similarity between two vectors, which is important in tasks like classification or regression.

- **Applications in Neural Networks:** Vectors are used to represent the input data in neural networks. For example, a dataset with $n$ features (such as height, weight, and age) for each data point can be represented as a vector of size $n$. Similarly, weights in a neural network layer are represented as vectors, and the input to each layer is typically a vector.

## 2. Matrices: Organizing Data in Two Dimensions

A matrix is a two-dimensional array of numbers, where each element is identified by its row and column indices. Matrices are widely used in neural networks to represent datasets, transformations, and operations between layers.

- **Definition:** A matrix is a rectangular array of numbers arranged in rows and columns. For instance, a matrix $\mathbf{A}$ with $m$ rows and $n$ columns is written as:

$$\mathbf{A} = \begin{bmatrix} a_{11} & a_{12} & \cdots & a_{1n} \\ a_{21} & a_{22} & \cdots & a_{2n} \\ \vdots & \vdots & \ddots & \vdots \\ a_{m1} & a_{m2} & \cdots & a_{mn} \end{bmatrix}$$

Where $a_{ij}$ represents the element in the $i$-th row and $j$-th column.

- **Matrix Operations:**

  - **Addition:** Two matrices of the same dimensions can be added by adding their corresponding elements. If $\mathbf{A}$ and $\mathbf{B}$ are matrices of the same size, then their sum is $\mathbf{A} + \mathbf{B}$, where $(a_{ij} + b_{ij})$ is computed for each element.

  - **Matrix Multiplication:** Matrix multiplication is an important operation where the number of columns in the first matrix must equal the number of rows in the second matrix. The element $c_{ij}$ of the product matrix $\mathbf{C} = \mathbf{A} \cdot \mathbf{B}$ is computed as the sum of products of corresponding elements from the rows of $\mathbf{A}$ and the columns of $\mathbf{B}$. This operation is essential in neural networks, where the input data is multiplied by a weight matrix in each layer.

    If $\mathbf{A}$ is a matrix with dimensions $m \times n$ and $\mathbf{B}$ is a matrix with dimensions $n \times p$, the resulting matrix $\mathbf{C}$ will have dimensions $m \times p$.

  - **Transpose:** The transpose of a matrix $\mathbf{A}$ is a new matrix $\mathbf{A}^T$, where the rows of $\mathbf{A}$ become the columns of $\mathbf{A}^T$. This operation is important for transforming data and adjusting dimensions in neural network operations.

**Applications in Neural Networks:** Matrices are fundamental in representing data batches, weights, and activation functions in neural networks. For example, a neural network layer takes a vector of inputs and multiplies it by a weight matrix to generate the output. Matrices help organize the data, manage complex operations, and facilitate efficient computation, especially when using batch processing (handling multiple inputs at once).

### 3. Tensors: Multi-dimensional Generalizations of Vectors and Matrices

A tensor is a generalization of vectors and matrices to higher dimensions. While vectors are one-dimensional arrays and matrices are two-dimensional, tensors can be multi-dimensional. Tensors are essential for handling complex data structures like images, videos, and higher-order representations in deep learning.

**Definition**: A tensor is a multi-dimensional array of numbers. The rank of a tensor refers to the number of dimensions it has:

- **Rank-0 tensor**: A scalar (a single number).
- **Rank-1 tensor**: A vector (one-dimensional array).
- **Rank-2 tensor**: A matrix (two-dimensional array).
- **Rank-3 tensor and higher**: Higher-dimensional arrays, often used to represent more complex data, such as multi-channel images (height, width, and color channels) or video data (height, width, time, and color channels).

**Tensor Operations**: Tensors support many of the same operations as vectors and matrices, such as addition, multiplication, and transposition. However, with multi-dimensional data, operations like element-wise multiplication, broadcasting, and contraction (summation across dimensions) become important.

- **Applications in Neural Networks**: Tensors are essential in deep learning frameworks like **TensorFlow** and **PyTorch**, which are designed to handle multi-dimensional data for tasks like image and video processing. For instance, a **color image** can be represented as a rank-3 tensor with dimensions $H \times W \times C$, where $H$ is the image height, $W$ is the image width, and $C$ is the number of color channels (typically 3 for RGB). As the complexity of data increases (e.g., with video or 3D objects), tensors are used to represent this high-dimensional data in neural networks.

## 4. Why These Concepts Matter for Neural Networks

Neural networks heavily rely on vectors, matrices, and tensors because they enable efficient mathematical operations that underlie the processes of forward propagation and backpropagation. The ability to perform operations like matrix multiplication and tensor transformations is key to representing and learning from high-dimensional data.

For example, in fully connected layers of a neural network, input vectors are multiplied by weight matrices to generate outputs, which are then passed through an activation function. Similarly, convolutional layers in CNNs use tensor operations to filter images, and recurrent layers in RNNs handle sequences of data as tensors.

By understanding these essential linear algebra concepts, you can begin to understand the inner workings of neural networks and how data flows through them, as well as how networks learn and make predictions. Mastery of vectors, matrices, and tensors is an essential foundation for understanding the mathematical machinery that powers deep learning models and algorithms.

In summary, vectors, matrices, and tensors are the fundamental building blocks of neural networks, enabling efficient data representation and manipulation. Vectors represent individual data points or features, matrices organize data into two-dimensional structures for batch processing and transformations, and tensors generalize these concepts to higher dimensions for complex data types. These mathematical tools allow neural networks to process vast amounts of data, perform calculations, and learn intricate patterns, making them essential for modern artificial intelligence applications.

## 2.2. Calculus for Neural Networks (Derivatives and Gradients)

Calculus plays a central role in the training of neural networks, particularly in optimization and backpropagation. In this section, we will explore the essential calculus concepts necessary for understanding neural networks—specifically derivatives and gradients—and how they are used to update the parameters (weights and biases) of a neural network during training. Understanding these concepts is vital for grasping how neural networks learn and improve their performance over time.

### 1. The Role of Calculus in Neural Networks

Neural networks learn by minimizing a loss function, which measures how far the model's predictions are from the true values. This is done by adjusting the network's parameters (such as weights and biases) based on feedback from the loss function. The process of minimizing the loss involves moving in the direction of the steepest decrease in the loss, which is where derivatives and gradients come into play.

**Derivative**: The derivative of a function describes the rate at which the function's output changes with respect to a change in the input. In simpler terms, it tells us how steep the function is at any given point. In the context of neural networks, derivatives help us understand how a small change in the model's parameters affects the loss.

**Gradient**: The gradient is a vector that contains all the partial derivatives of a function with respect to its parameters. In neural networks, the gradient points in the direction of the steepest ascent in the loss function. To minimize the loss, we adjust the model's parameters in the opposite direction of the gradient, a technique known as gradient descent.

## 2. Derivatives: Understanding the Rate of Change

A **derivative** measures how a function changes as its input changes. Mathematically, the derivative of a function $f(x)$ with respect to $x$ is written as $f'(x)$, and it represents the rate at which the output $f(x)$ changes when $x$ changes by a small amount. For a function $f(x)$, the derivative is defined as:

$$f'(x) = \lim_{\Delta x \to 0} \frac{f(x + \Delta x) - f(x)}{\Delta x}$$

**Interpretation in Neural Networks**: In neural networks, we often deal with multi-variable functions, where the output depends on several parameters (such as weights and biases). When we want to know how the output of a neural network changes with respect to a specific weight, we take the derivative of the loss function with respect to that weight. This helps us understand how sensitive the loss is to changes in the weight, and this information is used to update the weight in the correct direction during training.

## 3. Gradient: The Multivariable Derivative

In a neural network, the parameters (weights and biases) are typically more than one, meaning we need to compute derivatives with respect to multiple variables. For a function with multiple variables, the gradient is a vector that consists of all the partial derivatives of the function with respect to each of its variables.

For a function $f(x_1, x_2, \ldots, x_n)$ with multiple variables, the gradient is given by:

$$\nabla f(x_1, x_2, \ldots, x_n) = \left( \frac{\partial f}{\partial x_1}, \frac{\partial f}{\partial x_2}, \ldots, \frac{\partial f}{\partial x_n} \right)$$

**Interpretation in Neural Networks**: The gradient in neural networks tells us how the loss function changes as each parameter (weight or bias) changes. In the context of training a neural network, we compute the gradient of the loss function with respect to all the parameters in the network. This gradient vector is then used in optimization algorithms like gradient descent to adjust the weights and biases in such a way that the loss is minimized.

## 4. Backpropagation: Using Derivatives and Gradients to Update Weights

The key to training a neural network efficiently is backpropagation, which is an application of the chain rule of calculus. Backpropagation allows us to compute the gradient of the loss function with respect to each weight in the network by propagating the error backward through the network, starting from the output layer to the input layer.

Here's a step-by-step outline of how backpropagation works using derivatives and gradients:

**Forward Pass**: During the forward pass, the input data is passed through the network, and the output is computed using the current weights and biases. The loss function is then calculated based on the network's output and the true labels.

**Compute Gradients (Backward Pass):** Once the loss is computed, backpropagation is used to compute the gradient of the loss function with respect to each weight and bias in the network. This is done by applying the chain rule of calculus, which allows us to compute the derivative of the loss function with respect to each parameter in the network. The chain rule is essential because the loss function is indirectly dependent on the weights through the layers of the network.

- **Example:** Consider a simple neural network with an activation function $\sigma(x)$, a weight $w$, and an output $y$. The chain rule allows us to compute the gradient of the loss function $L$ with respect to $w$ as:

$$\frac{\partial L}{\partial w} = \frac{\partial L}{\partial y} \cdot \frac{\partial y}{\partial w}$$

This is applied recursively for each layer in the network.

**Update Weights Using Gradient Descent**: Once the gradients are computed, we use an optimization algorithm like gradient descent to update the weights and biases in the network. The weights are updated in the direction of the negative gradient to reduce the loss. This step is repeated iteratively across multiple training epochs until the model converges to a minimum of the loss function.

$$w_{\text{new}} = w_{\text{old}} - \eta \cdot \frac{\partial L}{\partial w}$$

Where:

- $w_{\text{new}}$ is the updated weight,

- $w_{\text{old}}$ is the previous weight,

- $\eta$ is the learning rate, and

- $\frac{\partial L}{\partial w}$ is the gradient of the loss with respect to the weight.

## 5. Gradient Descent: Optimizing the Loss Function

In practice, gradient descent is used to iteratively adjust the weights to minimize the loss function. The basic idea is to move in the direction opposite to the gradient in order to find the minimum of the loss function. There are several variants of gradient descent:

- **Batch Gradient Descent**: Computes the gradient using the entire dataset.
- **Stochastic Gradient Descent (SGD):** Computes the gradient using a single data point at a time.
- **Mini-batch Gradient Descent**: Computes the gradient using a small batch of data points, combining the advantages of both batch and stochastic gradient descent.

While gradient descent is the most commonly used method, there are more advanced techniques such as momentum, RMSProp, and Adam that adjust the learning rate during training to improve convergence speed and avoid getting stuck in local minima.

## 6. Practical Importance of Derivatives and Gradients in Training Neural Networks

The primary goal of training a neural network is to find the optimal set of weights that minimizes the loss function. The use of derivatives and gradients allows us to adjust the weights incrementally based on how much they influence the loss. Through this process, the network "learns" from the data and gradually improves its predictions. Without the use of derivatives and gradients, it would be impossible to efficiently train complex models with millions of parameters.

For example, in image classification tasks, the neural network learns the underlying patterns of the image data by adjusting the weights based on the gradients computed during backpropagation. Over time, the model improves its ability to recognize objects by minimizing the loss, and the predictions become more accurate.

In summary, calculus, specifically derivatives and gradients, is fundamental to understanding how neural networks learn. The derivative allows us to measure the rate of change of the loss function with respect to the parameters, while the gradient provides a vector that points in the direction of steepest ascent in the loss function. By using backpropagation and gradient descent, neural networks can adjust their parameters to minimize the loss function and learn from the data. Understanding these concepts is crucial for anyone who wants to delve deeper into the mechanics of neural networks and deep learning.

# 2.3. Probability & Statistics for Deep Learning

Probability and statistics form the backbone of many machine learning algorithms, especially in deep learning. These mathematical tools help us model uncertainty, make predictions, and understand the distribution of data. In the context of neural networks and deep learning, probability and statistics provide the framework for learning from data, evaluating models, and improving performance through optimization. In this section, we will explore how probability and statistics are applied in deep learning, with a focus on key concepts like probability distributions, Bayes' theorem, expectation, variance, and the concept of overfitting and underfitting.

### 1. Probability: Modeling Uncertainty in Deep Learning

In deep learning, we often deal with uncertain, noisy, or incomplete data. Probability theory allows us to model this uncertainty and make predictions about future data points, given the data we have observed so far.

**Probability Distributions**: A probability distribution defines the likelihood of different outcomes in a random experiment. In deep learning, probability distributions help us represent uncertainties in data and predictions.

**Discrete Distributions**: For example, the Bernoulli distribution represents binary outcomes (e.g., success or failure), and the Multinomial distribution is used to model outcomes with more than two possible outcomes, such as classification tasks.

**Continuous Distributions**: A common continuous distribution used in deep learning is the Gaussian distribution (also known as the normal distribution), which is often used to represent random variables that cluster around a mean value, such as the distribution of pixel values in images.

Conditional Probability: In deep learning, we frequently need to compute the probability of an event occurring given that another event has already occurred. This is expressed through conditional probability. For example, we might be interested in the probability of a certain class label $C$ given some input features $X$. This is written as $P(C|X)$, and it is a key component in algorithms like logistic regression and softmax classification.

Bayes' Theorem: Bayes' Theorem is a fundamental concept in probability theory that allows us to update our beliefs about the probability of an event, given new evidence. It is often used in machine learning for posterior inference, where we compute the probability of a model's parameters given some observed data. Mathematically, Bayes' Theorem is given by:

$$P(\theta|D) = \frac{P(D|\theta)P(\theta)}{P(D)}$$

Where:

- $P(\theta|D)$ is the posterior probability of the parameters $\theta$ given the data $D$,

- $P(D|\theta)$ is the likelihood of observing the data given the parameters,

- $P(\theta)$ is the prior probability of the parameters, and

- $P(D)$ is the marginal likelihood of the data.

Bayes' Theorem is used in Bayesian neural networks, where we model the uncertainty in the model parameters by treating them as random variables and updating our beliefs about these parameters as we observe more data.

## 2. Statistics: Describing Data in Deep Learning

Statistics allows us to summarize and describe datasets, and it is essential for understanding the structure of data before training a deep learning model. Key statistical measures are used to assess the performance of models, evaluate uncertainty, and tune models for better generalization.

**Expectation and Variance:**

Expectation (or mean) is a measure of the central tendency of a dataset and represents the average value of a random variable. In deep learning, the expected value of a random variable can represent the average prediction of a model or the expected output of a layer.

Variance measures how spread out the values of a dataset are around the mean. In deep learning, high variance can indicate that the model is too complex and overfitting the training data. Conversely, low variance might suggest underfitting. Variance is important for understanding the model's ability to generalize to new, unseen data.

**Covariance and Correlation:**

Covariance measures the relationship between two variables and indicates whether the variables tend to increase or decrease together. In deep learning, covariance is used to understand the relationship between different features in the data or between the input and output variables.

Correlation is a normalized version of covariance that measures the strength and direction of the linear relationship between two variables. The correlation coefficient, $\rho$, ranges from -1 (perfect negative correlation) to 1 (perfect positive correlation), with 0 indicating no linear relationship.

**Sampling and the Law of Large Numbers:**

- Sampling is the process of selecting a subset of data from a larger dataset, often used in mini-batch gradient descent to improve computational efficiency.
- The Law of Large Numbers states that as the size of a sample increases, the sample mean will converge to the true population mean. In deep learning, this concept is important when working with large datasets, as it ensures that the model's performance on a sample is representative of its performance on the entire dataset.

### 3. Evaluation Metrics: How Well is the Model Performing?

In deep learning, we use statistical measures to assess how well a model is performing. These metrics help us evaluate the accuracy, precision, recall, and generalization of the model.

**Accuracy**: Accuracy is a measure of how often the model makes correct predictions. It is calculated as the ratio of correct predictions to the total number of predictions. However, accuracy is not always the best metric, especially for imbalanced datasets.

**Precision, Recall, and F1-Score**: In classification tasks, we often use precision and recall to evaluate the model's performance:

- Precision is the proportion of true positive predictions out of all positive predictions made by the model.
- Recall (or sensitivity) is the proportion of true positive predictions out of all actual positive instances in the dataset.
- F1-Score is the harmonic mean of precision and recall and is often used when dealing with imbalanced classes, as it balances the trade-off between precision and recall.

**Confusion Matrix**: A confusion matrix is a table used to evaluate the performance of classification models. It summarizes the true positives, true negatives, false positives, and false negatives, providing a clear picture of how well the model is performing across different classes.

**Loss Functions**: Loss functions are used to quantify the difference between the predicted values and the true values. Common loss functions used in deep learning include:

- **Mean Squared Error (MSE):** Often used in regression tasks to minimize the squared differences between the predicted and actual values.
- **Cross-Entropy Loss**: Used in classification tasks to measure the difference between the predicted probability distribution and the true class distribution.

### 4. Overfitting and Underfitting: The Bias-Variance Tradeoff

In deep learning, models can either overfit or underfit the data, and understanding this is crucial for training effective models.

Overfitting occurs when a model learns the training data too well, including noise and outliers, and fails to generalize to new, unseen data. This typically happens when the model is too complex, and it memorizes the training data rather than learning the underlying patterns. Overfitting can be detected by comparing the training accuracy to the validation accuracy: if the model performs significantly better on the training set than on the validation set, overfitting is likely occurring.

Underfitting happens when a model is too simple and cannot capture the underlying patterns in the data. Underfitting is typically observed when the model has too few parameters or when training is stopped too early. A model that performs poorly on both the training and validation sets is likely underfitting.

**Bias-Variance Tradeoff**: The bias-variance tradeoff refers to the balance between underfitting and overfitting. A model with high bias tends to underfit, while a model with high variance tends to overfit. The goal is to find a model that achieves a low bias and low variance, allowing it to generalize well to unseen data.

### 5. Monte Carlo Methods and Bootstrapping

Monte Carlo methods are a class of algorithms that rely on repeated random sampling to estimate mathematical quantities, such as expectations or variances. In deep learning, these methods are used in tasks like Monte Carlo dropout for uncertainty estimation in neural networks.

Bootstrapping is a statistical method for estimating the distribution of a sample statistic by resampling with replacement from the original dataset. It is used in ensemble learning methods and can be applied to evaluate the stability of model predictions.

Probability and statistics are crucial tools for understanding, building, and optimizing deep learning models. Probability helps us handle uncertainty, model distributions, and make predictions, while statistics allows us to describe data, evaluate model performance, and ensure our models generalize well. Understanding key concepts such as probability distributions, Bayes' theorem, variance, and overfitting is essential for designing and training effective deep learning models. By leveraging these concepts, deep learning practitioners can improve model accuracy, prevent overfitting, and build more robust systems that perform well on real-world data.

# 2.4. Understanding High-Dimensional Spaces

In deep learning, neural networks often deal with high-dimensional data, and understanding high-dimensional spaces is crucial for grasping how neural networks learn, generalize, and process complex data. While the world we experience is inherently three-dimensional, much of the data used in deep learning exists in spaces with many more dimensions—often referred to as high-dimensional spaces. High-dimensional spaces are central to many deep learning models, including those used for image recognition, natural language processing, and time series forecasting.

In this section, we will explore the concept of high-dimensional spaces, their significance in deep learning, and some key mathematical and geometric ideas that help us understand them.

## 1. What Are High-Dimensional Spaces?

A high-dimensional space refers to a space with more than three dimensions. While humans can only visualize three-dimensional space (length, width, and height), computers can work with data that has thousands or even millions of dimensions. These high-dimensional spaces are abstract and difficult for us to directly visualize, but they are essential for understanding modern machine learning and deep learning models.

**Dimension**: The number of independent coordinates required to specify a point in a space defines the dimension of that space. In a 2D space, you need two coordinates (x and y) to define a point. In 3D space, you need three coordinates (x, y, and z), and in a high-dimensional space, the number of coordinates can be in the thousands or even millions.

**Example in Data**: A typical image, for instance, may have thousands or millions of pixels, and each pixel can be represented as a coordinate in a high-dimensional space. For a grayscale image with a resolution of 100x100, the image can be represented as a vector with 10,000 dimensions—one for each pixel. For colored images, the dimensionality increases even further because each pixel has multiple color channels (e.g., red, green, blue).

## 2. The Curse of Dimensionality

While high-dimensional spaces are powerful, they come with challenges. One of the biggest challenges is the curse of dimensionality. This term refers to various phenomena that arise when working with data in high-dimensional spaces, which can negatively affect the performance of machine learning models.

**Sparse Data**: As the dimensionality of the data increases, the data points become increasingly sparse. For example, in a 3D space, data points might be spread out across the space, but in a 1000-dimensional space, they are even more spread out. The result is that many machine learning algorithms struggle to capture meaningful patterns when the data is sparse because there is insufficient data to learn from.

**Distance Measures Lose Meaning**: In high-dimensional spaces, traditional distance metrics like Euclidean distance become less informative. In low dimensions, the distance between two points is relatively straightforward to compute and interpret, but as the number of dimensions increases, the distance between points becomes similar for most points in the space. This phenomenon is known as the concentration of measure, where distances between random points become almost the same, making it difficult to differentiate between close and far points.

**Overfitting**: High-dimensional spaces also increase the risk of overfitting in machine learning models. A high number of features (dimensions) increases the number of parameters the model must learn, and this can lead to a model that memorizes the training data instead of generalizing to new, unseen data.

## 3. Geometric Intuition in High Dimensions

Although we cannot directly visualize high-dimensional spaces, we can still develop an intuitive understanding by thinking about some basic geometric principles and how they apply to high-dimensional data.

**Vectors and Linear Algebra**: A point in a high-dimensional space can be represented as a vector. In deep learning, most operations—such as matrix multiplications, dot products, and vector transformations—are performed in high-dimensional spaces. Understanding how vectors behave in high-dimensional spaces is critical because these operations are central to how neural networks function.

**Hyperplanes and Linear Separation**: In machine learning, one of the key ideas is separating different classes of data points. In 2D, we might separate two classes of points with a straight line. In 3D, we use a plane. In high-dimensional spaces, we use hyperplanes—generalizations of lines and planes to higher dimensions. Neural networks, particularly support vector machines (SVMs), work by finding these hyperplanes to classify data.

In deep learning, neurons in the network act as hyperplanes that transform the input data into an output space that can more easily be classified or predicted. The transformation is done through a series of learned weights and biases.

**Curvature and Manifolds**: High-dimensional spaces are often described as manifolds, which are mathematical structures that look flat locally but may have curvature globally. This concept is important for understanding the geometry of neural network activations and the way neural networks map data from input to output. Deep learning models, especially autoencoders and generative models, are often designed to learn these complex manifolds.

## 4. Principal Component Analysis (PCA): Reducing Dimensionality

To combat the curse of dimensionality, we often perform dimensionality reduction. One of the most common techniques is Principal Component Analysis (PCA), which reduces the dimensionality of the data while retaining as much of the variation as possible.

PCA works by finding a new set of axes (called principal components) that capture the most variance in the data. These axes are ordered so that the first component captures the greatest variance, the second captures the second greatest variance, and so on. By keeping only the first few components, we can reduce the dimensionality of the data while still preserving much of the information.

**Application in Deep Learning**: PCA is often used for data preprocessing to reduce the dimensionality of inputs before they are fed into a neural network, especially when the data is very high-dimensional (e.g., images, text, or speech). This helps reduce computational complexity and mitigate the risk of overfitting.

## 5. The Role of High-Dimensional Spaces in Neural Networks

Neural networks are inherently designed to work in high-dimensional spaces. The concept of high-dimensional representations and transformations is fundamental to how neural networks learn and generalize. Here's how:

**High-Dimensional Representations in Neural Networks**: When data is fed into a neural network, the network transforms it through a series of layers and activations. Each layer in a neural network learns to map the input data into a higher-dimensional space where it is easier to classify or predict. These transformations allow the network to learn complex, non-linear relationships in the data that would be difficult to capture in a low-dimensional space.

**Hidden Layers and Feature Space**: The neurons in the hidden layers of a neural network can be thought of as mapping the input data into a higher-dimensional feature space. This transformation allows the network to learn more complex features, making it possible to solve non-linear problems like image recognition or natural language processing. The network can learn these high-dimensional representations from the data through optimization techniques like gradient descent.

**Activation Functions**: Activation functions (like the sigmoid, ReLU, and tanh) help create non-linearities in the network, which enables the model to learn complex patterns in high-dimensional spaces. Without activation functions, the neural network would only be able to perform linear transformations, limiting its ability to capture the complexity of real-world data.

## 6. Visualizing High-Dimensional Spaces

While we cannot directly visualize high-dimensional spaces, various techniques allow us to visualize them indirectly. t-SNE (t-Distributed Stochastic Neighbor Embedding) and UMAP (Uniform Manifold Approximation and Projection) are two popular methods used to reduce the dimensionality of high-dimensional data to 2D or 3D for visualization. These techniques help us understand the structure of the data, identify clusters, and interpret the results of deep learning models.

Understanding high-dimensional spaces is a key concept in deep learning and is essential for building and interpreting neural networks. While these spaces are difficult to visualize directly, we can understand their geometry and how deep learning algorithms operate in them. High-dimensional spaces allow neural networks to learn complex, non-linear relationships, which is what makes them so powerful. However, they also pose challenges, such as the curse of dimensionality and the risk of overfitting. Techniques like dimensionality reduction and proper regularization are essential for making deep learning models more efficient and effective when dealing with high-dimensional data. Understanding how to navigate these spaces is essential for anyone working with deep learning and machine learning algorithms.

# 3. Biological Inspiration & Perceptron Model

Neural networks are inspired by the human brain, mimicking the way biological neurons process information. This chapter explores the connection between neuroscience and artificial intelligence, explaining how brain-like structures influence deep learning models. You'll dive into the perceptron, the simplest artificial neuron, and understand how it makes decisions using weighted inputs and activation functions. By examining the perceptron's strengths and limitations, you'll see how it paved the way for more advanced neural network architectures, setting the stage for modern AI breakthroughs.

## 3.1. The Human Brain vs. Artificial Neural Networks

The development of Artificial Neural Networks (ANNs) is deeply inspired by the biological neural networks found in the human brain. The underlying concept of artificial neural networks draws from our understanding of how biological systems process information, but with notable differences in structure, function, and complexity. In this section, we'll explore the similarities and differences between the human brain and artificial neural networks to provide insights into the strengths, limitations, and future potential of both.

### 1. Basic Structure: Neurons in the Brain vs. Artificial Neurons

**Biological Neurons**: The human brain is composed of roughly 86 billion neurons, each of which is connected to thousands of other neurons via synapses. Neurons in the brain receive signals, process them, and transmit output to other neurons. Each neuron is a complex structure with several parts:

- **Dendrites**: Branch-like structures that receive input signals from other neurons.
- **Cell Body (Soma):** Contains the nucleus and is responsible for processing the input signals.
- **Axon**: The long extension that transmits the output signal to other neurons or muscles.
- **Synapses**: The connections between neurons where signals are passed chemically and electrically.

Neurons in the brain communicate with each other through electrical impulses, and the strength of the signal between neurons changes over time, depending on how frequently they fire together, a concept known as synaptic plasticity.

**Artificial Neurons**: In artificial neural networks, the artificial neuron (or perceptron) is a simplified mathematical model that imitates the behavior of biological neurons. An artificial neuron consists of:

- **Inputs**: Representing data or features fed into the network.
- **Weights**: Parameters that define the importance of each input.
- **Bias**: A constant value added to the input to adjust the output.
- **Activation Function**: A mathematical function that decides whether or not to fire the neuron by producing an output based on the weighted sum of inputs.

Unlike biological neurons, artificial neurons are much simpler and lack the complexity of dendrites, axons, and synapses. They also operate using mathematical operations, such as summation and nonlinear activation functions.

## 2. Signal Processing: Electrical vs. Mathematical Operations

**Biological Processing**: The brain's neurons communicate by firing action potentials (electrical signals) along axons. When a neuron receives a signal from its dendrites, it processes the incoming information and, if the signal is strong enough, sends an electrical impulse (action potential) to other neurons through the axon. This signal transmission involves intricate chemical processes that allow for adaptation over time, making the brain extremely flexible and capable of learning complex tasks.

**Artificial Processing**: Artificial neurons process information in a purely mathematical way. When inputs are fed into an artificial neuron, they are multiplied by weights, summed together, and then passed through an activation function. The output is then sent to other neurons in the network. The signal flow through artificial neural networks is defined by simple mathematical operations rather than the complex biochemical processes that occur in the brain.

While artificial neural networks use backpropagation and gradient descent to learn, the underlying mathematical framework is far less biologically complex than the brain's electrochemical processes.

## 3. Learning: Synaptic Plasticity vs. Backpropagation

**Synaptic Plasticity**: In the human brain, learning is achieved through synaptic plasticity, which is the ability of synapses to strengthen or weaken over time in response to repeated activity. The famous principle "cells that fire together, wire together" suggests that when two neurons are activated at the same time, the synapse between them becomes stronger, increasing the likelihood of their future activation together. This is the biological basis of learning and memory, and it allows the brain to adapt and improve over time.

Hebbian learning, a type of synaptic plasticity, is a well-known model of how learning occurs in the brain. It states that when one neuron repeatedly activates another, the connection between the two neurons becomes stronger. Over time, these neural connections allow the brain to form patterns, associations, and memories.

**Backpropagation in ANNs**: In contrast, artificial neural networks learn by adjusting the weights of connections between neurons using backpropagation. Backpropagation is a supervised learning algorithm where the network compares its output to the desired output, calculates the error, and propagates this error backward through the network. The error is then used to adjust the weights of the neurons via an optimization algorithm such as gradient descent. This process enables the network to reduce the error over time and improve performance.

While backpropagation is inspired by biological learning mechanisms, it is far simpler and mathematically structured. The brain, by comparison, is a much more complex and adaptive system, with learning occurring through many different mechanisms beyond synaptic plasticity, such as neurogenesis, long-term potentiation, and reinforcement learning.

### 4. Parallel Processing: The Brain's Massive Parallelism vs. Neural Network Architectures

**Brain's Parallelism**: One of the remarkable features of the human brain is its ability to process information in parallel. Neurons operate in parallel, meaning that multiple neurons can simultaneously process and send signals to other neurons. The brain's architecture allows for the efficient handling of diverse sensory inputs (sight, sound, touch) and enables the processing of complex cognitive tasks like thinking, reasoning, and problem-solving in real-time.

The brain can process sensory inputs, make decisions, and execute motor responses nearly instantaneously. Its parallel nature also enables multiple tasks to be handled simultaneously, such as thinking, feeling, and moving, all at once.

**Artificial Neural Networks**: Artificial neural networks also process information in parallel, but not to the same extent as the human brain. Each artificial neuron can operate in parallel during training and inference, particularly in large-scale networks. However, the true parallelism of the brain, where billions of neurons work simultaneously and interact in highly complex ways, is much more advanced than what current artificial networks can replicate.

The parallelism in deep learning networks comes from the fact that each layer of the network can process inputs simultaneously and compute outputs independently, allowing for faster computations and improved scalability. However, current artificial neural networks are still limited in terms of how they handle real-time data and multi-tasking compared to the brain.

## 5. Complexity: Brain's Unparalleled Sophistication vs. ANN's Simplicity

**Complexity of the Brain**: The human brain is an incredibly sophisticated organ that is capable of processing multimodal information, adapting to new situations, and exhibiting emotional intelligence, creativity, and reasoning. It is made up of specialized regions that handle different functions, such as memory, language, vision, and motor control. Additionally, the brain operates through highly complex networks of neurons that interact with each other in dynamic and flexible ways.

The brain's ability to learn from few examples, make sense of ambiguous information, and adapt to new environments is a testament to its complexity. Moreover, the brain is also energy-efficient, consuming roughly 20 watts of power, which is remarkably low compared to the computational resources needed for training modern neural networks.

**Artificial Neural Networks' Simplicity**: In contrast, artificial neural networks are far less complex. While they have proven to be very effective at tasks such as image recognition, language modeling, and game-playing, they are still limited by the quality and quantity of the data they are trained on. They require large amounts of labeled data, specialized hardware (e.g., GPUs), and significant computing power to achieve good performance. Furthermore, ANNs are still far from exhibiting the general-purpose intelligence, creativity, and adaptability of the human brain.

Current artificial neural networks are highly specialized, meaning they can perform specific tasks very well but struggle to generalize across domains (i.e., transfer learning is still a major challenge).

## 6. Conclusion: Inspiration vs. Imitation

The human brain has served as the primary inspiration for artificial neural networks, providing key ideas about how information can be processed and learned in networks of interconnected units. While artificial neural networks share some broad conceptual similarities with biological neural networks, they are far simpler and operate in a different way, both in terms of architecture and learning. The brain's capacity for parallel processing, its plasticity, and its ability to adapt to new situations make it an unparalleled model of intelligence, one that current artificial systems strive to imitate, but have yet to fully replicate.

As deep learning technologies evolve, there is growing interest in creating more brain-like systems, from neuromorphic computing (which mimics the brain's structure and function) to the development of more efficient learning algorithms. Though we still have a long way to go in replicating the complexity and adaptability of the human brain, artificial neural networks remain a powerful tool that has already revolutionized many fields, and they continue to improve with time and research. Understanding the similarities and differences between the brain and artificial networks helps us move toward creating more advanced and intelligent systems in the future.

## 3.2. The Perceptron: The First Neural Network Model

The perceptron is one of the foundational models in the history of neural networks and deep learning. Developed by Frank Rosenblatt in 1957, it is often considered the first artificial neural network, and its introduction marked a significant step forward in the field of machine learning. While simple compared to modern neural networks, the perceptron laid the groundwork for the more advanced, multilayer networks that followed. Understanding the perceptron helps us appreciate the evolution of artificial neural networks and the challenges faced in their development.

In this section, we will explore what a perceptron is, how it works, and its significance in the evolution of neural networks.

### 1. What is the Perceptron?

At its core, a perceptron is a single-layer neural network designed for binary classification tasks, where the goal is to classify inputs into one of two possible categories (e.g., yes/no, 1/0, true/false). It is composed of an input layer and an output layer, with no hidden layers in between. The perceptron can be viewed as a linear classifier, meaning it separates input data into two categories by drawing a straight line (or hyperplane in higher dimensions) between them.

**Inputs**: Each input to the perceptron is a feature of the data (e.g., pixel values for an image, measurements in a dataset). Each input is associated with a weight, which represents the importance of that particular feature in the classification process.

**Weights**: Weights are numerical values assigned to each input. The perceptron learns these weights during the training process. The higher the weight, the more influence a particular input has on the perceptron's decision.

**Bias**: In addition to the weighted sum of the inputs, a bias term is added. The bias allows the perceptron to adjust the decision boundary and helps make the model more flexible.

**Activation Function**: After the perceptron computes the weighted sum of inputs (plus bias), it applies an activation function to determine the output. In the original perceptron, the activation function is a step function that outputs one value (e.g., 1) if the sum of the inputs exceeds a certain threshold and another value (e.g., 0) otherwise. This step function makes the perceptron a binary classifier, meaning it assigns one of two possible output values.

**The perceptron can thus be expressed mathematically as:**

$$y = \begin{cases} 1 & \text{if } \sum w_i x_i + b > 0 \\ 0 & \text{otherwise} \end{cases}$$

Where:

- $y$ is the output (0 or 1).

- $w_i$ are the weights for each input $x_i$.

- $b$ is the bias term.

- The sum $\sum w_i x_i + b$ is the weighted sum of inputs.

## 2. The Perceptron Learning Rule

The perceptron model learns through a simple algorithm known as the perceptron learning rule. This algorithm allows the perceptron to adjust its weights and bias to minimize classification errors and improve its accuracy on training data. The learning rule works as follows:

**Initialize weights and bias**: Set the weights and bias to small random values, typically close to zero.

**For each training sample:**

- Compute the weighted sum of inputs and bias.
- Apply the step function to generate the predicted output.
- Compare the predicted output with the actual target label.

**Update weights**: If the perceptron's prediction is incorrect (i.e., the predicted output doesn't match the target label), update the weights and bias. The update is based on the difference between the predicted output and the target label. The weights are updated as follows:

$$w_i \leftarrow w_i + \Delta w_i$$

Where the change in weights $\Delta w_i$ is calculated as:

$$\Delta w_i = \eta(y_{\text{true}} - y_{\text{pred}})x_i$$

- $\eta$ is the learning rate, which controls how much the weights are adjusted with each update.

- $y_{\text{true}}$ is the true label.

- $y_{\text{pred}}$ is the predicted label.

- $x_i$ is the input feature.

**Repeat**: Continue the process of calculating the output and adjusting the weights until the perceptron converges or reaches a predefined number of iterations.

This process allows the perceptron to learn the best set of weights that minimize errors on the training data. However, the perceptron can only learn to classify linearly separable data, meaning data that can be separated by a straight line (or hyperplane) in its feature space.

### 3. Limitations of the Perceptron

While the perceptron was a groundbreaking invention in the 1950s, it has some fundamental limitations that became clear over time:

**Linear Separability**: The most significant limitation of the perceptron is that it can only solve problems where the data is linearly separable. This means that the data must be able to be separated into two classes using a straight line (or hyperplane in higher dimensions). If the data is not linearly separable (as is the case with more complex problems like XOR), the perceptron cannot learn an appropriate classification boundary.

**XOR Problem**: A classic example of a non-linearly separable problem is the XOR (exclusive OR) logic gate. The XOR function cannot be correctly modeled by a single perceptron because the data points representing the two output classes cannot be separated by a single line. This limitation led to the realization that more complex models, such as multi-layer networks, were needed.

**No Hidden Layers**: The original perceptron consists only of an input layer and an output layer, with no hidden layers to capture more complex patterns in the data. This lack of depth means that the perceptron is limited in its ability to model complex relationships between inputs and outputs.

## 4. The Impact of the Perceptron on Neural Networks

Despite its limitations, the perceptron played a pivotal role in the development of neural networks and machine learning. Several key ideas from the perceptron continue to be important in modern deep learning:

**Weights and Bias**: The concept of weights and bias as adjustable parameters is central to all neural networks, from the simple perceptron to deep convolutional networks. These parameters allow the network to adapt and improve its performance through learning.

**Activation Functions**: The perceptron introduced the idea of using an activation function to determine the output of a neuron based on the weighted sum of inputs. While the original perceptron used a step function, modern networks use more sophisticated activation functions such as sigmoid, ReLU, and softmax.

**Learning through Backpropagation**: While the perceptron uses a simple learning rule, the idea of adjusting weights based on error feedback laid the foundation for more advanced learning algorithms. Backpropagation—a technique that allows multi-layer networks to adjust weights based on error gradients—built upon the perceptron learning rule and enabled the training of deeper, more powerful networks.

## 5. The Perceptron's Revival: The Modern Neural Network

Although the perceptron had its limitations, it remains a critical part of the history of neural networks. Over the years, neural network research expanded to overcome the perceptron's drawbacks, most notably with the development of multilayer perceptrons (MLPs), which consist of multiple layers of neurons, including hidden layers that allow for more complex decision boundaries.

With the advent of deep learning and the use of large-scale datasets and powerful computational hardware, the perceptron's basic principles have been extended and refined into the sophisticated neural networks we use today.

The perceptron is a simple but powerful model that laid the foundation for the development of artificial neural networks. It introduced key ideas like weighted inputs, activation functions, and learning through feedback, which are still essential in deep learning today. However, its inability to solve non-linearly separable problems limited its practical use in complex tasks. Despite these limitations, the perceptron remains an important part of the neural network family and serves as a stepping stone to the more advanced models we use today. By understanding the perceptron, we gain insight into the evolution of neural networks and the foundational principles that continue to drive the field of artificial intelligence forward.

# 3.3. Limitations of the Perceptron (XOR Problem & Beyond)

While the perceptron was an important milestone in the development of artificial intelligence and neural networks, it is not without its limitations. One of the most well-known and foundational challenges associated with the perceptron is its inability to solve certain problems that are non-linearly separable. Among the most famous of these problems is the XOR problem, which became a key reason for the development of more advanced neural network architectures.

In this section, we'll delve into the limitations of the perceptron, focusing on the XOR problem, and explore other challenges that limit the perceptron's effectiveness in more complex tasks.

### 1. The XOR Problem: The Ultimate Demonstration of Linearity's Limits

The XOR problem (exclusive OR) is a classic example in computational theory and neural networks that illustrates the limitation of the perceptron's capacity to handle non-linearly separable data.

**XOR Logic**: The XOR gate is a logical operation that outputs true (1) when the number of true inputs is odd. For two binary inputs, the truth table for XOR looks like this:

| Input 1 | Input 2 | Output (XOR) |
|---------|---------|--------------|
| 0 | 0 | 0 |
| 0 | 1 | 1 |
| 1 | 0 | 1 |
| 1 | 1 | 0 |

The XOR operation returns 1 for inputs where one is 1 and the other is 0, and 0 for inputs where both are the same. The key challenge is that the outputs (0 or 1) cannot be separated by a single straight line in a 2D space when plotted graphically.

**Graphing XOR**: If you plot the XOR inputs on a graph, it becomes apparent that the points representing the output 1 (i.e., (0, 1) and (1, 0)) are not linearly separable from the points representing the output 0 (i.e., (0, 0) and (1, 1)). The two classes cannot be separated by a straight line, and hence, a perceptron fails to classify them correctly.

**Perceptron's Limitation**: The perceptron can only learn to classify data that is linearly separable, meaning there exists a straight line (or hyperplane) that can divide the two classes of data. Since the XOR problem is a non-linearly separable problem, the perceptron fails to find a decision boundary that correctly classifies all data points, resulting in poor performance for this problem.

The perceptron's failure to solve the XOR problem became a critical insight into the need for more sophisticated neural network architectures that could handle non-linear decision boundaries.

## 2. The Perceptron's One-Layer Limitation

The perceptron consists of a single-layer network with input neurons connected directly to an output neuron. While this structure is simple and effective for linearly separable problems, it lacks the ability to represent complex, non-linear relationships. Here's why:

**Single Layer Structure**: In the perceptron model, the input data is passed through a single layer of neurons, where each neuron computes a weighted sum and applies a threshold via an activation function. The decision boundary it creates is always a straight line (or hyperplane in higher dimensions), which means it can only separate data that is linearly separable.

**No Hidden Layers**: The perceptron lacks hidden layers, which are a crucial component in more powerful neural network models. Hidden layers allow the network to create more complex decision boundaries by transforming the data through non-linear functions. Without hidden layers, the perceptron is unable to learn any representations or complex patterns that would allow it to handle tasks like XOR or more complex image classification problems.

**Linear Transformations Only**: The perceptron only performs linear transformations on the input data. Without the ability to combine features in non-linear ways (such as through combinations of multiple neurons in hidden layers), it cannot represent functions that require non-linear separability.

### 3. The Need for Multilayer Networks

The failure of the perceptron to solve the XOR problem highlighted the need for multilayer neural networks that could learn complex, non-linear decision boundaries. This led to the development of Multilayer Perceptrons (MLPs), which consist of multiple layers of neurons, including hidden layers that enable more complex learning. Here's how multilayer networks overcome the perceptron's limitations:

**Hidden Layers**: The addition of hidden layers allows for the creation of non-linear transformations of the input data. This enables the network to learn non-linear relationships between inputs and outputs, making it capable of solving problems like XOR.

**Non-linear Activation Functions**: In addition to the structure of multilayer networks, the introduction of non-linear activation functions, such as sigmoid, ReLU, and tanh, allows the network to model more complex decision boundaries that cannot be captured by a linear function.

**Universal Approximation Theorem**: The universal approximation theorem states that a multilayer neural network with non-linear activation functions can approximate any continuous function to an arbitrary degree of accuracy. This ability to approximate non-linear functions is what allows deeper networks to tackle a broad range of real-world problems, from image recognition to natural language processing.

### 4. The Vanishing Gradient Problem

While the perceptron's inability to solve non-linearly separable problems was its most significant limitation, modern deep neural networks have their own set of challenges. One key problem that arose with the expansion to deeper networks is the vanishing gradient problem.

**Backpropagation and Gradients**: Backpropagation, the algorithm used for training neural networks, works by calculating gradients of the loss function with respect to the weights in the network. These gradients indicate how much each weight should be adjusted in order to minimize the error.

**Vanishing Gradients in Deep Networks**: In very deep neural networks (i.e., networks with many hidden layers), gradients can become very small as they are propagated back through each layer. This results in extremely slow learning or complete failure to update the weights in the earlier layers. This problem is exacerbated by the use of activation functions like sigmoid or tanh, which squash values into a small range, causing gradients to diminish.

**Solutions to Vanishing Gradients**: Techniques like ReLU activation (which does not saturate) and batch normalization have been developed to mitigate the vanishing gradient problem, allowing deeper networks to learn more effectively.

## 5. Limitations Beyond the XOR Problem

While the XOR problem is the classic demonstration of the perceptron's limits, there are other areas where the perceptron fails to meet the demands of modern machine learning tasks:

**Complex, Real-World Data**: In real-world problems, data is often messy, noisy, and complex. The perceptron's simple linear decision boundary is insufficient for accurately classifying data that does not conform to clean, separable patterns. Tasks like image classification, speech recognition, and natural language processing require far more powerful models capable of processing high-dimensional and non-linearly separable data.

**Non-Linearity in Data Relationships**: Many relationships in data are inherently non-linear. For example, in image recognition, the relationship between pixels and objects in the image is highly non-linear. The perceptron's linear decision boundary cannot capture such complex patterns, and more advanced neural networks, such as convolutional neural networks (CNNs), are required for these tasks.

The perceptron, despite being the first neural network model, has several critical limitations that hinder its ability to solve complex problems. Its inability to handle non-linearly separable problems, exemplified by the XOR problem, was a fundamental challenge that led to the development of more advanced neural network architectures, such as multilayer perceptrons and deep neural networks. The XOR problem highlighted the necessity for hidden layers and non-linear activation functions in learning complex patterns in data.

While the perceptron is a historical milestone, it is not sufficient for most modern machine learning tasks. Today, we rely on more sophisticated architectures capable of handling complex, high-dimensional data, enabling us to solve real-world problems across various fields, from computer vision to speech processing. The development of neural networks beyond the perceptron represents one of the most significant advancements in the field of artificial intelligence, paving the way for the deep learning revolution.

# 3.4. Introduction to Multilayer Perceptrons (MLP)

The Multilayer Perceptron (MLP) is a fundamental architecture in the field of artificial neural networks and a significant advancement over the single-layer perceptron. While the perceptron could only handle linearly separable problems, the introduction of multilayer networks revolutionized the field by enabling neural networks to solve far more complex, non-linear problems. The MLP, by incorporating multiple layers of neurons (input, hidden, and output layers), has the capability to model intricate patterns and relationships within data.

In this section, we will explore the core principles behind MLPs, their structure, how they solve problems that were impossible for single-layer perceptrons, and their application in modern machine learning tasks.

### 1. Structure of a Multilayer Perceptron

An MLP consists of three types of layers: the input layer, one or more hidden layers, and the output layer. Here's a breakdown of each layer:

**Input Layer**: The input layer receives the raw input features of the data. Each neuron in this layer corresponds to one feature of the input data. For example, in an image classification task, each pixel might correspond to a neuron in the input layer.

**Hidden Layers**: Between the input and output layers, the MLP has one or more hidden layers. These layers consist of neurons that do not directly interact with the external environment but instead process the input data. Each neuron in a hidden layer takes in weighted inputs from the previous layer and applies an activation function to produce an output, which is passed to the next layer. The more hidden layers an MLP has, the more complex the relationships it can model.

**Output Layer**: The output layer produces the final prediction of the network. The number of neurons in the output layer depends on the type of problem being solved. For example, in binary classification, there might be one output neuron, while for multi-class classification, there would be one neuron for each class.

The key innovation in the MLP is the use of multiple hidden layers that allow the network to learn and represent non-linear relationships in the data. Each hidden layer progressively extracts more abstract features from the input data, enabling the network to recognize complex patterns.

## 2. The Role of Activation Functions

The introduction of activation functions in the MLP is what makes it capable of solving non-linear problems, unlike the perceptron, which used a simple step function. Activation functions introduce non-linearity to the network, allowing it to approximate any continuous function and capture intricate data patterns.

Some commonly used activation functions in MLPs include:

**Sigmoid Function**: The sigmoid function squashes the input into a range between 0 and 1. It was widely used in early neural networks but has since been largely replaced by other functions due to issues like vanishing gradients during backpropagation.

$$\sigma(x) = \frac{1}{1 + e^{-x}}$$

**Hyperbolic Tangent (tanh):** The tanh function is similar to the sigmoid but outputs values between -1 and 1, making it more useful in certain contexts. However, it also suffers from the vanishing gradient problem.

$$\tanh(x) = \frac{e^x - e^{-x}}{e^x + e^{-x}}$$

**Rectified Linear Unit (ReLU):** ReLU has become the default activation function in many neural networks due to its simplicity and effectiveness. It outputs the input directly if it's positive; otherwise, it outputs zero. ReLU helps mitigate the vanishing gradient problem, making it suitable for deeper networks.

$$\text{ReLU}(x) = \max(0, x)$$

**Softmax:** The softmax function is commonly used in the output layer for multi-class classification problems. It converts raw scores (logits) into probabilities that sum to 1, representing the likelihood of each class.

$$\text{Softmax}(x_i) = \frac{e^{x_i}}{\sum e^{x_j}}$$

## 3. The Training Process: Backpropagation

The training of a Multilayer Perceptron relies on an algorithm called backpropagation. Backpropagation is a method for updating the weights of the network through the process of gradient descent, allowing the network to minimize the loss function and improve its predictions over time. Here's a breakdown of the process:

**Forward Pass:** During the forward pass, input data is passed through the input layer, then through each hidden layer, and finally to the output layer. Each layer computes a weighted sum of its inputs, applies an activation function, and passes the result to the next layer. The final output is the network's prediction.

**Loss Calculation:** After the forward pass, the loss function (also called the cost function) measures the difference between the network's predicted output and the true target values. Common loss functions include mean squared error for regression tasks and cross-entropy for classification tasks.

**Backward Pass (Backpropagation):** During the backward pass, the error is propagated back through the network. The gradient of the loss function with respect to each weight is computed using the chain rule of calculus. This tells us how much each weight contributed to the error, allowing us to adjust the weights to reduce the error.

**Weight Update**: Using an optimization algorithm like gradient descent, the weights are adjusted in the direction that minimizes the error. The learning rate controls how large each weight update is. There are variations of gradient descent, such as Stochastic Gradient Descent (SGD), Adam, and RMSprop, that aim to improve convergence speed and accuracy.

## 4. Why MLPs Work for Non-Linear Problems

The key advantage of Multilayer Perceptrons over single-layer perceptrons is their ability to learn non-linear decision boundaries. This is due to the hidden layers and the use of non-linear activation functions.

In a simple perceptron, the network is essentially performing a linear transformation on the input data, which can only separate linearly separable classes. The addition of hidden layers allows the network to create more complex decision boundaries. Here's how:

- Each hidden layer applies a non-linear transformation to the data. As the data moves through successive hidden layers, the network progressively captures more abstract features and non-linear relationships in the data.
- By combining these non-linear transformations, MLPs can model highly complex functions and approximate non-linear decision boundaries that are required for many real-world tasks, such as object recognition, speech recognition, and machine translation.

## 5. Applications of Multilayer Perceptrons

MLPs are versatile and have been applied to a wide range of machine learning tasks. Some key applications include:

**Image Classification**: MLPs can classify images by learning complex patterns in pixel values, often used in early image classification tasks before the rise of Convolutional Neural Networks (CNNs).

**Speech Recognition**: MLPs have been applied to recognizing spoken language by learning patterns in audio features, such as Mel-frequency cepstral coefficients (MFCCs).

**Natural Language Processing**: MLPs are used for tasks like sentiment analysis, language modeling, and machine translation, where they learn relationships between words and their meanings in a sequence.

**Function Approximation and Regression**: MLPs are used for tasks where the goal is to approximate a function that maps inputs to continuous outputs, such as predicting stock prices or weather forecasting.

## 6. Limitations of MLPs

Despite their advantages, MLPs also have limitations:

**Overfitting**: If the network has too many hidden layers or neurons, it may memorize the training data rather than learning general patterns. Regularization techniques such as dropout, L2 regularization, and early stopping can help mitigate overfitting.

**Scalability**: MLPs are not as efficient as Convolutional Neural Networks (CNNs) for tasks like image and video processing. CNNs are better suited for spatially structured data due to their use of convolutional layers, which reduce the number of parameters and make the network more computationally efficient.

**Vanishing Gradient Problem**: Like other deep networks, MLPs can suffer from the vanishing gradient problem, particularly when using activation functions like sigmoid or tanh. This issue can slow down or prevent the effective training of deep MLPs.

The Multilayer Perceptron (MLP) represents a major advancement in the development of artificial neural networks, enabling the ability to learn complex, non-linear relationships in data. With its layered structure and use of non-linear activation functions, MLPs can model intricate patterns that are impossible for simpler networks like the perceptron. While MLPs have limitations, particularly in handling large-scale and complex data, they laid the groundwork for more specialized architectures like CNNs and RNNs, and continue to be an important tool in machine learning and artificial intelligence.

# 4. Multilayer Perceptron (MLP) & Backpropagation

Building on the perceptron model, this chapter introduces the Multilayer Perceptron (MLP), a more powerful neural network architecture that can solve complex problems by using multiple layers of neurons. You'll learn how MLPs process data through hidden layers to capture intricate patterns and how they use backpropagation to adjust weights and minimize errors. The chapter breaks down the backpropagation algorithm step-by-step, showing how it enables the network to learn from its mistakes through gradient descent. By the end of this chapter, you'll understand how MLPs form the backbone of many deep learning applications, from image classification to natural language processing.

## 4.1. The Structure of an MLP (Layers, Neurons, Weights, and Biases)

The Multilayer Perceptron (MLP) is a type of feedforward neural network that is structured in layers, with each layer consisting of multiple neurons. These layers work together to process and transform input data, enabling the network to learn complex patterns and relationships. The core components of an MLP include layers, neurons, weights, and biases—each playing a crucial role in how the network learns and makes predictions.

In this section, we will break down the structure of an MLP, detailing how each element functions and contributes to the overall network.

### 1. Layers of an MLP

An MLP consists of three main types of layers: input layer, hidden layers, and output layer. Each layer serves a specific function in the network's learning process:

**Input Layer**: The input layer is the first layer of the network and receives the raw data. Each neuron in this layer corresponds to one feature in the input data. For example, in an image classification task, each pixel of the image might correspond to a neuron in the input layer. The input layer simply passes the data forward to the next layer without processing it, acting as the gateway into the network.

**Hidden Layers**: Hidden layers are intermediate layers between the input and output layers. They play a crucial role in learning patterns in the data. Each hidden layer consists of multiple neurons, each of which applies a weighted sum of inputs, followed by an activation function. The output of each hidden layer is passed to the next hidden layer or the output layer. Deep neural networks often have multiple hidden layers, allowing the network to capture increasingly abstract features from the input data.

**Output Layer**: The output layer is the final layer in the MLP, where the model produces its predictions. The number of neurons in the output layer depends on the type of problem the network is solving. For example:

- In binary classification, there may be one neuron with a sigmoid activation function that outputs a value between 0 and 1 (indicating the probability of the positive class).
- In multi-class classification, the output layer will have one neuron for each class, typically with a softmax activation function that outputs a probability distribution over all classes.
- In regression tasks, the output layer will have one or more neurons that provide continuous values.

## 2. Neurons: The Building Blocks of the Network

Neurons are the fundamental units within each layer of an MLP. Each neuron is responsible for performing a simple mathematical operation and passing its output to the next layer. The neuron receives inputs, computes a weighted sum, and applies an activation function to this sum. Here's how it works:

**Inputs**: A neuron receives inputs from the neurons in the previous layer. If the neuron is in the input layer, it receives the raw data features directly. If it's in a hidden or output layer, it receives the output values from the neurons in the previous layer.

**Weights**: Each input to a neuron is associated with a weight, which determines the importance of that input in the neuron's calculation. The weight reflects the strength of the connection between two neurons—larger weights mean that the input has more influence on the neuron's output. Initially, weights are usually set to random values and are adjusted during training through backpropagation to minimize the network's error.

**Bias**: Along with weights, each neuron has a bias. The bias allows the neuron to shift the output, even when all inputs are zero. This helps the neuron learn patterns that do not pass through the origin (i.e., the bias shifts the activation function along the x-axis). The bias is also updated during training along with the weights. Mathematically, the output of a neuron is calculated as:

$$\text{Output} = f\left(\sum_{i=1}^{n} w_i x_i + b\right)$$

Where:

- $x_i$ are the inputs to the neuron.

- $w_i$ are the weights associated with the inputs.

- $b$ is the bias.

- $f$ is the activation function applied to the weighted sum.

### 3. Weighted Sum and Activation Function

Each neuron in an MLP computes a weighted sum of its inputs. This sum is then passed through an activation function, which introduces non-linearity into the network and allows it to solve complex problems. The general process is as follows:

**Weighted Sum**: The inputs to a neuron are multiplied by their respective weights, and the results are summed together along with the bias term. The formula for this operation is:

$$z = \sum_{i=1}^{n} w_i x_i + b$$

Where:

- $z$ is the weighted sum.

- $x_i$ are the inputs to the neuron.

- $w_i$ are the weights associated with the inputs.

- $b$ is the bias.

**Activation Function**: After computing the weighted sum, the result is passed through an activation function to determine the output of the neuron. Common activation functions include:

**Sigmoid**: Maps values between 0 and 1, often used in binary classification tasks.

$$\sigma(z) = \frac{1}{1 + e^{-z}}$$

**Tanh (Hyperbolic Tangent):** Maps values between -1 and 1, often used in hidden layers.

$$\tanh(z) = \frac{e^z - e^{-z}}{e^z + e^{-z}}$$

**ReLU (Rectified Linear Unit):** Sets negative values to 0, making it computationally efficient and effective in preventing the vanishing gradient problem.

$$\text{ReLU}(z) = \max(0, z)$$

**Softmax**: Used in the output layer for multi-class classification, softmax converts logits into probabilities.

$$\text{Softmax}(z_i) = \frac{e^{z_i}}{\sum_j e^{z_j}}$$

The choice of activation function depends on the type of problem the MLP is being used for.

## 4. How Layers, Neurons, Weights, and Biases Work Together

The process begins in the input layer, where raw data is fed into the network. Each input feature is represented as a neuron, and the values of these features are passed to the neurons in the first hidden layer. The neurons in this hidden layer compute the weighted sum of the inputs, apply the activation function, and pass the result to the next hidden layer (if present) or the output layer. This process continues through all layers of the MLP until the final output is generated.

**Forward Propagation**: During forward propagation, each layer computes the weighted sum of its inputs, applies the activation function, and passes the output to the next layer. The output of the final layer is the network's prediction.

**Backpropagation and Learning**: After the forward pass, the network compares its output to the true labels (targets) using a loss function. The loss function quantifies how far the network's prediction is from the true values. The goal is to minimize this loss, and this is achieved by adjusting the weights and biases during the backpropagation process. The gradients of the loss function with respect to the weights and biases are computed, and the weights are updated to reduce the error.

The structure of an MLP is composed of layers, neurons, weights, and biases, all of which play essential roles in the network's learning process. The input layer provides the data, the hidden layers allow the network to learn complex patterns, and the output layer produces the final predictions. Neurons perform simple computations, but by combining them in multiple layers with non-linear activation functions, an MLP can model intricate, non-linear relationships. Through the process of forward propagation and backpropagation, the MLP adjusts its weights and biases to minimize the loss function, ultimately learning to make accurate predictions.

## 4.2. Forward Propagation: How Data Flows Through a Neural Network

Forward propagation is a crucial phase in the neural network's process, where input data is passed through the layers of the network to generate the final output. It is during forward propagation that the network processes input data, computes intermediate values through various layers, and makes predictions. This process serves as the foundation for the neural network's learning process, which is further refined by backpropagation (covered later). Understanding forward propagation is essential for comprehending how neural networks function and how they compute outputs from input data.

In this section, we will break down the steps involved in forward propagation, explaining the flow of data through the network, how neurons compute their outputs, and how the final predictions are made.

### 1. The Flow of Data in Forward Propagation

Forward propagation begins with the input data and ends with the network's output predictions. The data flows through each layer of the network, where each neuron performs computations and passes the results forward to the next layer.

Here is a high-level view of the data flow during forward propagation:

**Input Layer**: The process starts at the input layer, where the network receives raw data (features). Each feature is represented by a neuron in the input layer, and each neuron holds the corresponding input value.

**Hidden Layers**: The data moves from the input layer to the first hidden layer. Each neuron in the hidden layer performs a weighted sum of the inputs it receives from the previous layer (input or another hidden layer) and applies an activation function. The result is passed forward to the next layer.

**Activation Functions**: As the data flows through each neuron in the hidden layers, an activation function is applied to introduce non-linearity. The choice of activation function influences how well the network can learn complex patterns in the data. Popular activation functions include ReLU, sigmoid, and tanh.

**Output Layer**: Finally, after passing through all hidden layers, the data reaches the output layer. The output layer neurons compute the final predictions, and if necessary, apply a final activation function, such as softmax (for classification tasks) or no activation (for regression tasks). The output layer produces the final results, which are either class probabilities, continuous values, or any other form of prediction depending on the task.

## 2. Detailed Breakdown of Forward Propagation

To better understand how forward propagation works, let's walk through the detailed steps involved in the calculation at each layer:

Input Layer: The input layer is simply a collection of neurons that represent the raw data features. Suppose you have a dataset with 3 features $x_1, x_2, x_3$, and these are fed into the network. The input layer passes these values directly to the first hidden layer, without any computation or transformation.

$$\text{Input layer:} \quad x_1, x_2, x_3$$

**Hidden Layer Calculations**: Once the input data is passed to the hidden layer, each neuron in the hidden layer calculates a weighted sum of the inputs. The weighted sum for a neuron is computed as follows:

$$z = w_1 x_1 + w_2 x_2 + w_3 x_3 + b$$

Where:

- $w_1, w_2, w_3$ are the weights associated with each input $x_1, x_2, x_3$.
- $b$ is the bias term for the neuron, which allows the network to model more complex relationships.
- $z$ is the weighted sum.

The next step is to apply an **activation function** $f(z)$ to the weighted sum. This introduces non-linearity into the computation, allowing the network to model complex patterns. For example, if we use the **ReLU activation function**, we would compute:

$$a = \text{ReLU}(z) = \max(0, z)$$

This output $a$ is then passed to the next layer (either another hidden layer or the output layer). Each neuron in a hidden layer applies this process individually.

For multiple hidden layers, this process repeats: the output from one layer becomes the input to the next layer. For example, the output from the first hidden layer becomes the input for the second hidden layer.

**Output Layer**: Once the data reaches the output layer, the same weighted sum process occurs. However, the activation function used here depends on the nature of the task:

For binary classification, the output layer typically uses the sigmoid activation function, which outputs a probability value between 0 and 1.

$$y = \sigma(z) = \frac{1}{1 + e^{-z}}$$

For multi-class classification, the output layer uses the softmax function, which converts the raw scores (logits) into probabilities that sum to 1, representing the likelihood of each class.

$$\text{Softmax}(z_i) = \frac{e^{z_i}}{\sum_j e^{z_j}}$$

For regression tasks, there may be no activation function (or a linear activation), and the output would be a continuous value.

The final output from the output layer is the network's prediction for the given input data.

## 3. Matrix Representation of Forward Propagation

In practice, forward propagation is often expressed in matrix form for computational efficiency. For a network with multiple layers, the process involves performing matrix multiplications for each layer's calculations. This allows the model to handle large datasets efficiently, especially when training with batch processing.

For example, suppose the network has an input layer $X$ with multiple data points (a batch of inputs), weights $W$ for each layer, and biases $b$. The forward pass for a single layer in matrix form can be expressed as:

$$Z = XW + b$$

Where:

- $X$ is the input matrix, where each row represents a sample and each column represents a feature.
- $W$ is the weight matrix, which contains the weights for each neuron in the layer.
- $b$ is the bias vector, which is added to each neuron's calculation.

The output $Z$ is then passed through the activation function $f$, giving the activation $A$:

$$A = f(Z)$$

The process is repeated for each layer in the network until the final output is generated.

## 4. The Role of Activation Functions in Forward Propagation

As discussed earlier, activation functions play a key role in forward propagation by introducing non-linearity into the network. This enables the network to model more complex patterns and relationships than just linear transformations. The activation function applied to the weighted sum of inputs at each neuron determines the output of the neuron and influences how the network learns from the data.

Common activation functions include:

- **ReLU (Rectified Linear Unit):** Provides non-linearity by outputting zero for negative inputs and the input itself for positive values.
- **Sigmoid:** Squashes outputs between 0 and 1, making it ideal for binary classification tasks.
- **Tanh (Hyperbolic Tangent):** Squashes outputs between -1 and 1, often used in hidden layers.
- **Softmax:** Converts raw output values (logits) into probabilities for multi-class classification.

Each activation function has its own advantages and is chosen based on the problem at hand.

## 5. Summary of Forward Propagation

In summary, forward propagation is the process through which input data flows through the layers of a neural network to generate predictions. Here's a concise overview of the steps involved:

- The input data is passed into the network's input layer.
- Data flows through the hidden layers, where each neuron computes a weighted sum of inputs and applies an activation function.
- The process repeats layer by layer until the data reaches the output layer.
- The output layer generates the final predictions, applying an appropriate activation function based on the task (sigmoid, softmax, or none for regression).
- The result is the network's prediction or output.

Forward propagation is essential for making predictions once the network has been trained. Understanding how data flows through the network helps in building, debugging, and optimizing neural network models.

# 4.3. Backpropagation: Learning Through Error Correction

Backpropagation is the core algorithm that allows neural networks to learn from data and adjust their parameters (weights and biases) to minimize errors in predictions. Without backpropagation, a neural network would be unable to refine its model based on the feedback it receives from its predictions. It is a supervised learning method that works by calculating the gradient of the loss function with respect to each weight in the network, using this information to update the weights in the direction that reduces the loss.

This process is crucial for the network's learning because it enables the model to make gradual improvements in its performance by adjusting the weights and biases after each prediction. In this section, we will break down the concept of backpropagation, explain its key steps, and show how it helps the network learn from its mistakes.

## 1. The Goal of Backpropagation

The primary goal of backpropagation is to minimize the loss function, which measures the difference between the neural network's predicted output and the actual (true) output. The neural network is trained by updating its weights and biases to reduce the loss, thus improving its accuracy. Backpropagation helps determine how much each weight in the network contributed to the error, and it provides a way to adjust them effectively.

To achieve this, backpropagation calculates gradients (the partial derivatives of the loss function with respect to the weights) and uses them to adjust the weights and biases through an optimization technique like gradient descent. These steps are repeated iteratively, gradually decreasing the loss and improving the model's performance.

## 2. The Steps of Backpropagation

Backpropagation is typically broken down into two major phases: forward propagation and backward propagation.

### Step 1: Forward Propagation

In this first step, the data is passed through the network, as explained in the previous section on forward propagation. The input data is processed layer by layer until the network generates a prediction at the output layer. The output is compared to the true labels, and the loss (or error) is calculated using a loss function.

The loss function quantifies how far the network's prediction is from the true values. Common loss functions include mean squared error (MSE) for regression tasks and cross-entropy loss for classification tasks.

**For example:**

In a regression task, the loss function may be the mean squared error (MSE), defined as:

$$\text{MSE} = \frac{1}{n} \sum_{i=1}^{n} (y_{\text{true}} - y_{\text{pred}})^2$$

Where $y_{\text{true}}$ is the true value, $y_{\text{pred}}$ is the predicted value, and $n$ is the number of data points.

In a classification task, cross-entropy loss is typically used:

$$\text{Cross-Entropy Loss} = -\sum_{i=1}^{n} y_{\text{true}} \log(y_{\text{pred}})$$

Where $y_{\text{true}}$ represents the true labels (in one-hot encoded format), and $y_{\text{pred}}$ is the predicted probability of each class.

## Step 2: Backward Propagation

Once the forward pass is complete and the loss has been calculated, the next step is to propagate the error backward through the network to update the weights and biases. Backward propagation involves two key steps: calculating the gradients and updating the weights.

**Calculating Gradients (Partial Derivatives):** In backpropagation, we need to compute the gradient of the loss function with respect to each weight and bias in the network. This tells us how much each weight contributed to the error. The gradient is calculated using the chain rule from calculus.

The chain rule allows us to break down the calculation of the gradient of the loss with respect to each weight as a series of smaller steps. For each neuron, we calculate the derivative of the loss function with respect to the output of the neuron, and then multiply that by the derivative of the output with respect to the input (which involves the weights and activation function).

The gradient for a weight is the derivative of the loss function with respect to that weight, and it indicates how to change the weight to reduce the error. Mathematically, the gradient descent update rule for a weight $w$ is:

$$w \leftarrow w - \eta \cdot \frac{\partial \text{Loss}}{\partial w}$$

Where:

- $\eta$ is the **learning rate**, a hyperparameter that controls the size of the weight update.

- $\frac{\partial \text{Loss}}{\partial w}$ is the gradient of the loss function with respect to the weight.

By calculating these gradients for each weight and bias, the network can understand how each parameter should change to minimize the loss.

**Applying the Gradients**: Once the gradients have been computed, they are used to update the weights and biases through an optimization technique like gradient descent. The update rule for each weight involves subtracting a portion of the gradient (scaled by the learning rate) from the current value of the weight. This helps reduce the loss by gradually moving the weights in the direction that minimizes the error.

**The general update rule is:**

$$w = w - \eta \cdot \frac{\partial \text{Loss}}{\partial w}$$

Where:

- $w$ is the current weight.

- $\frac{\partial \text{Loss}}{\partial w}$ is the gradient of the loss function with respect to the weight.

- $\eta$ is the learning rate.

The biases are also updated similarly, with the gradient of the loss function with respect to each bias being computed and applied.

**Step 3: Repeating the Process**

The forward and backward propagation steps are repeated for each batch of data in the training set. After each pass through the network, the weights are updated based on the gradients, and the process continues for multiple epochs (iterations through the full training dataset). As the training progresses, the weights and biases converge to values that minimize the loss, and the neural network becomes better at making accurate predictions.

## 3. The Chain Rule: Core of Backpropagation

The chain rule in calculus is the key to backpropagation. It allows us to calculate the gradient of the loss function with respect to each parameter (weight or bias) in the network by breaking down the complex chain of functions involved in the calculation.

At each layer, we apply the chain rule to compute the gradient of the loss with respect to the parameters at that layer. Specifically, we use the following formula to compute the gradient of the loss with respect to a weight $w$ in a layer:

$$\frac{\partial \text{Loss}}{\partial w} = \frac{\partial \text{Loss}}{\partial a} \cdot \frac{\partial a}{\partial z} \cdot \frac{\partial z}{\partial w}$$

Where:

- $a$ is the output of the neuron (after applying the activation function).
- $z$ is the weighted sum before applying the activation function.
- The first term ($\frac{\partial \text{Loss}}{\partial a}$) represents how the loss changes with respect to the output of the neuron.
- The second term ($\frac{\partial a}{\partial z}$) is the derivative of the activation function, showing how the output changes with respect to the input.
- The third term ($\frac{\partial z}{\partial w}$) is simply the input value $x$, which tells us how the weighted sum depends on the weight.

## 4. Importance of Backpropagation in Training Neural Networks

Backpropagation allows the neural network to learn from its errors and adjust its parameters accordingly. This iterative process of forward and backward passes enables the network to progressively improve its ability to make accurate predictions.

**Efficiency**: By using the chain rule to calculate gradients, backpropagation allows the network to efficiently compute the necessary updates for each weight and bias, even in deep networks with many layers.

**Error Propagation**: One of the most powerful aspects of backpropagation is its ability to "propagate" the error backwards through the network. By doing so, the network can adjust all parameters, not just those in the output layer, making it capable of learning more complex patterns and representations.

Backpropagation is the cornerstone of neural network training, enabling the network to learn from its predictions by correcting errors. Through the process of calculating gradients and updating the weights using optimization techniques like gradient descent, backpropagation allows neural networks to improve their performance over time. Understanding backpropagation is crucial for designing and training deep neural networks, as it empowers the network to fine-tune its parameters to make accurate predictions and model complex patterns in data.

## 4.4. Vanishing & Exploding Gradients: Problems & Solutions

During the process of training deep neural networks, a significant challenge that arises is the issue of vanishing gradients and exploding gradients. These problems can severely hinder the network's ability to learn effectively and can lead to slow or failed convergence. Both problems occur during backpropagation and are tied to how gradients are propagated through the layers of a neural network. In this section, we will explore what vanishing and exploding gradients are, how they occur, why they are problematic, and the strategies used to mitigate or prevent them.

### 1. Vanishing Gradients: What It Is and Why It Happens

Vanishing gradients occur when the gradients of the loss function become extremely small as they are propagated backward through the network. This means that during backpropagation, the weight updates become very small, and as a result, the network's weights and biases hardly change. This leads to a very slow learning process, especially in deep neural networks with many layers.

The problem is most pronounced in networks with sigmoid or tanh activation functions. The key reason for vanishing gradients in these networks is the nature of their derivatives. These functions have a limited range of outputs (e.g., sigmoid outputs between 0 and 1, and tanh outputs between -1 and 1). When their derivatives are computed, they can be very small, particularly when the activation function is in the saturation region (close to 0 or 1 for sigmoid, or close to -1 or 1 for tanh). This results in gradients that shrink as they are propagated backward through each layer.

The chain rule used in backpropagation multiplies the gradients across each layer, and when the gradients are small, this multiplication results in exponentially smaller values as you move deeper into the network. By the time the gradients reach the initial layers, they can become so small that they are effectively zero, causing the model to stop learning.

## 2. Exploding Gradients: What It Is and Why It Happens

On the opposite end of the spectrum, exploding gradients occur when the gradients become extremely large during backpropagation. This typically happens when the derivatives of the activation functions or weights are too large, causing the gradients to grow exponentially as they are propagated back through the network. The exploding gradients problem can lead to numeric instability during training, where the weights may become too large, making the model's behavior unpredictable and difficult to optimize.

Exploding gradients are often observed in deep networks where weights are initialized too large, or in networks with ReLU activation functions. ReLU (Rectified Linear Unit) outputs values from 0 to infinity, and when gradients are propagated backward through ReLU units, they can accumulate large values, especially if weights are not initialized carefully. Similarly, recurrent neural networks (RNNs) are particularly susceptible to exploding gradients, especially in long sequences of data.

## 3. Why Vanishing & Exploding Gradients Are Problems

Both vanishing and exploding gradients pose significant challenges for training deep neural networks:

**Vanishing Gradients**: When the gradients become too small, the network cannot learn effectively. The weights and biases in the initial layers of the network may never be updated, meaning the network will fail to learn useful features from the input data. This can lead to very slow convergence and may cause the network to get stuck in a suboptimal state.

**Exploding Gradients**: When the gradients become too large, they cause the weights to grow uncontrollably, which can lead to unstable updates. This results in erratic weight changes that make the model fail to converge or cause numerical instability. In extreme cases, the weights may become NaN (not a number), halting the training process completely.

Both problems can occur in very deep networks, especially when using certain activation functions or inappropriate weight initialization methods. These issues are compounded by the fact that modern deep learning models are often quite large, with many layers and parameters, making them more prone to such gradient-related issues.

## 4. Solutions to Vanishing & Exploding Gradients

Several strategies have been developed to mitigate the effects of vanishing and exploding gradients. These strategies aim to ensure stable learning by controlling how gradients are propagated through the network and adjusting the architecture and training process.

## a. Weight Initialization Techniques

One of the most effective ways to combat both vanishing and exploding gradients is to initialize the weights of the network properly. If the weights are initialized too large, they may lead to exploding gradients; if they are initialized too small, vanishing gradients can occur.

**Xavier Initialization (Glorot Initialization):** For networks that use the sigmoid or tanh activation functions, Xavier initialization is a good choice. It initializes the weights with a distribution that considers the number of input and output units in the layer. This helps in maintaining a variance that is neither too large nor too small, reducing the risk of vanishing or exploding gradients.

**The weights are initialized according to:**

$$W \sim \mathcal{N}\left(0, \frac{2}{n_{in} + n_{out}}\right)$$

Where $n_{in}$ is the number of input units and $n_{out}$ is the number of output units.

**He Initialization:** For networks that use ReLU or its variants (like Leaky ReLU), He initialization is commonly used. It initializes the weights to have a variance that accounts for the fact that ReLU can output very large values, thus avoiding the issue of exploding gradients.

**The weights are initialized as:**

$$W \sim \mathcal{N}\left(0, \frac{2}{n_{in}}\right)$$

## b. Activation Function Choice

The choice of activation function significantly impacts the occurrence of vanishing or exploding gradients:

**ReLU and its variants (Leaky ReLU, Parametric ReLU):** ReLU is less prone to vanishing gradients compared to sigmoid or tanh. However, it can suffer from the "dying ReLU" problem (where neurons stop updating due to having zero gradients), which is addressed by using variants like Leaky ReLU, where a small slope is used for negative values, ensuring that the gradient is never exactly zero.

Swish Activation: Swish is a newer activation function that has been shown to mitigate both vanishing and exploding gradients in some cases. It is defined as $\text{Swish}(x) = x \cdot \sigma(x)$, where $\sigma(x)$ is the sigmoid function.

## c. Batch Normalization

Batch normalization is a technique that normalizes the activations of each layer to have zero mean and unit variance. By controlling the distribution of activations, batch normalization ensures that gradients do not vanish or explode as they are propagated back through the network. This method helps stabilize learning and improve the convergence rate, especially in very deep networks.

Batch normalization can be applied before or after the activation function and helps to mitigate both vanishing and exploding gradient problems by ensuring that the outputs of each layer are well-scaled and stable.

## d. Gradient Clipping

Gradient clipping is an effective technique for mitigating exploding gradients. When the gradients become too large, they are clipped to a predefined threshold before being used to update the weights. This ensures that the updates to the weights remain stable and prevents large, erratic changes.

Gradient clipping is often used in training recurrent neural networks (RNNs), where exploding gradients are a common issue due to long sequences.

## e. Skip Connections / Residual Networks

One of the most powerful architectural solutions to vanishing gradients is the use of skip connections, or residual networks (ResNets). Skip connections allow the gradient to flow directly through certain layers, bypassing intermediate layers. This helps gradients avoid becoming too small as they propagate back through the network.

In residual networks, each layer learns residual mappings (the difference between the input and output), making it easier for the network to learn identity mappings and improving training in very deep networks.

Vanishing and exploding gradients are critical issues that can hinder the training of deep neural networks. These problems arise from the behavior of gradients during backpropagation, and they can lead to slow or unstable learning. However, there are various solutions to address these challenges, such as proper weight initialization, choosing appropriate activation functions, using batch normalization, clipping gradients, and utilizing residual networks. By applying these techniques, deep learning practitioners can mitigate the effects of vanishing and exploding gradients, enabling more efficient and stable training of complex neural networks.

# 5. Activations & Loss Functions

Activation functions and loss functions are critical components that determine how a neural network learns and makes predictions. In this chapter, you will explore the role of activation functions, such as ReLU, Sigmoid, and Softmax, in introducing non-linearity to the model, allowing it to solve complex problems that linear models cannot. Additionally, you'll dive into the concept of loss functions, which measure how far a network's predictions are from the actual outcomes. You'll learn about popular loss functions like Mean Squared Error (MSE) and Cross-Entropy, and how they guide the network's learning process during training. By understanding these fundamental concepts, you'll be better equipped to design and optimize neural networks for a wide range of applications.

## 5.1. Role of Activation Functions in Neural Networks

Activation functions are a crucial component in the architecture of neural networks. They are mathematical functions that determine the output of a neuron in response to the input, and they play a vital role in enabling neural networks to model complex patterns in data. Without activation functions, a neural network would essentially be equivalent to a linear model, no matter how many layers it has, which would significantly limit its ability to perform complex tasks like image recognition, natural language processing, or time series forecasting.

In this section, we will delve into the role of activation functions, why they are necessary for deep learning models, and explore the different types of activation functions commonly used in neural networks.

### 1. What Are Activation Functions?

An activation function takes the weighted sum of the inputs to a neuron and applies a non-linear transformation to this sum. This transformation enables the neural network to capture and model complex, non-linear relationships between inputs and outputs. The output of the activation function determines whether the neuron should be activated, or fired, based on the input.

Mathematically, an activation function $f$ takes the input to a neuron $z$ (which is the weighted sum of inputs and biases) and returns an output $a$:

$$a = f(z)$$

The choice of activation function affects how the network learns, how it behaves during training, and the overall performance of the model.

## 2. The Necessity of Activation Functions

Without activation functions, the network would not be able to introduce non-linearity into the model. Consider a network where each layer applies only a linear transformation to its inputs. If every layer only performs a linear transformation, no matter how deep the network is, the entire network would still behave as if it were a single linear transformation.

For example, consider two linear layers in a network:

$$y = W_2 \cdot (W_1 \cdot x + b_1) + b_2$$

Here, $W_1$ and $W_2$ are weight matrices, $b_1$ and $b_2$ are biases, and $x$ is the input. If both transformations are linear, the composition of these two linear functions would still be a linear function. This severely limits the expressiveness of the model and its ability to solve complex tasks that involve non-linear relationships in the data.

Activation functions break this limitation by introducing non-linearity into the model, allowing it to learn more intricate patterns and relationships. This is why deep learning models rely heavily on activation functions to learn complex representations of the data.

## 3. Common Types of Activation Functions

There are several types of activation functions, each with its advantages and disadvantages. The choice of activation function depends on the problem at hand, the architecture of the network, and the nature of the data. Below are the most commonly used activation functions:

### a. Sigmoid Function (Logistic Function)

The sigmoid function is one of the earliest and simplest activation functions used in neural networks. It maps input values to a range between 0 and 1. Its formula is:

$$f(x) = \frac{1}{1 + e^{-x}}$$

Where $x$ is the input to the neuron.

**Pros:**

Sigmoid outputs values between 0 and 1, making it useful for models where the output needs to be interpreted as a probability (e.g., binary classification).
It is differentiable, which makes it suitable for backpropagation.

**Cons:**

- The sigmoid function suffers from the vanishing gradient problem, where gradients become very small for large positive or negative values of $x$, leading to slow or ineffective learning in deep networks.
- It is computationally expensive due to the exponential term.

**b. Tanh Function (Hyperbolic Tangent)**

The tanh function is similar to the sigmoid function but maps input values to a range between -1 and 1. Its formula is:

$$f(x) = \frac{e^x - e^{-x}}{e^x + e^{-x}}$$

**Pros:**

- Tanh is zero-centered, meaning it outputs values in the range (-1, 1), which can make optimization easier than the sigmoid function.
- It is differentiable, allowing it to be used in backpropagation.

**Cons:**

- Like the sigmoid function, tanh suffers from the vanishing gradient problem, where the gradients become very small for large input values, especially when the input is far from zero.

## c. Rectified Linear Unit (ReLU)

The ReLU activation function is one of the most popular activation functions used in modern neural networks. It outputs the input directly if it is positive; otherwise, it outputs zero. Its formula is:

$$f(x) = \max(0, x)$$

**Pros:**

- ReLU is computationally efficient because it only requires a thresholding operation, making it faster to compute than sigmoid and tanh.
- It has become the default activation function for many neural networks, particularly deep networks, due to its simplicity and efficiency.
- ReLU helps mitigate the vanishing gradient problem, as it does not saturate for positive values.

**Cons:**

- **Dying ReLU**: If a large number of neurons in a network have negative values for their inputs, they will always output zero, effectively "dying" and never updating during training. This issue can be addressed by using variants like Leaky ReLU.

## d. Leaky ReLU

Leaky ReLU is a variant of the ReLU function designed to address the "dying ReLU" problem. Instead of outputting zero for negative values, it allows a small, non-zero gradient. Its formula is:

$$f(x) = \begin{cases} x & \text{if } x > 0 \\ \alpha x & \text{if } x \leq 0 \end{cases}$$

Where $\alpha$ is a small constant (typically 0.01).

**Pros:**

- Leaky ReLU allows a small gradient when $x$ is negative, which helps prevent neurons from dying and allows for more stable training.

**Cons:**

- The choice of $\alpha$ is a hyperparameter that must be tuned for optimal performance.

### e. Softmax Function

The softmax function is often used in the output layer of classification networks, particularly when the network is tasked with multi-class classification. It converts the output values into a probability distribution over the classes, making the sum of the outputs equal to 1. Its formula is:

$$f(x_i) = \frac{e^{x_i}}{\sum_j e^{x_j}}$$

Where $x_i$ is the input to the $i$-th output neuron, and the denominator sums the exponential of all inputs.

**Pros:**

- Softmax outputs a probability distribution, which is useful for multi-class classification tasks where each class is mutually exclusive.

**Cons:**

- Softmax can be sensitive to the scale of the inputs, which can lead to numerical instability, especially when the input values are large.

### 4. Key Considerations for Choosing an Activation Function

Choosing the right activation function is crucial for the performance of a neural network. Some key considerations when selecting an activation function include:

- **Non-linearity**: The activation function must introduce non-linearity into the model to enable the network to learn complex patterns.
- **Gradient behavior**: Functions like ReLU are less prone to vanishing gradients, making them a popular choice for deep networks.

- **Computational efficiency**: ReLU and its variants are much more computationally efficient compared to sigmoid or tanh.
- **Task type**: For binary classification tasks, sigmoid might be a good choice for the output layer, while softmax is typically used for multi-class classification.

Activation functions play a vital role in enabling neural networks to learn complex patterns from data. They introduce the necessary non-linearity into the model, allowing it to solve problems that involve intricate relationships in the data. Choosing the right activation function is crucial for the success of a deep learning model, and understanding the characteristics and behaviors of different activation functions helps in selecting the best one for a given task.

## 5.2. Common Activation Functions: ReLU, Sigmoid, Tanh, Softmax

Activation functions are a cornerstone of deep learning architectures, allowing neural networks to model complex, non-linear relationships. In this section, we will focus on four of the most commonly used activation functions in neural networks: ReLU (Rectified Linear Unit), Sigmoid, Tanh (Hyperbolic Tangent), and Softmax. Each of these functions has unique properties, advantages, and limitations, and their use depends on the specific requirements of the model and task at hand.

### 1. Rectified Linear Unit (ReLU)

The ReLU function is one of the most widely used activation functions, especially in modern deep learning architectures. ReLU operates by applying a threshold to the input. If the input is positive, it returns the input value; if the input is negative, it outputs zero. Mathematically, it is expressed as:

$$f(x) = \max(0, x)$$

Where:

- $x$ is the input to the neuron.

**Advantages of ReLU:**

- **Non-linearity**: Despite being a simple threshold function, ReLU introduces non-linearity into the network, allowing it to learn complex patterns.
- **Computational Efficiency**: ReLU is computationally efficient because it involves only a simple comparison and is very fast to compute. It does not require exponentiation or division, unlike sigmoid or tanh.
- **Reduced Likelihood of Vanishing Gradients**: ReLU is less likely to suffer from the vanishing gradient problem, which is prevalent in other activation functions like sigmoid and tanh. This is because it does not saturate for positive values.

## Disadvantages of ReLU:

- **Dying ReLU Problem**: A major drawback of ReLU is the "dying ReLU" problem. When the input to a neuron is negative, ReLU outputs zero, which can lead to neurons that never activate and, therefore, do not contribute to learning. This problem can cause certain neurons to "die" and stop updating, reducing the capacity of the model.
- **Sensitive to Outliers**: Since ReLU is unbounded for positive values, very large input values can lead to large outputs, potentially destabilizing the training process.

## Variants of ReLU:

To address the dying ReLU problem, variants like Leaky ReLU and Parametric ReLU (PReLU) have been introduced. These variants allow a small, non-zero gradient for negative inputs, preventing neurons from becoming inactive.

## 2. Sigmoid Activation Function

The sigmoid function is one of the oldest activation functions, frequently used in early neural networks. It maps any input value to an output between 0 and 1, which is useful for problems where outputs need to be interpreted as probabilities. The sigmoid function is mathematically defined as:

$$f(x) = \frac{1}{1 + e^{-x}}$$

Where:

- $x$ is the input to the neuron.

- $e$ is Euler's number (approximately 2.718).

**Advantages of Sigmoid:**

- **Probability Interpretation**: Since sigmoid outputs values in the range (0, 1), it is commonly used for binary classification tasks where the output represents a probability that a given input belongs to a particular class.
- **Smooth Gradient**: Sigmoid has a smooth gradient, making it differentiable at all points, which is important for backpropagation during training.

**Disadvantages of Sigmoid:**

- **Vanishing Gradient Problem**: One of the main drawbacks of sigmoid is the vanishing gradient problem. For large positive or negative input values, the gradient of the sigmoid function becomes very small, leading to slow or ineffective learning, especially in deep networks. This occurs because the gradient of the sigmoid function is very small in the saturation regions (near 0 or 1).
- **Non-zero Centered**: Sigmoid outputs values between 0 and 1, which means its output is not zero-centered. This can lead to inefficient learning because, when gradients are backpropagated through layers, the updates to weights may be uneven, slowing down convergence.

### 3. Tanh (Hyperbolic Tangent) Function

The tanh (short for "hyperbolic tangent") function is similar to the sigmoid function, but it outputs values in the range of -1 to 1, instead of 0 to 1. The formula for tanh is:

$$f(x) = \frac{e^x - e^{-x}}{e^x + e^{-x}}$$

Where:

- $x$ is the input to the neuron.

**Advantages of Tanh:**

- **Zero-Centered**: Unlike the sigmoid function, tanh is zero-centered, meaning it outputs values in the range (-1, 1). This property can help with optimization since it ensures that the gradient will have both positive and negative values, leading to more balanced weight updates during backpropagation.

- **Smooth Gradient**: Like sigmoid, tanh has a smooth gradient and is differentiable, making it suitable for backpropagation in neural networks.

## Disadvantages of Tanh:

- **Vanishing Gradient Problem**: Despite being zero-centered, tanh suffers from the vanishing gradient problem. For large positive or negative values of $x$, the function saturates, and the gradients become very small. This can slow down or even stop training in deep networks.
- **Computational Complexity**: Tanh requires exponentiation, which makes it slightly more computationally expensive than ReLU.

## 4. Softmax Function

The softmax function is used primarily in the output layer of neural networks for multi-class classification problems. It converts the raw outputs (logits) of the network into a probability distribution, where the sum of the outputs equals 1. The formula for the softmax function is:

$$f(x_i) = \frac{e^{x_i}}{\sum_j e^{x_j}}$$

Where:

- $x_i$ is the raw output (logit) for the $i$-th class,

- The denominator sums the exponentials of all the logits, ensuring the output values lie between 0 and 1, forming a valid probability distribution.

## Advantages of Softmax:

- **Probability Distribution**: Softmax transforms the network's raw output values into probabilities, which makes it very useful for multi-class classification tasks where each class is mutually exclusive.
- **Interpretability**: The outputs of the softmax function can be interpreted as probabilities, making it easy to understand the likelihood of an input belonging to a particular class.

## Disadvantages of Softmax:

- **Sensitive to Input Scale**: Softmax is sensitive to the scale of the input values. If the logits are very large or very small, the function can become numerically unstable. This issue can be mitigated by normalizing the logits before applying softmax.
- **Requires Multi-class Setting**: Softmax is designed for multi-class classification tasks. It is not suitable for binary classification, where sigmoid would be a better choice.

## Summary of Key Differences

| Activation Function | Range of Output | Common Use Case | Advantages | Disadvantages |
| --- | --- | --- | --- | --- |
| ReLU | $[0, \infty)$ | Hidden layers in deep networks | Simple, efficient, mitigates vanishing gradient problem | Dying ReLU problem for negative values |
| Sigmoid | $(0, 1)$ | Binary classification | Smooth gradient, probability interpretation | Vanishing gradient problem, non-zero centered |
| Tanh | $(-1, 1)$ | Hidden layers in deep networks | Zero-centered, smoother gradients than sigmoid | Vanishing gradient problem, computationally expensive |
| Softmax | $(0, 1)$ | Multi-class classification | Converts raw scores to probabilities, useful for multi-class problems | Sensitive to input scale, not suitable for binary classification |

Each activation function serves a specific purpose in neural networks and should be selected based on the problem and the layer in which it is used. ReLU and its variants are commonly used for hidden layers due to their simplicity and efficiency, while sigmoid and tanh are often used when the output is expected to lie within a certain range, with sigmoid being ideal for binary classification. Softmax, on the other hand, is the go-to function for multi-class classification tasks, converting raw output scores into meaningful probabilities. Understanding the characteristics and limitations of these activation functions is key to building effective neural networks.

# 5.3. Loss Functions: MSE, Cross-Entropy, Hinge Loss

In neural networks and deep learning, the loss function (also called the cost function) is a fundamental concept that quantifies how well the model's predictions align with the actual labels in the training data. The purpose of a loss function is to guide the training process by providing feedback that helps the model adjust its parameters (weights and biases). The goal of training a neural network is to minimize the loss function, thereby improving the model's accuracy or performance.

This section will explore three commonly used loss functions: Mean Squared Error (MSE), Cross-Entropy Loss, and Hinge Loss. Each loss function is suited to different types of machine learning tasks, such as regression or classification.

## 1. Mean Squared Error (MSE)

Mean Squared Error (MSE) is one of the most widely used loss functions, particularly for regression problems. It measures the average squared difference between the predicted values and the actual values. MSE is effective in penalizing large errors more than small ones, which makes it highly sensitive to outliers.

**Mathematical Definition of MSE:**

$$\text{MSE} = \frac{1}{n} \sum_{i=1}^{n} (y_i - \hat{y}_i)^2$$

Where:

- $y_i$ is the actual value (ground truth),

- $\hat{y}_i$ is the predicted value from the model,

- $n$ is the total number of data points.

**Advantages of MSE:**

- **Simple and Intuitive**: MSE is easy to understand and straightforward to compute, making it a natural choice for regression tasks.
- **Differentiable**: MSE is continuously differentiable, which is important for gradient-based optimization methods like gradient descent. This allows for smooth updates to model parameters during training.
- **Penalizes Large Errors**: Because it squares the error, MSE heavily penalizes large deviations between the predicted and actual values, which is useful in many real-world applications where large errors are particularly undesirable.

**Disadvantages of MSE:**

- **Sensitivity to Outliers**: MSE is very sensitive to outliers. A small number of large errors can disproportionately affect the overall loss, leading to model performance that is skewed by these outliers.
- **Not Robust in Certain Scenarios**: For problems where data has non-Gaussian noise or the errors are not symmetrically distributed, MSE may not be the most effective loss function.

**Use Case:**

- **Regression Tasks**: MSE is most commonly used in regression problems, where the goal is to predict continuous values (e.g., predicting house prices, stock prices, etc.).

## 2. Cross-Entropy Loss

Cross-Entropy Loss is the most common loss function used for classification problems, particularly in tasks where the model outputs probabilities (e.g., through a Softmax activation function). It measures the difference between two probability distributions: the predicted probability distribution (output of the model) and the true distribution (the true labels).

For binary classification, where each input has one of two possible classes (e.g., 0 or 1), binary cross-entropy is used. For multi-class classification, categorical cross-entropy is used.

**Mathematical Definition of Cross-Entropy Loss:**

For binary classification, the binary cross-entropy loss function is given by:

$$\text{Binary Cross-Entropy} = -\frac{1}{n} \sum_{i=1}^{n} [y_i \cdot \log(\hat{y}_i) + (1 - y_i) \cdot \log(1 - \hat{y}_i)]$$

Where:

- $y_i$ is the true label (either 0 or 1),

- $\hat{y}_i$ is the predicted probability of class 1,

- $n$ is the total number of data points.

For multi-class classification, the categorical cross-entropy loss is computed as:

$$\text{Categorical Cross-Entropy} = -\frac{1}{n}\sum_{i=1}^{n}\sum_{c=1}^{C} y_{ic} \cdot \log(\hat{y}_{ic})$$

Where:

- $y_{ic}$ is 1 if the $i$-th example belongs to class $c$, and 0 otherwise,
- $\hat{y}_{ic}$ is the predicted probability of class $c$,
- $C$ is the number of classes.

**C is the number of classes.**

**Advantages of Cross-Entropy Loss:**

- **Probabilistic Interpretation**: Cross-entropy loss provides a clear interpretation by measuring how well the predicted probabilities match the actual class labels.
- **Effective for Classification**: It is designed specifically for classification tasks, and it works well with softmax or sigmoid outputs, where the goal is to predict the probability of each class.
- **Sensitive to Confident Misclassifications**: Cross-entropy loss punishes wrong predictions more severely if the model is confident about them. For example, if the model outputs a very high probability for the wrong class, the loss will be significantly larger than for a less confident misprediction.

**Disadvantages of Cross-Entropy Loss:**

- **Sensitive to Misclassification**: Cross-entropy loss is highly sensitive to incorrect confident predictions, which can lead to large gradients and potentially unstable training if not handled properly.
- **Requires Probabilities**: Cross-entropy loss assumes that the model outputs probabilities, meaning that the model must use activation functions like sigmoid or softmax that produce probability distributions.

**Use Case:**

- **Classification Tasks**: Cross-entropy loss is used extensively for classification problems, both for binary and multi-class classification tasks (e.g., image classification, text classification, etc.).

## 3. Hinge Loss

Hinge Loss is primarily used in Support Vector Machines (SVMs), but it can also be applied to neural networks in classification problems. It is a loss function that helps the model achieve large margins between classes. Hinge loss is particularly useful for binary classification tasks with the output of the model being either 1 or -1 (often encoded as -1 for one class and 1 for the other).

### Mathematical Definition of Hinge Loss:

For binary classification with true labels $y \in \{-1, +1\}$ and predicted scores $f(x)$, hinge loss is given by:

$$\text{Hinge Loss} = \frac{1}{n} \sum_{i=1}^{n} \max(0, 1 - y_i \cdot f(x_i))$$

Where:

- $y_i$ is the true label (either -1 or 1),

- $f(x_i)$ is the predicted score for the $i$-th example (before applying the sign function).

### Advantages of Hinge Loss:

- **Large Margin Optimization**: Hinge loss encourages the model to create a large margin between the classes, which can lead to better generalization and more robust models.
- **Effective for SVMs**: Hinge loss is specifically designed for SVMs and is effective when working with linear classifiers.
- **Penalty for Incorrect Predictions**: The hinge loss is zero when the model's prediction is correct and the margin is greater than 1. If the margin is smaller or the prediction is incorrect, the loss increases.

### Disadvantages of Hinge Loss:

- **Not Probabilistic**: Unlike cross-entropy loss, hinge loss does not provide a probabilistic interpretation of the output, which may not be suitable for problems that require probability estimates (e.g., when the model needs to give the probability of a class).

- **Sensitive to Margin**: The hinge loss is particularly sensitive to the margin, and tuning the margin can be challenging.

## Use Case:

**Binary Classification with Linear SVMs**: Hinge loss is commonly used in linear SVMs and is applied when the task requires creating a decision boundary with a large margin, such as in text classification or image classification tasks with linear models.

## Summary of Loss Functions

| Loss Function | Use Case | Mathematical Form | Advantages | Disadvantages |
|---|---|---|---|---|
| Mean Squared Error | Regression | $\frac{1}{n}\sum_{i=1}^{n}(y_i - \hat{y}_i)^2$ | Simple, differentiable, penalizes large errors | Sensitive to outliers, not ideal for non-Gaussian data |
| Cross-Entropy Loss | Binary or Multi-class Classification | Binary: $-\frac{1}{n}\sum_{i=1}^{n}[y_i \log(\hat{y}_i) + (1 - y_i)\log(1 - \hat{y}_i)]$ | Probability interpretation, effective for classification | Sensitive to confident misclassifications, requires probabilities |
| Hinge Loss | Binary Classification with Linear SVMs | $\frac{1}{n}\sum_{i=1}^{n}\max(0, 1 - y_i f(x_i))$ | Large margin optimization, works well with SVMs | Not probabilistic, margin-sensitive |

The choice of loss function is fundamental to the success of a neural network model. MSE is ideal for regression tasks, while cross-entropy loss is the go-to choice for classification tasks, particularly those that involve probabilistic outputs. Hinge loss is useful in SVMs and other linear classifiers that aim to maximize the margin between classes. Understanding the strengths and weaknesses of each loss function helps in selecting the most appropriate one for a given problem and can significantly impact the performance and generalization ability of the model.

## 5.4. Choosing the Right Activation & Loss Function for a Task

The selection of appropriate activation functions and loss functions plays a crucial role in the success of training neural networks. The right choice can accelerate convergence, improve model performance, and lead to better generalization. In contrast, poor choices can lead to issues such as slow training, overfitting, underfitting, or poor predictive accuracy. This section aims to guide you in choosing the right activation and loss functions based on the type of task you're tackling.

### 1. Task Type: Regression vs. Classification

The first step in choosing the right activation and loss function is to identify the type of machine learning task you are solving: regression or classification.

- **Regression Tasks**: These tasks involve predicting a continuous value. For example, predicting house prices, temperatures, or stock prices.
- **Classification Tasks**: These tasks involve predicting discrete class labels. For example, classifying images as either cats or dogs, or classifying emails as spam or non-spam.

### Activation Functions for Regression

**Linear Activation**: In regression tasks, especially when predicting continuous values, the linear activation function is commonly used in the output layer. The linear activation function allows the network to output any real value without any transformation, which is appropriate for regression where the output isn't limited to a specific range. For example, when predicting the price of a house, you want the model to be able to output a continuous range of values, so a linear activation is a natural choice.

**ReLU (Rectified Linear Unit):** While ReLU is typically used in hidden layers, it can also be used in the output layer for some regression tasks, particularly if the predicted value is always positive. For example, predicting the number of people visiting a website (which can't be negative) can be modeled using a ReLU output.

### Loss Functions for Regression

**Mean Squared Error (MSE):** MSE is the most widely used loss function for regression tasks. It computes the square of the difference between the predicted value and the true value, penalizing large errors more heavily. MSE is useful when you want the model to minimize the magnitude of errors and is most commonly used when the target variable follows a Gaussian (normal) distribution.

**Mean Absolute Error (MAE):** MAE is another loss function for regression tasks that calculates the absolute difference between predicted and actual values. While MSE penalizes large errors more heavily, MAE is less sensitive to outliers and is useful in cases where the data contains noisy or extreme values. It is often used when you want to treat all errors equally regardless of magnitude.

## Activation Functions for Classification

**Sigmoid Activation**: For binary classification problems (tasks where the goal is to predict one of two classes), the sigmoid activation function is commonly used in the output layer. The sigmoid function squashes the output into the range [0, 1], interpreting it as the probability of the positive class. This makes it suitable for tasks such as spam classification or medical diagnosis (e.g., predicting whether a tumor is malignant or benign).

**Softmax Activation**: For multi-class classification problems (where there are more than two possible classes), the softmax activation function is typically used in the output layer. Softmax converts the raw output scores (logits) into a probability distribution over the classes. The model's predicted class corresponds to the class with the highest probability. Softmax is commonly used in problems like image classification (e.g., recognizing handwritten digits or classifying images of animals).

## Loss Functions for Classification

**Binary Cross-Entropy Loss**: For binary classification tasks, binary cross-entropy is the most appropriate loss function. This loss function measures the difference between the true binary labels and the predicted probabilities. It penalizes incorrect predictions, especially when the model is highly confident about the wrong prediction. This loss function is particularly suitable for tasks like email spam classification or predicting whether a customer will churn.

**Categorical Cross-Entropy Loss**: For multi-class classification tasks, categorical cross-entropy is used. It compares the true label (usually represented as a one-hot encoded vector) with the predicted probability distribution. This loss function is useful when the model outputs a probability for each class, and the goal is to maximize the likelihood of the correct class.

**Activation Functions for Specialized Tasks**

**Tanh (Hyperbolic Tangent):** The tanh function is often used in tasks that require outputs within a bounded range, specifically between -1 and 1. It's commonly used in hidden layers of neural networks. While not typically used in the output layer for regression, it can be beneficial for certain tasks like generative models or reinforcement learning where the output needs to be constrained within this range.

**ReLU and Variants (Leaky ReLU, Parametric ReLU, ELU):** In deep learning models, ReLU and its variants are used in the hidden layers of the network. These activation functions help to introduce non-linearity, enabling the network to learn more complex patterns. Leaky ReLU allows a small gradient when the input is negative, which helps alleviate the vanishing gradient problem. Exponential Linear Unit (ELU) also helps to avoid the vanishing gradient issue and has the advantage of faster convergence compared to standard ReLU.

### 2. Task-Specific Considerations

Beyond simply knowing whether your task is a regression or classification problem, other considerations can affect your choice of activation and loss function. Let's look at some of these factors:

### Imbalanced Data

If you are working with imbalanced datasets (where one class has significantly fewer examples than the others), cross-entropy loss might not always be the best option as it can be biased toward the majority class. In such cases, you may need to use weighted loss functions, where the loss is adjusted to give more importance to the minority class, or you can use other strategies like oversampling or undersampling.

### Multilabel Classification

In multilabel classification, where each input can belong to multiple classes simultaneously (e.g., tagging an image with multiple labels like "cat," "animal," and "cute"), you should use binary cross-entropy for each class instead of categorical cross-entropy. Each label is treated as a separate binary classification task.

### Regression with Constraints

If your regression task involves predicting values with specific constraints (such as predicting probabilities or counts), it might be useful to apply ReLU activation to the output layer to ensure that the predictions are non-negative. If the output must fall within a specific range, you can use sigmoid activation (for a range between 0 and 1) or a scaled sigmoid for a broader range.

## 3. Conclusion: Matching Functions to Tasks

In summary, the choice of activation and loss functions is critical to the success of your neural network model. Here are some general guidelines for selecting the appropriate functions based on the task:

| Task Type | Activation Function | Loss Function |
| --- | --- | --- |
| Regression | Linear (Output Layer) | Mean Squared Error (MSE), Mean Absolute Error (MAE) |
| Binary Classification | Sigmoid (Output Layer) | Binary Cross-Entropy Loss |
| Multi-Class Classification | Softmax (Output Layer) | Categorical Cross-Entropy Loss |
| Multilabel Classification | Sigmoid (Output Layer) for each label | Binary Cross-Entropy for each label |
| Specialized Tasks (e.g., Generative Models) | Tanh, ELU, or ReLU (Hidden Layers) | Depends on specific model architecture |

It's essential to experiment and adapt based on the characteristics of your dataset and the complexity of the task. As you progress in your deep learning journey, you will gain a better understanding of the nuances of different activation and loss functions and how they affect the performance of your models.

# 6. Optimization Techniques

Optimization is at the heart of training neural networks, helping them learn faster and more effectively. In this chapter, you'll discover various optimization techniques that fine-tune the parameters of your network for better performance. Starting with the foundational Gradient Descent algorithm, you'll explore its variants, such as Stochastic Gradient Descent (SGD), Momentum, and Adam, each offering unique advantages for different types of problems. The chapter explains how these algorithms adjust learning rates, avoid local minima, and improve the speed and accuracy of the training process. By understanding these optimization techniques, you'll gain the tools to train efficient and high-performing neural networks.

## 6.1. Introduction to Optimization in Neural Networks

Optimization is the backbone of training neural networks, as it is the process through which the network learns and improves. The goal of optimization is to adjust the network's parameters—its weights and biases—to minimize the error or loss function. In this way, optimization techniques ensure that the neural network learns from its mistakes, progressively improving its performance over time.

Without optimization, neural networks would be unable to generalize well to new, unseen data. The right optimization techniques make it possible for neural networks to find the optimal values for their parameters and minimize the loss function efficiently, ultimately leading to better model performance.

This section will explore the fundamental concepts and methods involved in optimizing neural networks, providing a foundation for more advanced topics such as gradient descent, stochastic gradient descent, and modern optimization algorithms.

### 1. What is Optimization?

At its core, optimization is the process of finding the best possible parameters (weights and biases) that minimize a given objective function, typically the loss function. In the context of neural networks, this process involves adjusting the model's parameters to reduce the difference between its predictions and the actual outputs (i.e., the loss).

The loss function quantifies the model's performance. Common loss functions include:

- Mean Squared Error (MSE) for regression tasks,
- Cross-Entropy Loss for classification tasks,

Hinge Loss for classification with margin-based methods like Support Vector Machines. To optimize a neural network, we aim to minimize the loss function by adjusting the model's parameters, a process known as training.

## 2. Gradient Descent: The Core of Optimization

The most widely used optimization technique in deep learning is Gradient Descent. This iterative optimization algorithm works by calculating the gradient (i.e., the derivative) of the loss function with respect to each parameter and adjusting the parameters in the direction that reduces the loss.

### How Gradient Descent Works:

- **Initialize Parameters**: Start with random initial values for the weights and biases of the network.
- **Compute Gradients**: Use backpropagation to compute the gradient of the loss function with respect to each parameter.
- **Update Parameters**: Adjust the parameters by moving in the direction opposite to the gradient (since we are minimizing the loss). The size of the step taken is determined by the learning rate.
- **Repeat**: This process is repeated for multiple iterations or until the loss converges to a minimum value.

The key idea behind gradient descent is that it uses the information about the slope (gradient) to guide the model's parameters toward the optimal values that minimize the loss function.

### Mathematical Formula for Gradient Descent:

Given a loss function $L(\theta)$, where $\theta$ represents the model's parameters, the gradient descent update rule is:

$$\theta_{new} = \theta_{old} - \eta \cdot \nabla_\theta L(\theta)$$

Where:

- $\theta_{old}$ are the current parameter values,
- $\eta$ is the learning rate (step size),
- $\nabla_\theta L(\theta)$ is the gradient of the loss function with respect to the parameters.

## 3. Types of Gradient Descent

While standard gradient descent is widely used, there are several variations that differ in how they compute and update the gradients. These variations help improve convergence speed and stability in training neural networks.

**Batch Gradient Descent (BGD):** In batch gradient descent, the gradient is computed using the entire dataset. This approach can be very slow, especially with large datasets, because it requires processing the whole dataset at each iteration. However, it provides an accurate estimate of the gradient and often leads to more stable convergence.

**Stochastic Gradient Descent (SGD):** Unlike batch gradient descent, stochastic gradient descent computes the gradient using only one randomly chosen data point at each iteration. This makes SGD much faster and capable of handling large datasets efficiently. However, it introduces more variance in the gradient estimates, leading to noisier updates and less stable convergence.

**Mini-Batch Gradient Descent:** This approach is a compromise between batch gradient descent and SGD. In mini-batch gradient descent, the gradient is computed using a small subset of data (a mini-batch) instead of the entire dataset or a single data point. Mini-batch gradient descent combines the advantages of both methods by reducing computation time and providing more stable convergence than pure SGD.

## 4. The Role of the Learning Rate

The learning rate is a crucial hyperparameter that determines the size of the steps taken during each update in the gradient descent process. A learning rate that is too large may cause the optimization to overshoot the minimum, leading to instability and poor performance. On the other hand, a learning rate that is too small can slow down convergence, requiring many more iterations to reach the optimal solution.

To optimize training, it is important to choose an appropriate learning rate, and in some cases, to use learning rate schedules or adaptive learning rates to adjust the learning rate during training based on the progress.

## 5. Optimization Challenges

Optimizing neural networks is not without its challenges. Several factors can complicate the optimization process:

**Local Minima and Saddle Points**: In high-dimensional spaces, the loss function may have many local minima or saddle points (points where the gradient is zero, but they are not minima). Gradient descent can get stuck at these points, resulting in suboptimal solutions. This is particularly problematic for deep networks with many layers, where the loss surface is highly complex.

**Vanishing and Exploding Gradients**: In deep networks, gradients can become very small (vanishing gradients) or very large (exploding gradients) as they propagate back through the layers during training. Vanishing gradients can cause the network to stop learning, while exploding gradients can lead to instability and overflow in the parameter updates.

**Overfitting**: As the network gets better at minimizing the loss on the training data, it may start overfitting—learning patterns that are specific to the training data but do not generalize well to new, unseen data. Overfitting can be mitigated using techniques such as regularization, dropout, or early stopping.

## 6. Advanced Optimization Algorithms

To address some of the challenges posed by gradient descent, several more advanced optimization algorithms have been developed. These include:

**Momentum**: Momentum is a technique that accelerates gradient descent by adding a fraction of the previous update to the current update. This helps smooth out the optimization process and speeds up convergence.

**Adagrad**: Adagrad adapts the learning rate based on the historical gradient information. It increases the learning rate for parameters that have infrequent updates and decreases it for parameters that are updated frequently, leading to better performance in some cases.

**RMSprop**: RMSprop is an extension of Adagrad that includes a moving average of the squared gradients to maintain a more stable and consistent learning rate. This algorithm is well-suited for non-stationary objectives, such as in training recurrent neural networks (RNNs).

**Adam (Adaptive Moment Estimation):** Adam combines the benefits of momentum and RMSprop. It adapts the learning rate for each parameter and includes momentum to accelerate convergence. Adam is one of the most popular optimization algorithms and is widely used in deep learning tasks due to its efficiency and ease of use.

Optimization is a key component of neural network training. Gradient descent and its variants provide a powerful way to adjust model parameters based on the loss function. However, challenges like local minima, vanishing gradients, and overfitting can complicate the optimization process. Advanced optimization algorithms like Adam, RMSprop, and momentum help address these issues and ensure that the network converges quickly and effectively.

In practice, selecting the right optimization technique, tuning the learning rate, and understanding the specific challenges of your model will be critical to achieving good performance and ensuring that your neural network learns effectively. The next sections will dive deeper into these optimization methods and how to apply them effectively in real-world deep learning problems.

# 6.2. Gradient Descent & Its Variants (SGD, Momentum, NAG)

Optimization is the process through which neural networks "learn" from data by minimizing the loss function. The most widely used optimization technique for training deep learning models is Gradient Descent. However, the basic form of gradient descent—Stochastic Gradient Descent (SGD)—and its variants, such as Momentum and Nesterov Accelerated Gradient (NAG), play a crucial role in speeding up training, improving convergence, and dealing with issues like vanishing gradients and local minima.

In this section, we will explore Gradient Descent and its variants in detail, highlighting how they work and their advantages over standard gradient descent.

## 1. Basics of Gradient Descent (GD)

At the core of neural network optimization, Gradient Descent (GD) is an iterative algorithm used to minimize a loss function. The objective is to adjust the model's parameters (weights and biases) by moving them in the opposite direction of the gradient of the loss function.

**The general procedure involves:**

**Calculating the Gradient**: The gradient of the loss function is calculated with respect to the model's parameters. This gradient points in the direction of the steepest ascent, so to minimize the loss function, we need to update the parameters in the opposite direction.

**Updating the Parameters**: The parameters are updated based on the learning rate ($\eta$) and the gradient computed at the current iteration:

$$\theta_{new} = \theta_{old} - \eta \cdot \nabla_\theta L(\theta)$$

where:

- $\theta_{new}$ is the updated parameter,

- $\theta_{old}$ is the current parameter,

- $\eta$ is the learning rate, and

- $\nabla_\theta L(\theta)$ is the gradient of the loss function with respect to the parameters.

The basic gradient descent can be categorized into three types based on how the gradient is computed:

**Batch Gradient Descent (BGD):** The gradient is computed using the entire training dataset. While this leads to more stable and precise updates, it can be computationally expensive and slow for large datasets.

**Stochastic Gradient Descent (SGD):** In SGD, the gradient is calculated using a single random data point from the training dataset. This makes SGD faster but introduces a lot of noise, leading to more fluctuation in the updates.

**Mini-Batch Gradient Descent**: This is a compromise between BGD and SGD. The gradient is computed on a small, randomly selected subset of the data (mini-batch), balancing the efficiency of SGD and the stability of BGD.

## 2. Stochastic Gradient Descent (SGD)

Stochastic Gradient Descent (SGD) is the most commonly used variant of gradient descent, particularly in deep learning. Unlike batch gradient descent, which computes the gradient over the entire training dataset, SGD computes the gradient using a single data point at each iteration. This makes the algorithm much faster and capable of handling large datasets, but it can also result in noisy updates due to the inherent variance in estimating the gradient from just one data point.

**Advantages of SGD:**

- **Faster Updates**: Since the gradient is computed using a single sample, each update is much faster than in batch gradient descent.
- **Memory Efficient**: SGD requires less memory because it doesn't need to store the entire dataset in memory at once.

However, the noisy updates in SGD can make the convergence path much more erratic. This means that the algorithm might not directly converge to the global minimum, and might instead "oscillate" around the optimal value, which can delay convergence.

**Learning Rate**: The choice of learning rate is especially important for SGD. If the learning rate is too high, the updates can overshoot the minimum. If it is too low, the algorithm can take a long time to converge.

## 3. Momentum

Momentum is an optimization technique that aims to accelerate SGD by adding a fraction of the previous update to the current update. The idea is to use past gradients to smooth the updates, making the optimization process faster and more stable.

Momentum helps by allowing the algorithm to build up velocity in directions of consistent gradient and dampen oscillations in directions of less consistent gradient. This results in faster convergence and avoids the fluctuations caused by SGD.

**Mathematically, the momentum update rule is:**

$$v_t = \beta v_{t-1} + (1 - \beta)\nabla_\theta L(\theta)$$

$$\theta_t = \theta_{t-1} - \eta v_t$$

where:

- $v_t$ is the velocity at iteration $t$,

- $\beta$ is the momentum factor (usually close to 1, e.g., 0.9),

- $\nabla_\theta L(\theta)$ is the gradient of the loss function,

- $\eta$ is the learning rate,

- $\theta_t$ is the updated parameter.

**Advantages of Momentum:**

- **Faster Convergence**: Momentum helps accelerate convergence in directions where gradients are consistent and reduces oscillations where the gradient is noisy or changes direction.
- **Overcoming Local Minima**: By maintaining a "velocity" that carries the optimization through shallow local minima, momentum can help escape from poor local optima.
- **Stabilizing the Learning Process**: The inclusion of the previous update in the current one makes the optimization process smoother, reducing the instability seen in pure SGD.

**Disadvantages of Momentum:**

- **Requires Tuning**: The momentum term ($\beta$) must be carefully tuned. Too large a value can cause overshooting, while too small a value can make the updates too slow.

### 4. Nesterov Accelerated Gradient (NAG)

Nesterov Accelerated Gradient (NAG) is an improved version of momentum that introduces a correction step. Rather than applying momentum to the current parameters and then calculating the gradient, NAG first computes the gradient at the "look-ahead" position (i.e., the parameters adjusted by the momentum term) and then corrects the update.

**Mathematically, the NAG update rule is:**

$$v_t = \beta v_{t-1} + (1 - \beta)\nabla_\theta L(\theta + \beta v_{t-1})$$

$$\theta_t = \theta_{t-1} - \eta v_t$$

In this update, the gradient is calculated at the look-ahead position, taking into account the momentum from the previous step. This look-ahead step often leads to faster convergence than the traditional momentum method.

**Advantages of NAG:**

- **Faster Convergence**: By looking ahead and updating parameters based on future gradients, NAG can make more accurate updates, resulting in faster convergence.
- **Reduced Oscillations**: NAG can help reduce oscillations more effectively than momentum by providing a better estimate of the future gradient direction.

**Disadvantages of NAG:**

- **Computational Overhead**: NAG involves a slightly higher computational cost since it requires an additional gradient calculation at the "look-ahead" position.

## 5. Comparison Between SGD, Momentum, and NAG

| Optimization Algorithm | Description | Advantages | Disadvantages |
| --- | --- | --- | --- |
| SGD | Updates parameters using a single data point per iteration. | Faster than batch GD, efficient for large datasets. | Noisy updates, slow convergence, can get stuck in local minima. |
| Momentum | Adds a fraction of the previous update to smooth updates. | Speeds up convergence, reduces oscillations, escapes local minima. | Requires tuning of momentum factor. |
| NAG | Computes the gradient at the "look-ahead" position. | Faster convergence, reduces oscillations more effectively. | Computationally more expensive due to extra gradient computation. |

The choice of optimization algorithm can significantly impact the performance and efficiency of training a neural network. While SGD is a widely used baseline, Momentum and NAG offer significant improvements in terms of faster convergence and stability, especially in deeper networks or when dealing with large datasets.

In practice, NAG is often preferred over Momentum due to its superior performance in many scenarios. However, the choice of optimization method ultimately depends on the specific task, the architecture of the neural network, and the computational resources available.

In the following sections, we will explore more advanced optimization techniques and strategies, such as adaptive learning rates and optimizers like Adam, which combine the best features of these variants to further improve the training process.

## 6.3. Advanced Optimizers: Adam, RMSprop, AdaGrad

While Gradient Descent and its variants like SGD, Momentum, and Nesterov Accelerated Gradient (NAG) form the foundation of neural network optimization, more advanced optimizers have been developed to address some of the challenges encountered during training. These advanced optimizers, such as Adam, RMSprop, and AdaGrad, aim to improve the efficiency, speed, and stability of the learning process by adapting the learning rate based on the gradients.

In this section, we will explore three popular and powerful optimizers: Adam, RMSprop, and AdaGrad, detailing how they work, their advantages, and their specific use cases.

### 1. AdaGrad (Adaptive Gradient Algorithm)

AdaGrad is one of the earliest optimizers that adaptively adjusts the learning rate for each parameter. Unlike standard gradient descent, which uses a constant learning rate for all parameters, AdaGrad modifies the learning rate for each parameter based on its historical gradient.

The key idea behind AdaGrad is that it gives larger updates to parameters with small gradients and smaller updates to parameters with large gradients. This helps the model converge more efficiently by preventing large updates when gradients are steep, and increasing updates when gradients are small.

**How AdaGrad Works:**

AdaGrad stores the sum of the squared gradients for each parameter in a running accumulation, then uses this information to scale the learning rate for each parameter:

$$g_t = \nabla_\theta L(\theta) \quad \text{(the gradient of the loss function)}$$

$$r_t = r_{t-1} + g_t^2 \quad \text{(cumulative squared gradients)}$$

$$\theta_t = \theta_{t-1} - \frac{\eta}{\sqrt{r_t + \epsilon}} \cdot g_t$$

Where:

- $r_t$ is the sum of squared gradients up to time step $t$,

- $\epsilon$ is a small constant added for numerical stability,

- $\eta$ is the global learning rate,

- $\nabla_\theta L(\theta)$ is the gradient of the loss function with respect to the parameter $\theta$.

## Advantages of AdaGrad:

- **Adapts Learning Rate**: AdaGrad dynamically adjusts the learning rate, making it useful for sparse data or when certain features are more informative than others.
- **No Need for Manual Learning Rate Scheduling**: AdaGrad's adaptive nature means it does not require manual adjustment of the learning rate during training.

## Disadvantages of AdaGrad:

- **Rapidly Decaying Learning Rates**: While AdaGrad adapts the learning rate, its learning rate tends to decay too quickly, especially for tasks with a large number of iterations. This can lead to the optimizer becoming too conservative after a few updates, slowing down convergence.
- **Not Ideal for Non-Sparse Data**: AdaGrad works well when the data is sparse (e.g., natural language or certain types of image data), but may not be as effective for dense datasets.

## When to Use AdaGrad:

AdaGrad is often used for models where features have varying levels of importance, or in domains like natural language processing (NLP) or recommendation systems where data is sparse.

## 2. RMSprop (Root Mean Square Propagation)

RMSprop is an advanced optimization algorithm designed to overcome the problem of rapidly decaying learning rates in AdaGrad. Unlike AdaGrad, which accumulates all past gradients, RMSprop maintains a moving average of the squared gradients. This results in a more stable and consistent learning rate throughout the training process.

The idea behind RMSprop is to divide the learning rate for each parameter by the root of the moving average of its squared gradients, allowing the optimizer to adaptively adjust the learning rate in a way that improves convergence.

**How RMSprop Works:**

RMSprop updates the model's parameters as follows:

$$v_t = \beta v_{t-1} + (1 - \beta)g_t^2$$

$$\theta_t = \theta_{t-1} - \frac{\eta}{\sqrt{v_t + \epsilon}}g_t$$

Where:

- $v_t$ is the moving average of the squared gradients at time step $t$,

- $\beta$ is the decay factor (typically set to 0.9),

- $g_t$ is the gradient of the loss function with respect to the parameter $\theta$,

- $\eta$ is the learning rate,

- $\epsilon$ is a small constant for numerical stability.

**Advantages of RMSprop:**

- **Faster Convergence**: RMSprop's moving average of squared gradients prevents the rapid decay of the learning rate, allowing the model to converge faster and more consistently.

- **Adaptivity**: It adapts to the changing gradient information during training, which makes it especially useful for models trained on noisy or non-stationary data (e.g., in recurrent neural networks or reinforcement learning).

**Disadvantages of RMSprop:**

- **Sensitive to Hyperparameters**: RMSprop requires careful tuning of its hyperparameters, especially the learning rate $\eta$ and the decay factor $\beta$. If not tuned properly, it may still exhibit instability or slow convergence.
- **Relatively Complex:** While it's more advanced than AdaGrad, the algorithm introduces additional complexity compared to vanilla SGD or momentum-based methods.

**When to Use RMSprop:**

RMSprop is widely used in tasks that involve recurrent neural networks (RNNs) or reinforcement learning, where non-stationary gradients and high variance are common.

### 3. Adam (Adaptive Moment Estimation)

Adam is one of the most widely used and popular optimizers in deep learning. Adam combines the benefits of Momentum and RMSprop into a single optimization algorithm. It uses both the first moment (the mean) and the second moment (the uncentered variance) of the gradients to compute adaptive learning rates for each parameter.

By combining both momentum and adaptive learning rates, Adam provides efficient training that converges quickly and handles sparse gradients effectively.

**How Adam Works:**

Adam uses moving averages of the gradients and squared gradients to compute adaptive learning rates for each parameter:

1. **First moment (mean)**: $m_t = \beta_1 m_{t-1} + (1 - \beta_1)g_t$

2. **Second moment (uncentered variance)**: $v_t = \beta_2 v_{t-1} + (1 - \beta_2)g_t^2$

The parameter updates are then computed as:

$$\hat{m}_t = \frac{m_t}{1 - \beta_1^t} \quad \text{(bias correction for mean)}$$

$$\hat{v}_t = \frac{v_t}{1 - \beta_2^t} \quad \text{(bias correction for variance)}$$

$$\theta_t = \theta_{t-1} - \frac{\eta}{\sqrt{\hat{v}_t} + \epsilon}\hat{m}_t$$

Where:

- $m_t$ and $v_t$ are the first and second moment estimates at time $t$,

- $\beta_1$ and $\beta_2$ are the exponential decay rates for the moving averages (typically set to 0.9 and 0.999, respectively),

- $g_t$ is the gradient at time $t$,

- $\epsilon$ is a small constant for numerical stability.

## Advantages of Adam:

- **Efficient and Fast**: Adam adapts the learning rate for each parameter, improving both convergence speed and accuracy.
- **Handles Sparse Gradients Well**: Adam works well with sparse data, making it ideal for tasks like NLP, image classification, and more.
- **Less Memory Usage**: Compared to other optimizers like AdaGrad, Adam uses less memory and requires fewer parameters for updates.
- **Widely Used**: Adam is one of the most popular and robust optimizers in deep learning, often serving as the default choice for most neural network architectures.

## Disadvantages of Adam:

- **Sensitive to Hyperparameters**: While Adam works well in most cases, it is still sensitive to the choice of hyperparameters like learning rate, $\beta_1$, and $\beta_2$, and may not always work well without fine-tuning.

- **Can Overfit on Noisy Data**: Adam's adaptive learning rate can cause it to overfit, especially on small datasets or datasets with a lot of noise.

**When to Use Adam:**

Adam is a highly versatile optimizer that can be used for a wide range of deep learning tasks, from image recognition and text generation to reinforcement learning. It is particularly useful for models with large datasets and complex architectures, such as deep neural networks, CNNs, and RNNs.

## 4. Comparison Between Adam, RMSprop, and AdaGrad

| Optimizer | Main Advantage | Main Disadvantage | Best Use Case |
|---|---|---|---|
| AdaGrad | Adaptive learning rate based on historical gradients. | Learning rate decays too quickly. | Sparse data, NLP, and recommendation systems. |
| RMSprop | Moving average of squared gradients, preventing fast decay. | Sensitive to hyperparameters. | RNNs, reinforcement learning, and noisy data. |
| Adam | Combines Momentum and RMSprop, adapts learning rates for each parameter. | Sensitive to hyperparameters, may overfit with noisy data. | General-purpose deep learning, CNNs, RNNs, NLP tasks. |

The optimization techniques discussed in this chapter—AdaGrad, RMSprop, and Adam—are powerful tools for training deep learning models more efficiently and accurately. While each optimizer has its own strengths and weaknesses, Adam has become the go-to optimizer for most deep learning tasks due to its adaptability, speed, and stability. However, understanding when and why to use each optimizer is crucial for obtaining the best results in your specific use case.

In the next section, we will explore how to further improve model training with advanced techniques like learning rate schedules, weight decay, and early stopping.

# 6.4. Learning Rate Schedulers & Warm-up Strategies

Optimizing a neural network requires careful tuning of the learning rate—one of the most crucial hyperparameters that significantly affects model performance. Too high a learning rate may cause the model to diverge, while too low a learning rate can result in slow convergence. To address these challenges, learning rate schedulers and warm-up strategies are used to dynamically adjust the learning rate during training, improving both convergence speed and stability.

In this section, we will explore different learning rate scheduling techniques, the concept of warm-up strategies, and best practices for applying them to deep learning models.

## 1. Why Adjust the Learning Rate?

A fixed learning rate throughout training is often inefficient because:

- A high learning rate early in training helps the model make rapid progress.
- A lower learning rate later in training helps fine-tune the model and avoid overshooting the optimal solution.
- Some architectures require a gradual learning rate increase at the start to prevent unstable updates.

Thus, learning rate scheduling strategies allow us to adjust the learning rate dynamically to optimize training efficiency.

## 2. Learning Rate Schedulers

A learning rate scheduler is a function that adjusts the learning rate during training based on a predefined schedule. Several popular learning rate scheduling techniques are commonly used in deep learning:

### 2.1 Step Decay

Step decay reduces the learning rate at predefined intervals (e.g., after every few epochs). The learning rate is typically reduced by a constant factor (e.g., 0.1) at specific epochs.

$$\eta_t = \eta_0 \cdot \gamma^{\lfloor t/s \rfloor}$$

Where:

- $\eta_t$ is the learning rate at epoch $t$,

- $\eta_0$ is the initial learning rate,

- $\gamma$ is the decay factor (e.g., 0.1),

- $s$ is the step size (number of epochs before decay).

**Pros:**

- Simple to implement.
- Works well for models that benefit from sudden learning rate drops.

**Cons:**

- Sudden drops in learning rate may not always be optimal.
- Requires careful selection of decay steps.

**Use Case**: Common in classical deep learning architectures like ResNet.

### 2.2 Exponential Decay

Exponential decay continuously reduces the learning rate following an exponential function:

$$\eta_t = \eta_0 \cdot e^{-\lambda t}$$

Where:

- $\lambda$ is the decay rate, which controls how fast the learning rate decreases.

**Pros:**

- Provides a smooth, gradual reduction in learning rate.
- Helps prevent sudden drops that could disrupt training.

**Cons:**

- Needs careful tuning of $\lambda$ to avoid reducing the learning rate too quickly.

**Use Case**: Useful in scenarios where a steady decline in learning rate is beneficial, such as NLP tasks.

### 2.3 Cosine Annealing

Cosine Annealing gradually reduces the learning rate using a cosine function, allowing a smooth decay followed by restarts:

$$\eta_t = \eta_{\min} + \frac{1}{2}(\eta_{\max} - \eta_{\min})\left(1 + \cos\left(\frac{t}{T}\pi\right)\right)$$

Where:

- $\eta_{\max}$ and $\eta_{\min}$ are the maximum and minimum learning rates,

- $T$ is the total number of training steps.

**Pros:**

- Provides a cyclical learning rate reduction that can escape local minima.
- Allows for learning rate restarts, which can improve convergence.

**Cons:**

- Can be complex to tune properly.

**Use Case**: Effective for training deep networks with long training schedules, such as Transformer models.

### 2.4 ReduceLROnPlateau

Instead of using a predefined decay schedule, ReduceLROnPlateau monitors the validation loss and reduces the learning rate when improvements stagnate.

**Pros:**

- Automatically adapts learning rate based on model performance.
- Prevents unnecessary learning rate reductions when improvement is still occurring.

**Cons:**

- Requires proper patience setting (i.e., how many epochs to wait before reducing the learning rate).

**Use Case**: Works well in cases where loss plateauing is unpredictable, such as reinforcement learning.

### 3. Learning Rate Warm-up Strategies

While learning rate decay strategies focus on reducing the learning rate during training, learning rate warm-up does the opposite—it gradually increases the learning rate at the beginning of training.

### 3.1 Why Use Warm-up?

- Helps stabilize training at the start, especially for batch normalization models or Transformer-based architectures.
- Prevents large, unstable gradient updates when training begins.
- Useful when using adaptive optimizers like Adam.

### 3.2 Linear Warm-up

The learning rate increases linearly from a small value to a target learning rate over a predefined number of iterations.

$$\eta_t = \eta_{\text{init}} + t \cdot \frac{\eta_{\text{max}} - \eta_{\text{init}}}{T}$$

Where:

- $\eta_{\text{init}}$ is the initial learning rate,

- $\eta_{\text{max}}$ is the maximum learning rate,

- $T$ is the number of warm-up steps.

**Use Case**: Commonly used in Transformer models (e.g., BERT, GPT) to prevent instability in early training.

### 3.3 Exponential Warm-up

Exponential warm-up gradually increases the learning rate following an exponential function:

$$\eta_t = \eta_{\text{init}} \cdot e^{\lambda t}$$

This approach allows a more aggressive learning rate increase compared to linear warm-up.

**Use Case**: Effective for models that require rapid early adjustments.

### 4. Combining Warm-up & Learning Rate Schedules

For best results, learning rate warm-up is often combined with learning rate schedulers. A common approach is:

- **Warm-up phase**: Gradually increase the learning rate.
- **Training phase**: Apply step decay, cosine annealing, or ReduceLROnPlateau.

For example, Transformer models like BERT use linear warm-up followed by cosine decay.

### 5. Choosing the Right Learning Rate Strategy

The best strategy depends on your model and dataset:

| Scenario | Recommended Strategy |
| --- | --- |
| Small datasets, stable loss | Step Decay |
| Long training schedules, deep networks | Cosine Annealing |
| Unpredictable loss plateauing | ReduceLROnPlateau |
| Transformer-based models | Warm-up + Cosine Decay |
| Reinforcement learning | Exponential Decay or RMSprop |

Learning rate scheduling and warm-up strategies play a crucial role in optimizing deep learning models. Schedulers like step decay, cosine annealing, and ReduceLROnPlateau help models converge efficiently, while warm-up techniques prevent instability in early training. By choosing the right approach, you can significantly improve training stability, speed, and final model performance.

In the next section, we will explore regularization techniques to further enhance generalization and prevent overfitting.

# 7. Building a Neural Network from Scratch

In this chapter, you'll put everything you've learned into practice by building a simple neural network from the ground up. Using Python and NumPy, you will implement the key components of a neural network, including layers, activation functions, and backpropagation. Step by step, you'll create a fully functional network that can learn from data and make predictions, all without relying on high-level libraries like TensorFlow or PyTorch. This hands-on approach will deepen your understanding of how neural networks operate internally, providing you with the confidence to build and experiment with more complex models in the future.

## 7.1. Understanding the Neural Network Pipeline

Building a neural network from scratch requires a systematic approach that involves multiple stages, from data preprocessing to model evaluation. This structured workflow, known as the neural network pipeline, ensures that data flows efficiently through the network while allowing for effective learning. In this chapter, we will break down each stage of the pipeline, explaining how data is prepared, how the model is constructed, trained, and optimized, and how it is finally evaluated.

### 1. Overview of the Neural Network Pipeline

A complete neural network pipeline consists of the following stages:

- Data Collection & Preprocessing
- Dataset Splitting (Training, Validation, and Testing)
- Model Architecture Design
- Forward Propagation (Data Flow Through the Network)

### Loss Calculation

- Backward Propagation & Weight Updates
- Optimization & Hyperparameter Tuning
- Model Evaluation & Performance Metrics

### Deployment & Inference

Each of these stages plays a crucial role in ensuring the network learns effectively and generalizes well to unseen data. Let's explore each stage in detail.

## 2. Data Collection & Preprocessing

The first step in any machine learning project is data acquisition. Data can be collected from various sources, such as:

- Public datasets (e.g., ImageNet, MNIST, CIFAR-10)
- Web scraping and APIs
- Sensor data or real-time streaming sources

### 2.1 Data Cleaning

Raw data is often noisy, incomplete, or inconsistent. Data cleaning techniques include:

- Handling missing values (e.g., imputation, removal)
- Removing duplicate entries
- Normalizing text data (for NLP tasks)
- Fixing incorrect labels

### 2.2 Feature Scaling & Normalization

Neural networks perform better when numerical features are scaled to a consistent range. Common techniques include:

- **Min-Max Scaling**: Rescales features to a range [0,1] or [-1,1].
- **Standardization (Z-score normalization):** Converts data to have a mean of 0 and standard deviation of 1.
- **Log Transformation**: Useful for skewed data distributions.

### 2.3 Data Augmentation (for Image & Text Data)

For image and text-based neural networks, data augmentation helps artificially increase the dataset size by applying transformations such as:

- Image rotation, flipping, cropping, and color jittering
- Text synonym replacement, back-translation, and random word dropout

## 3. Dataset Splitting (Training, Validation, and Testing)

Once the data is preprocessed, it is split into three parts:

- **Training Set (70-80%)** – Used to train the neural network.
- **Validation Set (10-15%)** – Used to fine-tune hyperparameters and prevent overfitting.
- **Test Set (10-15%)** – Used to evaluate the final model's generalization ability.

## Why Split Data?

- The training set allows the model to learn.
- The validation set ensures hyperparameter tuning does not bias the final performance.
- The test set provides an unbiased estimate of model performance.

## 4. Model Architecture Design

Designing a neural network involves defining:

- **Number of Layers** – A simple feedforward network may have an input layer, one or more hidden layers, and an output layer.
- **Number of Neurons per Layer** – Too few neurons may underfit, while too many may overfit.
- **Activation Functions** – Common choices include ReLU, Sigmoid, Tanh, and Softmax.
- **Loss Function** – Chosen based on the task (e.g., cross-entropy for classification, mean squared error for regression).

## Example of a Simple Feedforward Neural Network

```
import tensorflow as tf
from tensorflow.keras.models import Sequential
from tensorflow.keras.layers import Dense

model = Sequential([
    Dense(64, activation='relu', input_shape=(input_dim,)),
    Dense(32, activation='relu'),
    Dense(output_dim, activation='softmax')  # Softmax for classification
])
```

## 5. Forward Propagation (Data Flow Through the Network)

Forward propagation refers to how input data flows through the neural network:

- Each neuron receives input data.
- The neuron processes the input using weights and biases.
- The activation function determines whether the neuron activates.
- The output is passed to the next layer.
- The final output is computed.

This process happens in every layer and ultimately produces an output prediction.

## 6. Loss Calculation

The model's predictions are compared against the actual values using a loss function. The loss quantifies how well (or poorly) the model is performing.

### Common loss functions:

- Classification: Cross-entropy loss
- Regression: Mean squared error (MSE)
- Ranking tasks: Hinge loss

### Example of computing loss:

*loss = tf.keras.losses.SparseCategoricalCrossentropy()*

## 7. Backpropagation & Weight Updates

After loss calculation, the model adjusts weights and biases using backpropagation:

- The gradient of the loss function is computed for each parameter.
- The optimizer (e.g., Adam, SGD) updates the weights accordingly.
- The model gradually improves by minimizing the loss.

### Gradient Descent in Action

*optimizer = tf.keras.optimizers.Adam(learning_rate=0.001)*
*model.compile(optimizer=optimizer, loss='categorical_crossentropy',*
*metrics=['accuracy'])*

## 8. Optimization & Hyperparameter Tuning

Hyperparameters such as the learning rate, batch size, and number of epochs need careful tuning.

**Common tuning techniques:**

- **Grid Search**: Tries all possible combinations.
- **Random Search**: Randomly selects hyperparameters.
- **Bayesian Optimization**: Uses probabilistic models to find the best set.

**Automated tuning example using KerasTuner:**

```
import keras_tuner as kt

def build_model(hp):
   model = Sequential([
      Dense(hp.Int('units', 32, 128, step=32), activation='relu'),
      Dense(10, activation='softmax')
   ])
   model.compile(optimizer='adam', loss='sparse_categorical_crossentropy',
metrics=['accuracy'])
   return model

tuner = kt.RandomSearch(build_model, objective='val_accuracy', max_trials=5)
```

## 9. Model Evaluation & Performance Metrics

Once training is complete, the model is evaluated using performance metrics:

- Accuracy, Precision, Recall, **F1-score** (for classification)
- Mean Squared Error (MSE), **R² Score** (for regression)
- Confusion Matrix, **ROC-AUC** (for imbalanced datasets)

**Example:**

```
from sklearn.metrics import classification_report

y_pred = model.predict(X_test)
```

*print(classification_report(y_test, y_pred))*

**10. Deployment & Inference**

Once trained, the model can be deployed using:

- **Flask/FastAPI** for web applications
- **TensorFlow** Serving for large-scale inference
- **Edge AI** Deployment for mobile & IoT devices

**Example Flask API:**

*from flask import Flask, request, jsonify*

*app = Flask(__name__)*

```
@app.route('/predict', methods=['POST'])
def predict():
    data = request.json['input']
    prediction = model.predict(data)
    return jsonify({'prediction': prediction.tolist()})

if __name__ == '__main__':
    app.run()
```

The neural network pipeline is a structured workflow that transforms raw data into a trained deep learning model. Each step—from data preprocessing to deployment—plays a critical role in ensuring efficient learning and accurate predictions. By mastering this pipeline, you can build, train, and deploy powerful AI models from scratch. In the next section, we will explore regularization techniques to further improve model performance and prevent overfitting.

# 7.2. Implementing a Simple Neural Network Using NumPy

Building a neural network from scratch using NumPy is a great way to understand the fundamental mechanics of deep learning. While frameworks like TensorFlow and PyTorch abstract many details, coding a neural network manually gives insight into forward propagation, backpropagation, and optimization techniques. In this section, we will implement a simple feedforward neural network with one hidden layer using only NumPy.

## 1. Understanding the Neural Network Structure

We will implement a basic neural network with:

- **Input layer**: Takes in features from the dataset.
- **Hidden layer**: Contains a set of neurons with activation functions.
- **Output layer**: Produces predictions based on input data.

**For this example, we will:**

- Train the network on a simple dataset.
- Use sigmoid activation for both hidden and output layers.
- Optimize weights using gradient descent.

## 2. Importing Dependencies

Since we are not using any deep learning frameworks, we only need NumPy for matrix operations.

*import numpy as np*

## 3. Generating Sample Data

We will create a small dataset with inputs (X) and corresponding binary outputs (Y).

*# Sample dataset: XOR problem*
*X = np.array([[0, 0], [0, 1], [1, 0], [1, 1]])  # Inputs*
*Y = np.array([[0], [1], [1], [0]])  # Expected outputs*

## 4. Initializing Weights and Biases

Weights and biases are crucial for determining how the network learns.

*# Set random seed for reproducibility*
*np.random.seed(42)*

*# Define layer sizes*

```
input_size = 2
hidden_size = 4
output_size = 1

# Initialize weights and biases
W1 = np.random.randn(input_size, hidden_size)  # Weights for input to hidden
b1 = np.zeros((1, hidden_size))  # Bias for hidden layer
W2 = np.random.randn(hidden_size, output_size)  # Weights for hidden to output
b2 = np.zeros((1, output_size))  # Bias for output layer
```

## 5. Defining Activation Functions

We will use the sigmoid function, which outputs values between 0 and 1.

```
def sigmoid(x):
    return 1 / (1 + np.exp(-x))

def sigmoid_derivative(x):
    return x * (1 - x)
```

## 6. Forward Propagation

In forward propagation, data flows through the network, and activations are computed.

```
def forward_propagation(X):
    global Z1, A1, Z2, A2
    Z1 = np.dot(X, W1) + b1  # Compute hidden layer linear transformation
    A1 = sigmoid(Z1)  # Apply activation
    Z2 = np.dot(A1, W2) + b2  # Compute output layer transformation
    A2 = sigmoid(Z2)  # Apply activation
    return A2
```

## 7. Backpropagation & Weight Updates

Backpropagation calculates the error gradient and updates weights.

```
def backpropagation(X, Y, learning_rate=0.1):
    global W1, b1, W2, b2

    # Compute output error
```

```
output_error = A2 - Y  # Difference between actual and predicted output
output_delta = output_error * sigmoid_derivative(A2)  # Apply derivative

# Compute hidden layer error
hidden_error = output_delta.dot(W2.T)
hidden_delta = hidden_error * sigmoid_derivative(A1)

# Update weights and biases
W2 -= A1.T.dot(output_delta) * learning_rate
b2 -= np.sum(output_delta, axis=0, keepdims=True) * learning_rate
W1 -= X.T.dot(hidden_delta) * learning_rate
b1 -= np.sum(hidden_delta, axis=0, keepdims=True) * learning_rate
```

## 8. Training the Neural Network

We train the network by repeatedly performing forward and backward propagation.

```
epochs = 10000
for epoch in range(epochs):
    forward_propagation(X)
    backpropagation(X, Y)

    # Print loss every 1000 epochs
    if epoch % 1000 == 0:
        loss = np.mean(np.abs(A2 - Y))
        print(f"Epoch {epoch}, Loss: {loss:.4f}")
```

## 9. Making Predictions

After training, we can test the network with new inputs.

```
predictions = forward_propagation(X)
print("Predictions after training:")
print(predictions.round())  # Rounding to get binary output
```

We successfully built and trained a simple neural network using NumPy. This exercise provides an intuitive understanding of forward propagation, backpropagation, and optimization. In the next section, we will explore regularization techniques to improve generalization and reduce overfitting.

## 7.3. Training the Network: Forward Pass, Backpropagation, and Weight Updates

Training a neural network involves three fundamental steps: forward propagation, backpropagation, and weight updates. These steps ensure that the network learns from its mistakes and improves over time. In this section, we will break down each step in detail and implement them using NumPy.

### 1. Overview of the Training Process

The training of a neural network follows these steps:

**Forward Propagation:**

- Data is passed through the network layer by layer.
- Neurons compute weighted sums and apply activation functions.
- The final layer outputs predictions.

**Loss Calculation:**

The difference between predictions and actual values is measured using a loss function. Backpropagation:

- The gradient of the loss function is computed with respect to each weight.
- The chain rule of calculus is used to propagate errors backward.

**Weight Updates:**

- Weights and biases are updated using gradient descent or other optimization algorithms.
- The learning process repeats over multiple epochs.

### 2. Forward Propagation: How Data Flows Through the Network

Forward propagation refers to the feedforward pass where input data moves through the network, producing outputs.

**Mathematical Formulation**

For a simple two-layer neural network:

**Compute the hidden layer activations:**

$$Z_1 = XW_1 + b_1$$

$$A_1 = \sigma(Z_1)$$

**Compute the output layer activations:**

$$Z_2 = A_1 W_2 + b_2$$

$$A_2 = \sigma(Z_2)$$

Where:

- $X$ is the input matrix.

- $W_1, W_2$ are weight matrices.

- $b_1, b_2$ are biases.

- $\sigma$ is the activation function (sigmoid in this case).

**Implementation in NumPy**

*import numpy as np*

```
# Activation function
def sigmoid(x):
    return 1 / (1 + np.exp(-x))

# Forward propagation function
def forward_propagation(X, W1, b1, W2, b2):
    Z1 = np.dot(X, W1) + b1
    A1 = sigmoid(Z1)
    Z2 = np.dot(A1, W2) + b2
    A2 = sigmoid(Z2)
    return Z1, A1, Z2, A2
```

## 3. Loss Calculation: Measuring Model Performance

The loss function measures the difference between the predicted and actual outputs.

**For binary classification, we use binary cross-entropy:**

$$L = -\frac{1}{N} \sum \left( Y \log(A_2) + (1 - Y) \log(1 - A_2) \right)$$

**Implementation in NumPy**

```
def compute_loss(Y, A2):
    m = Y.shape[0]
    loss = -np.sum(Y * np.log(A2) + (1 - Y) * np.log(1 - A2)) / m
    return loss
```

## 4. Backpropagation: Learning Through Error Correction

Backpropagation computes how much each weight and bias contributed to the error.

**Mathematical Formulation**

Using the chain rule, we compute gradients:

**Output layer gradients:**

$$dZ_2 = A_2 - Y$$

$$dW_2 = \frac{1}{m} A_1^T dZ_2$$

$$db_2 = \frac{1}{m} \sum dZ_2$$

**Hidden layer gradients:**

$$dZ_1 = dZ_2 W_2^T \cdot \sigma'(Z_1)$$

$$dW_1 = \frac{1}{m} X^T dZ_1$$

$$db_1 = \frac{1}{m} \sum dZ_1$$

**Implementation in NumPy**

```
def sigmoid_derivative(x):
    return x * (1 - x)

def backpropagation(X, Y, W1, b1, W2, b2, A1, A2, learning_rate):
    m = X.shape[0]

    # Compute gradients
    dZ2 = A2 - Y
    dW2 = np.dot(A1.T, dZ2) / m
    db2 = np.sum(dZ2, axis=0, keepdims=True) / m

    dZ1 = np.dot(dZ2, W2.T) * sigmoid_derivative(A1)
    dW1 = np.dot(X.T, dZ1) / m
    db1 = np.sum(dZ1, axis=0, keepdims=True) / m

    # Update weights and biases
    W2 -= learning_rate * dW2
    b2 -= learning_rate * db2
    W1 -= learning_rate * dW1
    b1 -= learning_rate * db1

    return W1, b1, W2, b2
```

## 5. Training the Neural Network

We run multiple epochs where we perform forward propagation, compute loss, backpropagate, and update weights.

**Implementation**

```
# Initialize parameters
np.random.seed(42)
input_size = 2
hidden_size = 4
output_size = 1
learning_rate = 0.1
epochs = 10000

W1 = np.random.randn(input_size, hidden_size)
b1 = np.zeros((1, hidden_size))
W2 = np.random.randn(hidden_size, output_size)
b2 = np.zeros((1, output_size))

# Input and output data
X = np.array([[0, 0], [0, 1], [1, 0], [1, 1]])  # XOR dataset
Y = np.array([[0], [1], [1], [0]])  # Expected output

# Training loop
for epoch in range(epochs):
    Z1, A1, Z2, A2 = forward_propagation(X, W1, b1, W2, b2)
    loss = compute_loss(Y, A2)
    W1, b1, W2, b2 = backpropagation(X, Y, W1, b1, W2, b2, A1, A2, learning_rate)

    if epoch % 1000 == 0:
        print(f"Epoch {epoch}, Loss: {loss:.4f}")
```

## 6. Making Predictions

After training, we can use the model for predictions.

```
predictions = forward_propagation(X, W1, b1, W2, b2)[-1]
print("Predictions:")
print(predictions.round())  # Rounding to get binary output
```

In this section, we implemented training for a simple neural network using NumPy. We explored:

- Forward propagation for computing predictions.
- Loss functions for measuring model performance.
- Backpropagation to compute weight updates.

- Gradient descent for optimization.

This hands-on approach provides a deep understanding of how neural networks learn, making it easier to transition to more advanced frameworks like TensorFlow and PyTorch. In the next section, we will explore regularization techniques to improve model generalization.

# 7.4. Debugging Neural Networks: Common Errors & Fixes

Training neural networks can be challenging, especially when things don't go as expected. Debugging is a crucial skill in deep learning, helping identify and resolve issues related to weight initialization, learning rates, overfitting, underfitting, and more. In this section, we will cover common errors that arise while training neural networks and provide practical solutions to fix them.

### 1. Model Not Learning (Loss Not Decreasing)

**Problem:**

- The loss remains constant or does not decrease significantly over epochs.
- The model is unable to improve its predictions.

**Possible Causes:**

Learning Rate Too High or Too Low

- A very high learning rate causes erratic updates, preventing convergence.
- A very low learning rate results in slow or no learning.

**Poor Weight Initialization**

- If weights are initialized too large or too small, they can cause vanishing or exploding gradients.

**Wrong Activation Function**

- Some activation functions (like sigmoid) can lead to saturation, where gradients become too small to update weights.

**Fixes:**

✅ **Adjust the Learning Rate**

- Try different learning rates: 0.01, 0.001, 0.0001.
- Use learning rate schedules like decay or adaptive optimizers (Adam, RMSprop).

✅ **Use Proper Weight Initialization**

- Use Xavier (Glorot) initialization for sigmoid/tanh activations.
- Use He initialization for ReLU-based networks.

✅ **Use Better Activation Functions**

Replace sigmoid with ReLU or Leaky ReLU to avoid saturation.

```
def relu(x):
    return np.maximum(0, x)
```

## 2. Exploding or Vanishing Gradients

**Problem:**

- Gradients explode (become very large), making training unstable.
- Gradients vanish (become too small), causing slow learning.

**Possible Causes:**

- Deep Networks Without Proper Initialization
- Use of Sigmoid/Tanh Activation in Deep Networks
- Poor Weight Scaling in Backpropagation

**Fixes:**

✅ **Use Proper Initialization**

- Xavier initialization for sigmoid/tanh networks.
- He initialization for ReLU networks.

## ✅ Use Batch Normalization

- Normalizes activations to prevent large/small gradient values.

## ✅ Use Gradient Clipping for Exploding Gradients

```
def clip_gradients(gradients, clip_value=1.0):
    return np.clip(gradients, -clip_value, clip_value)
```

## 3. Overfitting: Model Performs Well on Training but Poorly on Test Data

### Problem:

- The model achieves low loss on training data but has high loss on test data.
- The model memorizes training data instead of generalizing.

### Possible Causes:

- Too Many Parameters (Too Complex Model)
- Not Enough Training Data
- No Regularization Used

### Fixes:

## ✅ Use Regularization Techniques

L2 Regularization (Weight Decay): Penalizes large weights.

```
L2_penalty = np.sum(W ** 2) * 0.01  # Example for L2 regularization
```

**Dropout**: Randomly drops neurons during training to prevent reliance on specific patterns.

```
def dropout(A, dropout_rate=0.5):
    mask = np.random.rand(*A.shape) > dropout_rate
    return A * mask
```

✅ Increase Training Data

- Use data augmentation or transfer learning if data is limited.

✅ Simplify the Model

- Reduce the number of hidden layers or neurons to prevent overfitting.

## 4. Underfitting: Model Not Capturing Patterns in Data

**Problem:**

- The model has high training and test loss.
- The model is too simple and does not capture patterns in the data.

**Possible Causes:**

- Not Enough Neurons/Layers
- Too Strong Regularization
- Not Enough Training Time (Too Few Epochs)

**Fixes:**

✅ Increase Model Complexity

- Add more neurons/layers to the network.

✅ Train for More Epochs

- Use an early stopping technique to prevent overfitting.

✅ Reduce Regularization Strength

- If L2 regularization is too strong, reduce its coefficient.

## 5. Mismatched Input Shapes (Shape Errors in NumPy)

**Problem:**

- ValueError: shapes (x, y) and (a, b) not aligned

**Possible Causes:**

- Incorrect Matrix Multiplication Dimensions
- Mismatched Data and Weight Shapes

**Fixes:**

✅ **Check Input and Weight Shapes**

*print("X shape:", X.shape)*
*print("W1 shape:", W1.shape)*

✅ **Transpose Matrices Where Needed**

*If A = np.dot(X, W), ensure X.shape[1] == W.shape[0].*

**6. Poor Convergence Due to Incorrect Batch Size**

**Problem:**

- Model is unstable when batch size is too small.
- Model takes too long to converge when batch size is too large.

**Possible Causes:**

- Batch Size Too Small: Noisy updates.
- Batch Size Too Large: Fewer updates per epoch.

**Fixes:**

✅ **Use an Optimal Batch Size**

- Recommended batch sizes: 16, 32, 64, or 128.

✅ **Try Mini-Batch Gradient Descent**

- Uses a subset of data per update, balancing performance and efficiency.

## 7. Output Predictions Always the Same (No Learning Occurring)

**Problem:**

- The model always predicts one class (e.g., always 0 or always 1).

**Possible Causes:**

- Wrong Activation Function in Output Layer
- Learning Rate Too High (Diverging Updates)

**Fixes:**

✅ **Use the Right Activation Function**

- For binary classification: Use sigmoid.
- For multi-class classification: Use softmax.

✅ **Use Cross-Entropy Loss for Classification**

```
def cross_entropy_loss(y_true, y_pred):
    return -np.sum(y_true * np.log(y_pred))
```

Debugging neural networks requires careful observation of loss trends, activation outputs, and weight updates. Common errors include exploding/vanishing gradients, overfitting, underfitting, shape mismatches, and poor convergence. By applying techniques like batch normalization, weight initialization, regularization, gradient clipping, and learning rate adjustments, we can resolve most issues effectively.

In the next section, we will explore regularization and generalization techniques to build more robust neural networks.

# 8. Regularization & Generalization

To build neural networks that perform well on new, unseen data, we must ensure they generalize effectively—avoiding the common pitfall of overfitting to the training data. In this chapter, you'll explore regularization techniques that help improve model generalization. You'll learn about L1 and L2 regularization, which penalize large weights, and dropout, which randomly disables neurons during training to prevent the model from becoming too reliant on any single feature. The chapter also covers early stopping and batch normalization, additional methods that stabilize training and reduce overfitting. By the end of this chapter, you'll have the tools to create neural networks that perform well on both training and test data, ensuring their success in real-world applications.

## 8.1. Overfitting & Underfitting in Neural Networks

Building an effective neural network is not just about increasing layers and neurons; it's about striking a balance between learning patterns from data and generalizing to unseen examples. Two common issues arise when training models: overfitting and underfitting. Overfitting occurs when a model memorizes training data instead of generalizing, while underfitting happens when the model is too simple to capture meaningful patterns. In this section, we will explore the causes of these problems, how to identify them, and techniques to mitigate them.

### 1. Understanding Overfitting

### What is Overfitting?

Overfitting occurs when a neural network learns the noise and details in training data rather than just the underlying pattern. This results in a model that performs exceptionally well on training data but fails to generalize to new data.

### Signs of Overfitting:

✓ Very low training loss but high validation loss.

✓ Large gap between training accuracy and validation accuracy.

✓ The model performs well on seen data but poorly on new data.

**Causes of Overfitting:**

- **Too Many Parameters** – A very complex model captures noise instead of patterns.
- **Too Few Training Examples** – The model memorizes the small dataset instead of learning general features.
- **Lack of Regularization** – No constraints on weight values allow the model to over-adapt to training data.

## 2. Techniques to Prevent Overfitting

### ✅ Regularization (L1 & L2)

Regularization techniques add constraints to prevent excessively large weights.

- **L1 Regularization (Lasso Regression):** Encourages sparsity by adding the absolute value of weights as a penalty.
- **L2 Regularization (Ridge Regression):** Penalizes large weight values to prevent overfitting.

**Example**: L2 Regularization in Neural Networks

*L2_penalty = lambda_value * np.sum(weights ** 2)*

### ✅ Dropout Regularization

Dropout randomly disables neurons during training, forcing the network to learn more robust features.

*import tensorflow as tf*

*layer = tf.keras.layers.Dropout(0.5)  # 50% of neurons are dropped during training*

### ✅ Early Stopping

Monitor validation loss and stop training when the model starts to overfit.

*callback = tf.keras.callbacks.EarlyStopping(monitor='val_loss', patience=5)*

## ✅ Data Augmentation

Artificially increase dataset size by modifying existing samples.

*from tensorflow.keras.preprocessing.image import ImageDataGenerator*

*datagen = ImageDataGenerator(rotation_range=30, width_shift_range=0.2)*

## ✅ Batch Normalization

Normalizes activations between layers to reduce overfitting and stabilize training.

*layer = tf.keras.layers.BatchNormalization()*

## 3. Understanding Underfitting

### What is Underfitting?

Underfitting happens when a model is too simple to capture the complexity of the data, leading to poor performance on both training and validation data.

### Signs of Underfitting:

✔ High training and validation loss.

✔ No significant improvement in performance even with more training.

✔ The model fails to capture patterns, making overly simplistic predictions.

### Causes of Underfitting:

- **Model Too Simple** – Not enough layers, neurons, or features.
- **Training for Too Few Epochs** – The model has not learned enough patterns.
- **Too Much Regularization** – Constraints prevent the model from capturing useful information.

## 4. Techniques to Prevent Underfitting

## ✅ Increase Model Complexity

If a model is too simple, adding more layers, neurons, or using a deeper architecture can help.

*model.add(tf.keras.layers.Dense(128, activation='relu'))*
*model.add(tf.keras.layers.Dense(256, activation='relu'))*

### ✅ Train for More Epochs

If the model hasn't seen enough data, increasing epochs can improve learning.

*model.fit(X_train, y_train, epochs=100)*

### ✅ Reduce Regularization Strength

If L2 regularization or dropout is too strong, reduce its impact.

*layer = tf.keras.layers.Dropout(0.2)  # Use a lower dropout rate*

### ✅ Use Better Feature Engineering

Ensure that the dataset includes relevant features that help the model learn effectively.

## 5. Comparing Overfitting & Underfitting

| Feature | Overfitting | Underfitting |
|---|---|---|
| Training Loss | Very low | High |
| Validation Loss | High | High |
| Generalization | Poor | Poor |
| Model Complexity | Too complex | Too simple |
| Solution | Regularization, Dropout, Data Aug. | Increase model size, Train longer |

## 6. Finding the Right Balance

The key to training a well-generalized neural network is finding the sweet spot between overfitting and underfitting. The ideal model:

✓ Has a low training loss and a slightly higher validation loss.

✓ Shows stable learning curves without sudden jumps.

✓ Uses regularization techniques effectively.

Overfitting and underfitting are two major obstacles in deep learning. By using regularization, dropout, data augmentation, early stopping, and batch normalization, we can mitigate overfitting, while increasing model complexity, training longer, and improving features can help reduce underfitting. In the next section, we will explore advanced regularization and generalization techniques to further improve deep learning models.

# 8.2. Dropout: Preventing Overfitting by Neuron Removal

Overfitting is a common challenge in deep learning, where a model learns patterns from the training data so well that it fails to generalize to new, unseen data. Dropout is one of the most effective techniques to combat overfitting by randomly removing neurons during training, preventing the model from relying too heavily on specific neurons. This forces the network to learn robust features that generalize better. In this section, we will explore what dropout is, how it works, why it is useful, and how to implement it in practice.

### 1. Understanding Dropout

### What is Dropout?

Dropout is a regularization technique where, during each training iteration, a fraction of the neurons in the network are randomly dropped (set to zero). These neurons do not participate in forward or backward propagation in that specific iteration. This prevents over-reliance on specific neurons and ensures that multiple independent patterns are learned.

### How Dropout Works:

- During training, a certain percentage (dropout rate) of neurons is randomly turned off in each layer.
- The remaining active neurons adjust their weights to compensate for the missing ones.

- In testing (inference), all neurons are used, but their activations are scaled to match the expected behavior from training.

**Example**: Dropout with 50% Probability

If a fully connected layer has 10 neurons, with dropout = 0.5, then in each iteration, roughly 5 out of 10 neurons are randomly disabled.

## 2. Why Use Dropout?

### ✅ Prevents Overfitting

Dropout forces neurons to learn redundant and independent features, preventing the network from over-relying on specific patterns.

### ✅ Improves Generalization

By learning multiple representations of the data, the model generalizes better to unseen data.

### ✅ Acts Like an Ensemble Model

Dropout creates a different network structure in each training iteration. This is similar to training multiple models and averaging their results, improving stability.

### ✅ Reduces Co-adaptation of Neurons

When certain neurons dominate during training, the network fails to learn diverse features. Dropout prevents this by making each neuron independently contribute to learning.

## 3. Implementing Dropout in Neural Networks

Dropout is typically applied to fully connected (dense) layers in a neural network. It is not recommended for convolutional layers (CNNs) because convolutional layers already share weights and have fewer parameters compared to dense layers.

**Example**: Dropout in TensorFlow/Keras

```
import tensorflow as tf
from tensorflow.keras.models import Sequential
from tensorflow.keras.layers import Dense, Dropout

# Define a neural network with dropout
model = Sequential([
    Dense(128, activation='relu', input_shape=(784,)),  # Input layer
    Dropout(0.5),  # Drop 50% of neurons
    Dense(64, activation='relu'),
    Dropout(0.3),  # Drop 30% of neurons
    Dense(10, activation='softmax')  # Output layer
])

# Compile model
model.compile(optimizer='adam', loss='categorical_crossentropy', metrics=['accuracy'])
```

- Dropout(0.5) means 50% of the neurons are randomly dropped during training.
- The final layer does not use dropout, as it's only needed for learning robust features in hidden layers.

## 4. Choosing the Right Dropout Rate

The dropout rate should not be too high or too low:

✔ **0.2 - 0.5**: Recommended range for most networks.

✔ **< 0.2:** May not be effective in preventing overfitting.

✔ **> 0.5:** May lead to underfitting, as too many neurons are removed.

💡 **Best Practice**: Experiment with different dropout values and monitor validation accuracy.

## 5. Dropout in Different Neural Networks

◆ **Fully Connected Networks (MLP)** – Dropout is highly effective in dense layers to prevent overfitting.

◆ **Convolutional Neural Networks (CNNs)** – Dropout is typically applied only in fully connected layers after convolutions.

◆ **Recurrent Neural Networks (RNNs, LSTMs, GRUs)** – Special dropout techniques like Variational Dropout or DropConnect are used.

### Example: Dropout in CNNs

*from tensorflow.keras.layers import Conv2D, Flatten*

```
model = Sequential([
    Conv2D(32, (3,3), activation='relu', input_shape=(28,28,1)),
    Flatten(),
    Dense(128, activation='relu'),
    Dropout(0.5),  # Dropout applied before the final layer
    Dense(10, activation='softmax')
])
```

📌 Dropout is used after the fully connected (Dense) layer, not in convolutional layers.

### 6. Limitations of Dropout

🚫 **Not Always Needed** – If the dataset is very large or has strong regularization (like batch normalization), dropout may not be necessary.

🚫 **Does Not Work Well with Small Networks** – If the model is already simple, dropping neurons might lead to underfitting.

🚫 **Computational Overhead** – More iterations are needed to learn properly due to the random dropping of neurons.

### 7. Combining Dropout with Other Regularization Techniques

### Dropout is often used alongside:

✓ L1/L2 Regularization (Weight Decay) – Adds penalties to large weights.

✓ Batch Normalization – Normalizes activations, making training more stable.

✓ Data Augmentation – Increases training data diversity, improving generalization.

### Example: Dropout + L2 Regularization

*from tensorflow.keras.regularizers import l2*

```
model.add(Dense(128, activation='relu', kernel_regularizer=l2(0.01)))
model.add(Dropout(0.4))
```

## 8. Key Takeaways

✅ Dropout randomly removes neurons during training to prevent overfitting.

✅ It helps in learning robust and independent features, improving generalization.

✅ The optimal dropout rate is between 0.2 and 0.5 for most networks.

✅ It is not used in convolutional layers but is effective in dense layers.

✅ Works best when combined with L2 regularization, batch normalization, and data augmentation.

By implementing dropout effectively, neural networks can generalize better and perform well on unseen data. In the next section, we will explore other regularization techniques like L1/L2 weight decay and early stopping to further improve deep learning models. 🚀

# 8.3. Batch Normalization & Layer Normalization

Training deep neural networks can be challenging due to internal covariate shift, where the distribution of activations changes as training progresses. This makes learning inefficient and slows down convergence. Batch Normalization (BN) and Layer Normalization (LN) are two powerful techniques that help stabilize and accelerate training, improving model performance. In this section, we will explore how these techniques work, their advantages, and when to use each.

## 1. The Need for Normalization in Neural Networks

### What is Internal Covariate Shift?

Internal covariate shift refers to changes in the distribution of activations during training, making it harder for the model to learn effectively. This leads to:

✓ Slower training due to unstable gradients.

✓ Higher sensitivity to weight initialization.

✓ The need for lower learning rates, making training inefficient.

**How Normalization Helps:**

✓ **Stabilizes activations** – Keeps values in a fixed range, reducing sudden jumps in training.

✓ **Speeds up convergence** – Enables the use of higher learning rates, reducing training time.

✓ **Reduces dependency on weight initialization** – Improves model robustness.

✓ **Acts as a regularizer** – Helps prevent overfitting by introducing noise to activations.

**2. Batch Normalization (BN)**

**What is Batch Normalization?**

Batch Normalization (BN) normalizes activations across the mini-batch at each training step. It ensures that activations in each layer follow a standard normal distribution (mean = 0, variance = 1), making learning more stable.

**How Batch Normalization Works:**

- **Compute Mean & Variance** – Calculate the mean and variance for each feature in a batch.
- **Normalize** – Subtract the mean and divide by the standard deviation.
- **Scale & Shift** – Introduce learnable parameters $\gamma$ (scale) and $\beta$ (shift) to allow the model to learn optimal activation distributions.

**Mathematically:**

$$\hat{x}_i = \frac{x_i - \mu_B}{\sqrt{\sigma_B^2 + \epsilon}}$$

$$y_i = \gamma \hat{x}_i + \beta$$

Where:

- $\mu_B$ = Mean of batch

- $\sigma_B^2$ = Variance of batch

- $\epsilon$ = Small constant for numerical stability

- $\gamma, \beta$ = Trainable parameters

**Implementing Batch Normalization in TensorFlow/Keras**

*import tensorflow as tf*
*from tensorflow.keras.layers import Dense, BatchNormalization*

*model = tf.keras.Sequential([*
    *Dense(128, activation='relu'),*
    *BatchNormalization(),  # Normalizes activations*
    *Dense(64, activation='relu'),*
    *BatchNormalization(),*
    *Dense(10, activation='softmax')*
*])*

✓ BN is typically applied after a dense or convolutional layer before applying the activation function.

**Advantages of Batch Normalization**

✓ **Accelerates training** – Allows for higher learning rates without causing instability.

✓ **Reduces dependence on initialization** – Helps train deep networks without careful weight initialization.

✓ **Improves generalization** – Acts as a regularizer by adding noise to activations.

**Limitations of Batch Normalization**

🚫 **Not effective for very small batch sizes** – Needs a reasonable batch size (>16) to compute stable statistics.

🚫 **Adds computational overhead** – Extra computation per layer increases training time.

🚫 **Doesn't work well in RNNs** – Due to sequential dependencies in recurrent models.

**3. Layer Normalization (LN)**

**What is Layer Normalization?**

Layer Normalization (LN) normalizes activations across neurons within a layer, rather than across the batch. Unlike BN, which depends on the mini-batch statistics, LN computes normalization for each individual training example, making it more suitable for sequential models like RNNs.

**How Layer Normalization Works:**

- Compute mean & variance across the neurons in a layer for a single training example.
- Normalize activations by subtracting the mean and dividing by standard deviation.
- Scale and shift using learnable parameters $\gamma$ and $\beta$.

**Mathematically:**

$$\hat{x}_i = \frac{x_i - \mu_L}{\sqrt{\sigma_L^2 + \epsilon}}$$

$$y_i = \gamma \hat{x}_i + \beta$$

Where:

- $\mu_L$ = Mean of layer neurons

- $\sigma_L^2$ = Variance of layer neurons

- $\gamma, \beta$ = Trainable parameters

**Implementing Layer Normalization in TensorFlow/Keras**

```
from tensorflow.keras.layers import LayerNormalization

model = tf.keras.Sequential([
    Dense(128, activation='relu'),
    LayerNormalization(),  # Normalizes across neurons in the layer
    Dense(64, activation='relu'),
    LayerNormalization(),
    Dense(10, activation='softmax')
])
```

✓ LN is applied after fully connected or recurrent layers and works well in NLP models.

## Advantages of Layer Normalization

✓ **Works well with small batch sizes** – Doesn't rely on batch statistics.

✓ **Effective for RNNs & Transformers** – Handles sequential dependencies better.

✓ **Consistent across batches** – Since normalization happens per example, there are no batch-to-batch variations.

## Limitations of Layer Normalization

⃠ **Slower convergence than Batch Norm** – Doesn't reduce internal covariate shift as effectively.
⃠ **Less effective in CNNs** – Spatial dependencies make BN more useful in convolutional networks.

## 4. Batch Normalization vs. Layer Normalization

| Feature | Batch Normalization (BN) | Layer Normalization (LN) |
|---|---|---|
| Normalization Across | Batch (mini-batch samples) | Layer (neurons in a layer) |
| Works Well With | CNNs, MLPs, Large Batch Training | RNNs, Transformers, Small Batches |
| Relies on Batch Size? | Yes (needs sufficient batch size) | No (independent of batch size) |
| Regularization Effect? | Acts as implicit regularization | Less regularization effect |
| Computation Overhead? | Moderate | Lower than BN |
| Best Used In | Vision models (CNNs), Deep MLPs | NLP models, RNNs, Transformers |

### 5. Choosing Between BatchNorm and LayerNorm

✅ Use Batch Normalization if:

- You're working with CNNs or fully connected networks.
- You have large batch sizes (>16).
- You want faster convergence with minimal tuning.

✅ Use Layer Normalization if:

- You're working with RNNs, Transformers, or NLP models.
- You have very small batch sizes (<16).
- You need consistent normalization across different batches.

### 6. Key Takeaways

✔ **Batch Normalization (BN)** normalizes activations across a batch, making training faster and more stable.

✔ **Layer Normalization (LN)** normalizes across neurons in a layer, making it more suitable for RNNs and Transformers.

✔ BN is preferred for CNNs and large-batch training, while LN is better for sequential models and small-batch training.

✔ Both techniques improve model generalization and reduce sensitivity to weight initialization.

Batch Normalization and Layer Normalization are crucial tools in deep learning that improve training efficiency and model performance. In the next section, we will explore other regularization techniques, such as L1/L2 weight decay, early stopping, and data augmentation, to further enhance deep learning models. 🚀

# 8.4. Weight Decay (L1 & L2 Regularization)

Deep neural networks often suffer from overfitting, where they perform well on training data but fail to generalize to unseen data. One of the most effective ways to combat overfitting is weight decay, also known as L1 and L2 regularization. These techniques add a penalty to the loss function, encouraging the model to learn simpler, more generalizable patterns instead of memorizing the training data.

In this section, we will explore how L1 and L2 regularization work, their mathematical foundations, and how to implement them effectively in deep learning models.

## 1. The Problem of Overfitting and the Role of Weight Decay

### What is Overfitting?

Overfitting happens when a model becomes too complex and captures noise in the training data rather than meaningful patterns. This leads to:

⊘ High training accuracy but poor test accuracy
⊘ Sensitivity to small variations in input data
⊘ Inability to generalize well to unseen data

### How Weight Decay Helps

Weight decay works by adding a penalty to large weights, which discourages the model from assigning too much importance to any particular feature.

✓ Prevents excessive reliance on specific neurons

✓ Encourages simpler models with better generalization

✓ Reduces the risk of overfitting without requiring additional data

## 2. L1 Regularization (Lasso Regression)

### What is L1 Regularization?

L1 regularization (also known as Lasso) adds the absolute value of weights to the loss function. This forces some weights to become exactly zero, effectively performing feature selection by removing less important connections in the neural network.

### Mathematical Formula:

For a given loss function $L$, L1 regularization modifies it as follows:

$$L' = L + \lambda \sum |w_i|$$

where:

- $\lambda$ = Regularization strength (controls the penalty)

- $w_i$ = Weight of each neuron

## Key Characteristics of L1 Regularization:

✓ Produces sparse weight matrices (some weights are zero).

✓ Helps in feature selection by removing irrelevant inputs.

✓ Works well when only a few input features are relevant.

## Implementation in TensorFlow/Keras:

*from tensorflow.keras.regularizers import l1*
*from tensorflow.keras.layers import Dense*

*model.add(Dense(64, activation='relu', kernel_regularizer=l1(0.01)))  # Applying L1 regularization*

◆ The higher the value of 0.01, the more weights will be forced to zero.

## When to Use L1 Regularization?

✓ When you want feature selection (eliminate irrelevant inputs).

✓ When dealing with high-dimensional data (text, genetics, finance).

✓ When sparsity is desired (fewer active neurons).

## 3. L2 Regularization (Ridge Regression)

## What is L2 Regularization?

L2 regularization (also known as Ridge Regression) adds the squared values of the weights to the loss function. Unlike L1, which forces some weights to zero, L2 shrinks all weights but doesn't remove them entirely.

**Mathematical Formula:**

$$L' = L + \lambda \sum w_i^2$$

where:

- $\lambda$ = Regularization strength

- $w_i$ = Weight of each neuron

**Key Characteristics of L2 Regularization:**

✓ Prevents large weights but does not set them to zero.

✓ Works well when all input features are relevant.

✓ Helps models generalize better by reducing sensitivity to specific inputs.

**Implementation in TensorFlow/Keras:**

*from tensorflow.keras.regularizers import l2*

*model.add(Dense(64, activation='relu', kernel_regularizer=l2(0.01)))  # Applying L2 regularization*

◆ A larger 0.01 value will enforce stronger regularization.

**When to Use L2 Regularization?**

✓ When all input features contribute to the output.

✓ When you want smooth weight distributions (rather than sparse ones).

✓ When you are training deep networks where L1 might be too aggressive.

## 4. Combining L1 & L2: Elastic Net Regularization

Sometimes, neither L1 nor L2 alone is sufficient. Elastic Net Regularization combines both by adding a weighted sum of L1 and L2 penalties to the loss function.

$$L' = L + \alpha(\lambda_1 \sum |w_i| + \lambda_2 \sum w_i^2)$$

where $\alpha$ balances the importance of L1 vs. L2 regularization.

### Implementation in TensorFlow/Keras:

*from tensorflow.keras.regularizers import l1_l2*

*model.add(Dense(64, activation='relu', kernel_regularizer=l1_l2(l1=0.01, l2=0.01)))*

◆ Elastic Net is useful when dealing with high-dimensional data with some irrelevant features.

## 5. Choosing the Right Regularization Technique

| Feature | L1 (Lasso) | L2 (Ridge) | Elastic Net |
|---------|-----------|-----------|-------------|
| Effect on Weights | Some weights become zero | Shrinks weights but keeps them nonzero | Combines L1 & L2 effects |
| Feature Selection? | ☑ Yes (Removes unnecessary features) | ✗ No | ☑ Yes (to some extent) |
| Works Best When | Sparse features are important | All features contribute to output | There is a mix of relevant & irrelevant features |
| Best For | High-dimensional data (text, genetics, NLP) | General deep learning models | Complex data with mixed relevance |

## Regularization Strength (λ) Matters!

Too small → Minimal effect, overfitting persists.

Too large → Too much weight reduction, underfitting occurs.

Best approach → Use cross-validation to find the optimal λ.

## 6. Key Takeaways

✓ L1 regularization (Lasso) encourages sparsity by forcing some weights to zero.

✓ L2 regularization (Ridge) penalizes large weights without setting them to zero.

✓ Elastic Net combines L1 and L2 to balance feature selection and smooth learning.

✓ Regularization prevents overfitting, leading to better generalization.

✓ The optimal $\lambda$ value should be fine-tuned using validation experiments.

Weight decay (L1 & L2) is a fundamental tool in deep learning to improve model robustness and avoid overfitting. In the next section, we will explore Dropout and its role in preventing over-reliance on specific neurons in neural networks. 🚀

# 9. Convolutional Neural Networks (CNNs)

Convolutional Neural Networks (CNNs) are a specialized type of neural network designed for processing grid-like data, such as images. In this chapter, you'll dive into the architecture of CNNs, understanding the role of convolutional layers, pooling layers, and fully connected layers in feature extraction and classification. You'll learn how CNNs automatically detect patterns like edges, textures, and shapes in images, making them ideal for tasks like image recognition and object detection. Through hands-on examples, you'll implement a basic CNN and explore how it can outperform traditional neural networks on visual data, setting the stage for advanced computer vision applications.

## 9.1. Understanding Image Data & Why CNNs Work

Images are one of the most complex types of data in machine learning. Unlike traditional numerical datasets, image data is high-dimensional, structured in a way that standard machine learning algorithms struggle to interpret. This is where Convolutional Neural Networks (CNNs) excel. CNNs are designed to efficiently process, analyze, and extract meaningful patterns from images, making them the backbone of modern computer vision applications.

In this section, we will explore how image data is structured, the challenges in handling image-based tasks, and why CNNs outperform traditional machine learning models when dealing with images.

### 1. What is Image Data?

An image is essentially a grid of numerical values, where each number represents the intensity of a pixel in a specific color channel. The key components of an image are:

### 1.1 Pixels and Resolution

- An image is composed of tiny dots called pixels.
- Each pixel holds numerical values representing brightness or color.
- The resolution of an image refers to the number of pixels (e.g., 28×28, 256×256).

For example, a 28×28 grayscale image has 784 pixels, each with an intensity value between 0 (black) and 255 (white).

## 1.2 Color Channels (RGB Representation)

- Grayscale images have only one channel (intensity values from 0-255).
- Color images are represented using three channels: Red, Green, and Blue (RGB).
- Each pixel in an RGB image has three values, one for each channel, typically ranging from 0 to 255.

**Example**: A 256×256 color image has 256×256×3 = 196,608 pixel values.

## 1.3 Image Representation in a Computer

When stored in a computer, images are represented as multi-dimensional arrays (tensors):

- **Grayscale image**: Shape → (Height × Width)
- **Color image**: Shape → (Height × Width × 3)

## Example:

A 32×32 RGB image is represented as:

*image.shape  # Output: (32, 32, 3)*

This structure makes images high-dimensional and computationally expensive to process using traditional methods.

## 2. Challenges in Image Processing

## 2.1 High Dimensionality

Unlike tabular data, where features are limited, image data consists of thousands or even millions of pixels, making computations expensive and models prone to overfitting.

## 2.2 Spatial Hierarchies in Images

- Objects in images have spatial relationships (e.g., eyes are above the nose in a face).
- Traditional machine learning models treat pixels as independent features, ignoring spatial structures.

- CNNs solve this by preserving local patterns through convolutional layers.

### 2.3 Viewpoint & Scale Variability

- Objects appear different based on angle, size, lighting, and occlusions.
- A cat in one image might be smaller, rotated, or partially hidden in another.
- CNNs handle these variations using translation-invariant feature extraction.

## 3. Why Traditional Machine Learning Fails for Images

### 3.1 Flattening the Image Loses Important Features

Traditional machine learning models like logistic regression or support vector machines (SVMs) require 1D feature vectors.

- Flattening a 28×28 image into a 784-length vector destroys spatial relationships.
- The model fails to recognize objects effectively when shifted or resized.

### 3.2 Too Many Parameters for Dense Networks

Fully connected neural networks require one weight per connection, which quickly becomes infeasible.

**Example**: A 256×256 RGB image has 196,608 features → requires millions of parameters in a fully connected model!

### 3.3 No Hierarchical Feature Learning

- Traditional models learn individual pixels rather than patterns like edges, textures, or objects.
- CNNs automatically detect hierarchical patterns (edges → shapes → objects).

## 4. How CNNs Solve These Problems

### 4.1 Local Connectivity (Convolutions)

CNNs process images using convolutional layers, which apply filters to small patches of an image rather than treating all pixels equally.

- **Filters (Kernels):** Small matrices (e.g., 3×3, 5×5) slide over the image, capturing local features.
- **Stride:** Defines how much the filter moves at each step.

**Receptive Field:** The area of the image a filter interacts with at a time.

💡 **Benefit:** CNNs detect patterns regardless of their position in the image.

## 4.2 Hierarchical Feature Extraction

CNNs learn low-level and high-level features in stages:

- **First layers:** Detect edges and simple textures.
- **Deeper layers:** Identify shapes, parts of objects.
- **Final layers:** Recognize complex objects like faces or cars.

## 4.3 Shared Weights & Parameter Efficiency

Unlike fully connected networks where every pixel has an independent weight, CNNs reuse the same filters across the image → dramatically reduces the number of parameters.

**Example:**

- A fully connected model for a 256×256 image requires millions of parameters.
- A CNN using 3×3 filters needs only a few thousand parameters, making training feasible.

## 4.4 Pooling Layers for Spatial Invariance

CNNs use pooling layers (e.g., max pooling, average pooling) to:

✓ Reduce image size (downsampling)

✓ Retain important features

✓ Improve computational efficiency

**Example:**

- A 2×2 max-pooling layer reduces a 32×32 image to 16×16, keeping the most important pixel values.

### 4.5 Fully Connected Layer for Final Predictions

After extracting features, CNNs use a fully connected layer to classify objects.

### Example:

A CNN trained on cats vs. dogs will output:

- **Class 0** → Cat (Probability: 0.89)
- **Class 1** → Dog (Probability: 0.11)

## 5. Summary: Why CNNs Work for Images

| Feature | Traditional ML | CNNs |
|---|---|---|
| Spatial Awareness | ✕ No | ✓ Yes |
| Handles Large Images | ✕ No | ✓ Yes |
| Feature Engineering | Manual | Automatic |
| Translation Invariance | ✕ No | ✓ Yes |
| Hierarchical Learning | ✕ No | ✓ Yes |
| Computational Efficiency | ✕ Poor | ✓ Efficient |

### Key Takeaways

✓ CNNs are specifically designed for images, unlike traditional ML models.

✓ They preserve spatial structures using convolutions.

✓ CNNs automatically extract hierarchical features (edges → shapes → objects).

✓ Pooling layers help reduce size while keeping important features.

✓ CNNs are the foundation of modern computer vision applications.

# 9.2. Convolutional Layers, Filters, and Feature Extraction

At the core of Convolutional Neural Networks (CNNs) lies the convolutional layer, a powerful mechanism designed to extract meaningful patterns from image data. Unlike traditional neural networks, which treat every pixel as a separate input, CNNs leverage filters (kernels) to scan an image and capture spatial hierarchies such as edges, textures, and objects.

In this section, we will explore how convolutional layers work, the role of filters, and how CNNs automatically learn important features from images, making them ideal for computer vision tasks.

## 1. What is a Convolutional Layer?

A convolutional layer is a specialized layer in a CNN that applies filters (also called kernels) to an input image to extract features. Instead of analyzing every pixel independently, a convolutional layer captures local patterns by sliding a filter over the image and computing weighted sums.

### 1.1 How Convolution Works

Convolution is a mathematical operation that combines two functions to produce a third function. In CNNs, it involves:

- **Placing a small filter** (e.g., 3×3, 5×5) over an input image.
- **Multiplying filter values** (weights) with the corresponding pixel values.
- Summing up the results to generate a feature map.
- Sliding the filter across the image and repeating the process.

This process helps CNNs detect features like edges, corners, and textures, which are later combined into more complex patterns.

## 2. Understanding Filters (Kernels) in CNNs

### 2.1 What is a Filter?

A filter (kernel) is a small matrix (e.g., 3×3, 5×5) that is used to extract features from an image. Filters move across an image and perform element-wise multiplications followed by summation to generate a new representation of the image.

**Example of a 3×3 edge detection filter:**

$$\begin{bmatrix} -1 & -1 & -1 \\ -1 & 8 & -1 \\ -1 & -1 & -1 \end{bmatrix}$$

When this filter is applied to an image, it enhances edges by highlighting areas where pixel intensity changes significantly.

## 2.2 Types of Filters in CNNs

CNNs learn various filters during training, but some common types include:

✅ **Edge detection filters**: Detect outlines and contours.
✅ **Blur filters**: Reduce noise and smooth images.
✅ **Sharpening filters**: Enhance contrast and detail.
✅ **Gabor filters**: Capture texture and orientation information.

Each convolutional layer learns multiple filters, enabling the network to recognize different aspects of an image.

## 3. Feature Extraction: Understanding Feature Maps

A feature map is the output of a convolutional layer. It highlights specific patterns detected by a filter.

### 3.1 How Feature Extraction Works

- An image is passed through a convolutional layer.
- Different filters detect edges, textures, or shapes.
- Each filter produces a unique feature map.
- The CNN stacks multiple feature maps to capture multiple levels of detail.

**For example, in a face recognition model:**

- Early layers detect edges (nose, eyes, lips).
- Middle layers identify shapes (mouth, nose bridge).
- Deeper layers recognize full objects (entire faces).

This hierarchical learning allows CNNs to develop robust feature representations without needing manual feature engineering.

## 4. Key Hyperparameters in Convolutional Layers

To control how filters interact with an image, CNNs use several hyperparameters:

### 4.1 Stride

Defines how much a filter moves at each step.

**Common values:**

- **Stride = 1** → Moves one pixel at a time (fine-grained features).
- **Stride = 2** → Moves two pixels at a time (faster computation, reduces resolution).

Larger strides create smaller feature maps but reduce computational cost.

### 4.2 Padding

Determines how the edges of an image are handled.

Two common types:

✓ Valid Padding (No Padding): Feature map size shrinks after convolution.

✓ Same Padding (Zero Padding): Extra pixels are added to keep the same size.

Padding ensures that edge pixels are not ignored during convolution.

### 4.3 Number of Filters

- More filters = better feature extraction but higher computational cost.
- Early layers have a few filters (basic edges/textures).
- Deeper layers have many filters (complex patterns/objects).

## 5. Why CNNs Learn Better Features Than Traditional Methods

## 5.1 Automatic Feature Learning

Unlike traditional methods that require manual feature extraction, CNNs learn filters automatically through gradient-based training.

### Example:

- Instead of defining "what an edge looks like," CNNs learn edge-detecting filters from data.
- As CNNs get deeper, they learn abstract features like object parts and entire objects.

## 5.2 Translational Invariance

- Since filters scan the image locally, CNNs can recognize objects regardless of their position.
- This allows CNNs to detect objects even if they are shifted, rotated, or scaled.

## 5.3 Parameter Sharing = Fewer Parameters

- Unlike fully connected layers, where each neuron has a unique weight, CNNs share filter weights across the image.
- This reduces the number of parameters, making CNNs efficient for large images.

## 6. Summary: Why Convolutional Layers Matter

| Feature | Traditional ML | CNNs |
|---|---|---|
| Feature Engineering | Manual | Automatic |
| Spatial Awareness | ✗ No | ✓ Yes |
| Handles Large Images | ✗ No | ✓ Yes |
| Translation Invariance | ✗ No | ✓ Yes |
| Number of Parameters | High | Lower due to weight sharing |

## Key Takeaways

✓ CNNs use convolutional layers to extract important features from images.

✓ Filters (kernels) detect edges, textures, and complex patterns automatically.

✓ Feature maps capture meaningful representations, making CNNs highly effective for image-based tasks.

✓ Hyperparameters like stride, padding, and filter size control how features are extracted.

✓ CNNs reduce computational complexity by sharing weights, making them ideal for large-scale image processing.

# 9.3. Pooling Layers & Dimensionality Reduction

While convolutional layers extract features from an image, they often produce large feature maps, which can be computationally expensive and may lead to overfitting. To address this, pooling layers help reduce the dimensionality of feature maps while preserving essential information. Pooling layers make CNNs more efficient, robust to noise, and translation-invariant, ensuring that small variations in an image do not drastically change the network's predictions.

**In this section, we will explore:**

✓ What pooling layers are and why they are important.

✓ The different types of pooling operations (Max Pooling, Average Pooling, Global Pooling).

✓ How pooling helps with dimensionality reduction and overfitting prevention.

**1. What is a Pooling Layer?**

A pooling layer is a type of layer in CNNs that reduces the spatial dimensions (height and width) of a feature map while keeping the depth the same. This helps in:

◆ Reducing computational cost by decreasing the number of parameters.
◆ Extracting dominant features while discarding minor variations.
◆ Providing spatial invariance, meaning the network can recognize objects even if they appear in different locations.

Pooling layers operate independently on each feature map by applying an operation (like max or average pooling) over small regions of the image.

## 2. Types of Pooling Layers

### 2.1 Max Pooling

Max pooling is the most common type of pooling in CNNs. It selects the maximum value from each region of the feature map.

### ◆ Process:

- A window (e.g., 2×2 or 3×3) slides over the feature map.
- The maximum value in each window is retained.
- The rest of the values are discarded, reducing the size of the feature map.

### ✅ Advantages of Max Pooling:

✓ Helps in picking the most prominent features.

✓ Reduces noise and prevents overfitting.

✓ Works well for object detection tasks.

### Example of Max Pooling (2×2 filter, stride = 2):

| Before Pooling | After Max Pooling (2×2) |
|---|---|
| 1, 3, 2, 1 | 3, 4 |
| 2, 4, 3, 2 | 4, 5 |
| 1, 1, 5, 3 | 5, 6 |
| 3, 2, 6, 6 | 6, 6 |

◆ Notice how the largest number in each 2×2 region is retained while the others are discarded.

### 2.2 Average Pooling

Instead of selecting the maximum value, Average Pooling computes the average value within each window.

### ✅ Advantages of Average Pooling:

✔ Retains more spatial information than max pooling.

✔ Works well in tasks where fine details are important (e.g., medical imaging).

However, it is less commonly used because it preserves less contrast, making it less effective in object recognition tasks.

### 2.3 Global Pooling (Global Average & Global Max Pooling)

Instead of applying pooling to small regions, global pooling compresses the entire feature map into a single value per feature map.

- ◆ **Global Average Pooling (GAP):** Computes the average of all values in a feature map.
- ◆ Global Max Pooling (GMP): Picks the maximum value from the entire feature map.

### ✅ Why Use Global Pooling?

✔ Reduces a feature map to a single vector, making CNNs more efficient.

✔ Often used before fully connected layers in classification networks like ResNet and MobileNet.

✔ Helps prevent overfitting by minimizing parameters.

### Example:

- If a feature map is 7×7, Global Average Pooling would return a 1×1 value by averaging all 49 pixels.

### 3. Benefits of Pooling Layers

### 3.1 Dimensionality Reduction

- Pooling layers reduce the size of feature maps, decreasing the number of computations required. This helps CNNs run faster without significantly impacting performance.

**Example:**

- If an input image is 256×256, after two 2×2 pooling layers, its dimensions shrink to 64×64, significantly reducing computational cost.

## 3.2 Overfitting Prevention

Pooling introduces a form of regularization by removing less significant details, making the network more generalizable to new data. This prevents the model from memorizing exact pixel patterns, reducing overfitting.

## 3.3 Translation Invariance

Pooling layers help CNNs become robust to small shifts in images. If an object moves slightly in an image, a traditional neural network might misclassify it. But with pooling, CNNs can still recognize the object, making them highly effective for tasks like object recognition.

## 4. Hyperparameters in Pooling Layers

Pooling layers have several important hyperparameters:

- **Pool Size**: The size of the window used for pooling (e.g., 2×2, 3×3).
- **Stride**: How much the window moves after each operation. A stride of 2 is common.
- **Padding**: Whether to pad the image before pooling. Usually, pooling doesn't require padding.

**Example:**

- A 2×2 max pooling with stride 2 will reduce a 32×32 feature map to 16×16.
- A 3×3 average pooling with stride 1 will reduce a 32×32 feature map to 30×30.

## 5. Pooling in Action: A Simple Example

**Step 1: Input Feature Map**

**Imagine a 4×4 feature map:**

$$\begin{bmatrix} 1 & 2 & 3 & 4 \\ 5 & 6 & 7 & 8 \\ 9 & 10 & 11 & 12 \\ 13 & 14 & 15 & 16 \end{bmatrix}$$

## Step 2: Apply 2×2 Max Pooling (Stride 2)

$$\begin{bmatrix} 6 & 8 \\ 14 & 16 \end{bmatrix}$$

The result is a 2×2 feature map, reducing computation by 75% while retaining key information.

## 6. Summary: Why Pooling Matters in CNNs

| Feature | Max Pooling | Average Pooling | Global Pooling |
|---|---|---|---|
| Purpose | Extracts dominant features | Retains more overall information | Compresses entire feature map |
| Common Usage | Object detection, classification | Medical imaging, signal processing | Last layer before fully connected layers |
| Effect on Overfitting | Helps prevent overfitting | Less effective at preventing overfitting | Strong regularization effect |

## Key Takeaways

✓ Pooling layers reduce feature map size while keeping important patterns.

✓ Max pooling is the most commonly used technique due to its effectiveness in feature extraction.

✓ Average pooling is useful for applications requiring more detail retention.

✓ Global pooling drastically reduces dimensions and helps prevent overfitting.

✓ Pooling layers improve translation invariance, ensuring CNNs recognize objects regardless of slight changes in position.

# 9.4. Implementing a CNN from Scratch in Python

Convolutional Neural Networks (CNNs) are widely used for image classification, object detection, and various computer vision tasks. In this section, we will build a CNN from scratch using NumPy and implement a basic model without using deep learning frameworks like TensorFlow or PyTorch.

## 1. Understanding CNN Components

Before diving into implementation, let's summarize the key components of a CNN:

- **Convolutional Layer**: Extracts features using filters (kernels).
- **Activation Function (ReLU):** Introduces non-linearity to improve learning.
- **Pooling Layer**: Reduces spatial dimensions to prevent overfitting.
- **Fully Connected Layer**: Connects extracted features to final classification.

## CNN Architecture for Implementation

We will build a simple CNN to classify handwritten digits (MNIST dataset):

1 **Conv Layer** (3×3 filter, 8 filters, ReLU activation)

2 **Max Pooling** (2×2 window, stride 2)

3 **Conv Layer** (3×3 filter, 16 filters, ReLU activation)

4 **Max Pooling** (2×2 window, stride 2)

5 **Fully Connected Layer** with Softmax for classification

## 2. Import Required Libraries

Since we are implementing CNNs from scratch, we will only use NumPy and Matplotlib for visualization.

```
import numpy as np
import matplotlib.pyplot as plt
from keras.datasets import mnist
from sklearn.preprocessing import OneHotEncoder
```

## 3. Load & Preprocess the MNIST Dataset

The MNIST dataset consists of 28×28 grayscale images of handwritten digits (0-9). We will normalize the images and one-hot encode the labels.

```
# Load MNIST dataset
(X_train, y_train), (X_test, y_test) = mnist.load_data()

# Normalize pixel values (0-255) to (0-1)
X_train = X_train / 255.0
X_test = X_test / 255.0

# Reshape images to (28, 28, 1) for CNN input
X_train = X_train.reshape(-1, 28, 28, 1)
X_test = X_test.reshape(-1, 28, 28, 1)

# One-hot encode labels
encoder = OneHotEncoder(sparse=False)
y_train = encoder.fit_transform(y_train.reshape(-1, 1))
y_test = encoder.transform(y_test.reshape(-1, 1))

print("Dataset shape:", X_train.shape, y_train.shape)
```

## 4. Implementing Convolutional Layer

A convolution operation slides a filter (kernel) over an image, computing a dot product at each position.

### 4.1 Convolution Function

```
def convolve(image, kernel, stride=1, padding=0):
    """
    Perform 2D convolution operation on an image.
    """
    # Pad the image with zeros
    if padding > 0:
        image = np.pad(image, [(padding, padding), (padding, padding)], mode='constant')

    h, w = image.shape
    kh, kw = kernel.shape
    output_size = ((h - kh) // stride) + 1
```

```
result = np.zeros((output_size, output_size))

for i in range(0, h - kh + 1, stride):
    for j in range(0, w - kw + 1, stride):
        result[i // stride, j // stride] = np.sum(image[i:i+kh, j:j+kw] * kernel)

return result
```

## 5. Implementing Max Pooling Layer

Pooling reduces spatial dimensions while retaining essential features.

```
def max_pooling(image, pool_size=2, stride=2):
    """
    Apply Max Pooling operation.
    """
    h, w = image.shape
    output_size = h // pool_size
    pooled = np.zeros((output_size, output_size))

    for i in range(0, h, stride):
        for j in range(0, w, stride):
            pooled[i // stride, j // stride] = np.max(image[i:i+pool_size, j:j+pool_size])

    return pooled
```

## 6. Implementing Fully Connected Layer

A fully connected layer maps CNN features to final class predictions.

```
def fully_connected(inputs, weights, biases):
    """
    Compute output of a fully connected (dense) layer.
    """
    return np.dot(inputs, weights) + biases
```

## 7. Forward Pass of CNN

We now combine convolution, pooling, and fully connected layers to implement the forward pass of our CNN.

```python
# Initialize random filters for convolution
conv1_filter = np.random.randn(3, 3)  # 3×3 filter for first Conv layer
conv2_filter = np.random.randn(3, 3)  # 3×3 filter for second Conv layer

# Fully connected layer weights
fc_weights = np.random.randn(64, 10)  # 64 features to 10 output classes
fc_bias = np.random.randn(10)

def forward_pass(image):
    """
    Perform forward propagation through CNN.
    """
    # Step 1: First Convolution + ReLU
    conv1 = convolve(image, conv1_filter)
    conv1 = np.maximum(0, conv1)  # ReLU Activation

    # Step 2: First Pooling Layer
    pooled1 = max_pooling(conv1)

    # Step 3: Second Convolution + ReLU
    conv2 = convolve(pooled1, conv2_filter)
    conv2 = np.maximum(0, conv2)  # ReLU Activation

    # Step 4: Second Pooling Layer
    pooled2 = max_pooling(conv2)

    # Flatten pooled output
    flat_output = pooled2.flatten()

    # Step 5: Fully Connected Layer (Dense Layer)
    output = fully_connected(flat_output, fc_weights, fc_bias)

    return output

# Test with a sample image
sample_image = X_train[0].reshape(28, 28)
output = forward_pass(sample_image)
print("CNN Output Shape:", output.shape)
```

## 8. Implementing Softmax for Classification

The final layer of our CNN uses the Softmax function to convert raw outputs into probabilities.

```python
def softmax(x):
    """
    Compute softmax values for predictions.
    """
    exp_x = np.exp(x - np.max(x))
    return exp_x / np.sum(exp_x)


# Apply softmax to output layer
probabilities = softmax(output)
print("Predicted Class Probabilities:", probabilities)
```

## 9. Training the CNN (Basic Framework)

While a full training loop requires backpropagation, here's a simple loop structure:

```python
def train_cnn(X_train, y_train, epochs=10, learning_rate=0.01):
    for epoch in range(epochs):
        loss = 0
        for i in range(len(X_train)):
            image, label = X_train[i], y_train[i]

            # Forward pass
            output = forward_pass(image.reshape(28, 28))

            # Compute loss (Cross-Entropy)
            loss += -np.sum(label * np.log(softmax(output)))

            # Backpropagation (to be implemented)

        print(f"Epoch {epoch+1}, Loss: {loss:.4f}")

# Run training
train_cnn(X_train[:100], y_train[:100], epochs=3)
```

✓ We built a CNN from scratch using NumPy.

✓ Implemented Convolution, Pooling, Fully Connected Layers, and Softmax.

✓ Created a forward pass function for prediction.

# 10. Recurrent Neural Networks (RNNs) & LSTMs

Recurrent Neural Networks (RNNs) are designed to handle sequential data, making them ideal for tasks like time-series forecasting, speech recognition, and natural language processing. In this chapter, you'll explore how RNNs process data in sequences, maintaining memory of previous inputs to make predictions for the next element in the sequence. You'll also learn about Long Short-Term Memory (LSTM) networks, an advanced type of RNN that solves the problem of vanishing gradients, allowing the model to remember long-term dependencies. With hands-on examples, you'll see how RNNs and LSTMs excel in tasks like text generation, language modeling, and stock price prediction, giving you the tools to work with temporal data effectively.

## 10.1. The Need for Sequence Models: Time Series, Speech, & Text Data

Neural networks have revolutionized the way we process data, but not all data is the same. Unlike traditional datasets where inputs are independent of each other, many real-world problems involve sequential data—where past information affects future predictions. This is where sequence models like Recurrent Neural Networks (RNNs), Long Short-Term Memory (LSTM) networks, and Transformers become crucial.

In this chapter, we explore the importance of sequence models, why traditional models fail with sequential data, and how neural networks are adapted for tasks such as time series forecasting, speech recognition, and natural language processing (NLP).

### 1. What is Sequential Data?

Sequential data refers to data points that are ordered in a particular way, where the order of occurrence matters. Unlike independent samples used in traditional machine learning, sequential data relies on past values to make future predictions. Some key examples of sequential data include:

- **Time Series Data**: Stock prices, weather patterns, financial transactions, and IoT sensor readings.
- **Speech Data**: Audio signals where sound waves form a continuous sequence.
- **Text Data**: Sentences, paragraphs, and entire documents where words follow grammatical structures.

**Why Can't Traditional Models Handle Sequential Data?**

Traditional neural networks like fully connected networks (MLPs) and CNNs struggle with sequential data because:

- **Fixed Input-Output Structure**: Traditional models expect a fixed-length input and output, whereas sequence data can vary in length (e.g., sentences of different lengths).
- **Lack of Memory**: Fully connected layers process all inputs independently, meaning they don't retain previous information. But in tasks like speech recognition, a model needs to remember past words to understand the context.

**Poor Generalization on Long Sequences**: As sequence length increases, standard neural networks fail to capture long-term dependencies, making them ineffective for complex tasks like machine translation or sentiment analysis.
To overcome these challenges, sequence models were introduced.

**2. The Importance of Sequence Models**

Sequence models are designed to process and understand data where the order of elements matters. These models have unique architectures that allow them to remember past information and make decisions based on the entire context.

**Key Properties of Sequence Models**

✓ **Handles Variable-Length Sequences**: Unlike traditional models, sequence models can process inputs of different lengths (e.g., sentences in a chatbot).
✓ **Captures Temporal Dependencies**: These models maintain memory, meaning they can understand patterns that unfold over time.
✓ **Enables Contextual Learning**: Unlike feedforward models, sequence models take previous states into account, which is essential for understanding human language, stock trends, or speech signals.

**Types of Sequence Models**

Some of the most commonly used sequence models include:

- **Recurrent Neural Networks (RNNs):** Maintain a hidden state to remember past inputs.

- **Long Short-Term Memory Networks (LSTMs):** Improve upon RNNs by handling long-term dependencies.
- **Gated Recurrent Units (GRUs):** A simpler alternative to LSTMs with similar performance.
- **Transformers**: Use attention mechanisms instead of recurrence, enabling faster training and better long-range dependencies.

Now, let's examine how sequence models apply to three major domains: time series, speech, and text processing.

### 3. Time Series Forecasting with Sequence Models

### What is Time Series Data?

Time series data is a collection of observations recorded at regular time intervals, such as:

- **Stock Market Prices** (Predicting future stock prices based on historical trends)
- **Weather Forecasting** (Predicting rainfall, temperature, or storm patterns)
- **IoT Sensor Data** (Predicting failures in industrial equipment)

### Why Do We Need Sequence Models for Time Series?

Traditional models like regression struggle with time-dependent patterns. Sequence models like RNNs, LSTMs, and Transformers help capture trends, seasonality, and irregularities in time series data.

**Example**: Stock Price Prediction with LSTMs

LSTMs are widely used for stock price prediction because they:

- Remember past stock prices.
- Capture long-term trends.
- Filter out noise and irrelevant fluctuations.

A typical LSTM-based stock prediction model would take past 5–10 days of prices as input and predict the next day's price.

*model = Sequential()*
*model.add(LSTM(50, activation='relu', return_sequences=True, input_shape=(10, 1)))*

```
model.add(LSTM(50, activation='relu'))
model.add(Dense(1))
model.compile(optimizer='adam', loss='mse')
```

This model uses two LSTM layers to process stock prices over the past 10 days and predict future trends.

## 4. Speech Recognition with Sequence Models

### Why is Speech Data Challenging?

Speech signals are continuous waveforms where sound patterns change over time. Unlike simple classification tasks, speech recognition requires:

- **Understanding phonetics**: Mapping raw waveforms to phonemes (smallest units of sound).
- **Recognizing words and sentences**: Understanding word boundaries.
- **Handling background noise**: Separating speech from surrounding noise.

### How Do Sequence Models Help?

Sequence models like RNNs, LSTMs, and Transformers (e.g., Wav2Vec) convert speech signals into text by:

- Taking raw waveforms as input.
- Learning phoneme structures through long-term dependencies.
- Generating text output using a decoder.

**Example**: Speech-to-Text Using Deep Learning

A Recurrent Neural Network (RNN) can be trained to convert an audio signal into a text sequence:

```
model = Sequential()
model.add(SimpleRNN(128, input_shape=(None, 13), activation='relu'))
model.add(Dense(64, activation='relu'))
model.add(Dense(num_classes, activation='softmax'))
```

Here, SimpleRNN processes a sequence of Mel-frequency cepstral coefficients (MFCCs) extracted from audio files.

## 5. Natural Language Processing (NLP) with Sequence Models

**Why is Text Processing Hard?**

Natural Language Processing (NLP) deals with human language, which is inherently sequential and context-dependent. Challenges include:

- **Word Order Matters**: "John hit Tom" and "Tom hit John" mean different things.
- **Variable-Length Sentences**: Different inputs require models that can handle varying input lengths.
- **Long-Range Dependencies**: Some words depend on earlier words in a sentence.

**How Do Sequence Models Help?**

Sequence models like LSTMs and Transformers process text by:

- Learning word relationships and context.
- Using attention mechanisms to focus on important words.
- Generating coherent text in tasks like machine translation and chatbots.

**Example**: Sentiment Analysis Using LSTMs

```
model = Sequential()
model.add(Embedding(vocab_size, 100, input_length=max_length))
model.add(LSTM(64, return_sequences=True))
model.add(LSTM(64))
model.add(Dense(1, activation='sigmoid'))
```

This model learns sentiment polarity (positive/negative) from text.

## 6. Conclusion: The Power of Sequence Models

In this chapter, we explored why traditional models struggle with sequential data and how sequence models have transformed time series forecasting, speech recognition, and NLP. Key takeaways:

✓ Traditional models fail with sequence data due to lack of memory and context.

✓ Sequence models like RNNs, LSTMs, and Transformers overcome these limitations.

☑ Time series forecasting, speech recognition, and text processing benefit significantly from sequence models.

🚀 As deep learning advances, newer architectures like Transformers are replacing traditional RNNs, leading to breakthroughs in AI-driven chatbots, virtual assistants, and automated stock trading.

# 10.2. Basics of Recurrent Neural Networks (RNNs)

Artificial Neural Networks (ANNs) have proven highly effective for many machine learning tasks, including image classification and structured data analysis. However, standard ANNs struggle when dealing with sequential data, such as time series, speech, and text. This is because traditional feedforward networks do not retain past information, making them ineffective for tasks where context matters.

To address this limitation, Recurrent Neural Networks (RNNs) were introduced. RNNs are a class of neural networks specifically designed to process sequential data by maintaining memory of previous inputs. This chapter will cover the fundamental architecture of RNNs, their working principles, advantages, limitations, and practical applications.

## 1. Why Do We Need RNNs?

Many real-world problems require a model that can remember past inputs while making predictions. Consider the following scenarios:

- **Time Series Forecasting**: Predicting future stock prices based on previous trends.
- **Speech Recognition**: Understanding spoken words by analyzing past phonemes.
- **Machine Translation**: Translating sentences by considering prior words in a sequence.
- **Chatbots and Conversational AI**: Maintaining context in multi-turn conversations.

Traditional feedforward networks process each input independently, without any memory of previous computations. In contrast, RNNs introduce a feedback loop that allows information to persist over multiple time steps, enabling them to understand and predict sequential patterns.

## 2. Architecture of a Recurrent Neural Network (RNN)

The key innovation of RNNs is their ability to maintain an internal memory state, allowing them to process variable-length sequences. This is achieved through recurrent connections, where the output of a neuron at a given time step is fed back as an input in the next time step.

### Basic Structure of an RNN

A simple RNN cell consists of:

- **Input Layer**: Accepts the current input at time step $t$ Hidden Layer (Memory State): Maintains information from previous time steps.
- **Output Layer**: Produces a prediction for the current time step.

Mathematically, the hidden state $h_t$ at time step $t$ is updated as:

$$h_t = f(W_h h_{t-1} + W_x x_t + b)$$

Where:

- $x_t$ = Input at time step $t$

- $h_t$ = Hidden state at time step $t$

- $W_h$ = Weight matrix for hidden state

- $W_x$ = Weight matrix for input

- $b$ = Bias term

- $f$ = Activation function (commonly tanh or ReLU)

The final output at time step $t$ is computed as:

$$y_t = W_y h_t + b_y$$

Where $W_y$ and $b_y$ are the weight and bias for the output layer.

### 3. How RNNs Process Sequences

Unlike feedforward networks, RNNs process input sequentially, one step at a time. Let's consider a simple example of text processing:

**Example**: Predicting the Next Word in a Sentence

If the input sentence is:

"I love deep learning because it is ..."

1. At $t = 1$, input "I" is fed into the network.
2. At $t = 2$, input **"love"** is processed along with the hidden state from $t = 1$.
3. At $t = 3$, input **"deep"** is processed along with information from previous words.
4. The model continues until it generates a prediction for the next word.

The ability of RNNs to carry information across time steps makes them ideal for text and speech-related tasks.

### 4. Advantages of RNNs

#### ✓ Handles Sequential Data Efficiently

RNNs can process variable-length sequences, making them suitable for speech, text, and time series applications.

#### ✓ Captures Temporal Dependencies

By maintaining a hidden state, RNNs can understand relationships between past and present inputs.

#### ✓ Parameter Sharing

Unlike traditional neural networks, RNNs use the same set of weights across all time steps, reducing computational complexity.

## 5. Limitations of Basic RNNs

Despite their advantages, vanilla RNNs have several limitations:

### ✖ Vanishing Gradient Problem

During training, as errors propagate back through time (using backpropagation through time, or BPTT), gradients can become extremely small. This makes it difficult for RNNs to learn long-range dependencies.

### ✖ Exploding Gradient Problem

Conversely, gradients can grow excessively large, causing unstable updates to the model parameters.

### ✖ Short-Term Memory

Basic RNNs struggle to retain information from distant time steps, making them ineffective for long sequences.

To address these challenges, advanced RNN variants like Long Short-Term Memory (LSTM) networks and Gated Recurrent Units (GRUs) were developed.

## 6. Applications of RNNs

Despite their limitations, RNNs have been successfully applied in various domains:

### ◆ Time Series Forecasting

- Predicting weather conditions
- Forecasting stock prices
- Monitoring heart rate signals in healthcare

### ◆ Speech Recognition

- Converting spoken language into text (e.g., Siri, Google Assistant)
- Real-time voice translation

◆ **Natural Language Processing (NLP)**

- Sentiment analysis
- Text summarization
- Machine translation (Google Translate)

◆ **Video Analysis**

- Action recognition in video frames
- Automatic video captioning

## 7. Implementing a Simple RNN in Python

Let's implement a simple RNN using TensorFlow and Keras to predict a sequence.

```python
import numpy as np
import tensorflow as tf
from tensorflow.keras.models import Sequential
from tensorflow.keras.layers import SimpleRNN, Dense

# Generate sample data (sequence of numbers)
X = np.array([[i, i+1, i+2] for i in range(10)])
y = np.array([i+3 for i in range(10)])

# Reshape for RNN input
X = X.reshape((10, 3, 1))

# Build RNN model
model = Sequential([
    SimpleRNN(10, activation='relu', input_shape=(3, 1)),
    Dense(1)
])

# Compile and train the model
model.compile(optimizer='adam', loss='mse')
model.fit(X, y, epochs=100, verbose=0)

# Predict next value
print("Prediction:", model.predict(np.array([[[10], [11], [12]]])))
```

This simple example demonstrates how an RNN can learn a numerical pattern and predict the next value in a sequence.

Recurrent Neural Networks (RNNs) are a powerful tool for processing sequential data. They introduce a memory mechanism that allows models to learn temporal dependencies, making them effective for tasks such as speech recognition, time series forecasting, and NLP.

However, basic RNNs face challenges like the vanishing gradient problem, limiting their ability to capture long-term dependencies. These challenges are addressed by more advanced architectures like LSTMs and GRUs, which will be covered in the next section.

In summary:

✅ RNNs excel at handling variable-length sequential data.

✅ They capture temporal dependencies, unlike traditional neural networks.

✅ Vanishing gradients limit their ability to learn long-term dependencies.

✅ They form the foundation for advanced models like LSTMs, GRUs, and Transformers.

# 10.3. Vanishing Gradient Problem & Long Short-Term Memory (LSTMs)

Deep learning models, particularly Recurrent Neural Networks (RNNs), are highly effective for processing sequential data. However, standard RNNs suffer from a significant limitation known as the vanishing gradient problem, which hampers their ability to learn long-term dependencies. To address this issue, Long Short-Term Memory (LSTM) networks were introduced, offering a more robust approach to sequential learning.

This chapter delves into the vanishing gradient problem, its impact on RNNs, and how LSTMs mitigate these challenges, enabling deep learning models to process long sequences efficiently.

## 1. The Vanishing Gradient Problem in RNNs

### 1.1. Understanding Gradients in Neural Networks

In any deep learning model, the training process relies on gradient-based optimization using backpropagation. This technique updates weights by calculating gradients of the loss function with respect to model parameters.

For RNNs, this process is called Backpropagation Through Time (BPTT), which involves computing gradients across multiple time steps. However, as the number of time steps increases, the gradients can become extremely small (vanish) or large (explode).

## 1.2. Why Do Gradients Vanish?

The core reason for **vanishing gradients** in RNNs lies in their recurrent structure. At each time step $t$, the hidden state $h_t$ is updated based on the previous state $h_{t-1}$ and the current input $x_t$:

$$h_t = f(W_h h_{t-1} + W_x x_t + b)$$

Where:

- $W_h$ and $W_x$ are weight matrices,
- $b$ is the bias term,
- $f$ is an activation function (typically **tanh** or **sigmoid**).

When performing **BPTT**, gradients are computed at each time step and multiplied sequentially. If $W_h$ has small eigenvalues (e.g., between 0 and 1), repeated multiplication causes gradients to shrink exponentially. This results in **earlier time steps having negligible impact on the final updates**, making it difficult for the model to learn long-range dependencies.

## 1.3. Symptoms of Vanishing Gradients

- The model struggles to remember earlier inputs in a long sequence.
- Weights update very slowly, leading to prolonged training times.
- The model fails to capture long-term dependencies, making predictions unreliable.

While tuning hyperparameters (e.g., changing activation functions or initialization methods) can mitigate the problem to some extent, a more fundamental solution is required—this is where LSTMs come in.

## 2. Long Short-Term Memory (LSTM) Networks

## 2.1. Introduction to LSTMs

Long Short-Term Memory (LSTM) networks, introduced by Hochreiter & Schmidhuber (1997), are a special type of RNN designed to handle long-term dependencies by mitigating the vanishing gradient problem.

LSTMs achieve this by introducing a memory cell and three key mechanisms:

- **Forget Gate**: Determines which information should be discarded.
- **Input Gate**: Decides what new information should be stored.
- **Output Gate**: Controls what part of the memory should be used for the current output.

This architecture allows LSTMs to selectively retain and discard information, ensuring that relevant context is preserved over long sequences.

## 2.2. Architecture of an LSTM Cell

Each LSTM unit contains a **cell state** $C_t$, which acts as a memory, and three types of gates:

1. **Forget Gate ($f_t$)**

$$f_t = \sigma(W_f[h_{t-1}, x_t] + b_f)$$

- Uses a **sigmoid** function to decide how much of the previous memory should be **forgotten**.
- If $f_t$ is close to 0 → forget past information.
- If $f_t$ is close to 1 → retain past memory.

2. **Input Gate ($i_t$) & Candidate Memory ($\tilde{C}_t$)**

$$i_t = \sigma(W_i[h_{t-1}, x_t] + b_i)$$
$$\tilde{C}_t = \tanh(W_c[h_{t-1}, x_t] + b_c)$$

- The input gate determines how much new information should be added.
- The candidate memory stores potential new information.

## 3. Updating the Cell State

$$C_t = f_t \cdot C_{t-1} + i_t \cdot \tilde{C}_t$$

- The **old memory** is scaled by $f_t$.

- The **new candidate memory** is scaled by $i_t$ and added.

4. **Output Gate ($o_t$) & Final Hidden State ($h_t$)**

$$o_t = \sigma(W_o[h_{t-1}, x_t] + b_o)$$

$$h_t = o_t \cdot \tanh(C_t)$$

- The output gate determines **how much of the cell state** should be exposed.

- The final **hidden state** $h_t$ is derived from the memory cell.

## 2.3. Advantages of LSTMs

✅ **Solves the vanishing gradient problem**: The memory cell allows gradients to flow unimpeded, retaining long-term dependencies.
✅ **Efficient memory storage**: The forget gate ensures that irrelevant information is discarded, preventing unnecessary memory clutter.
✅ **Better handling of variable-length sequences**: Ideal for speech recognition, text generation, and machine translation.

## 3. Implementing an LSTM in Python

Let's build a simple LSTM-based text predictor using TensorFlow and Keras.

```
import numpy as np
import tensorflow as tf
from tensorflow.keras.models import Sequential
from tensorflow.keras.layers import LSTM, Dense

# Generate dummy sequential data
X = np.array([[i, i+1, i+2] for i in range(10)])
y = np.array([i+3 for i in range(10)])

# Reshape for LSTM input
X = X.reshape((10, 3, 1))
```

```
# Build LSTM model
model = Sequential([
    LSTM(10, activation='tanh', input_shape=(3, 1)),
    Dense(1)
])

# Compile and train the model
model.compile(optimizer='adam', loss='mse')
model.fit(X, y, epochs=100, verbose=0)

# Predict the next value
print("Prediction:", model.predict(np.array([[[10], [11], [12]]])))
```

This LSTM model processes sequential data and predicts the next value, demonstrating its ability to retain information over time.

The vanishing gradient problem severely limits the ability of standard RNNs to learn long-range dependencies. LSTMs solve this issue by incorporating a memory cell and gating mechanisms that selectively retain important information.

**Key Takeaways:**

✅ RNNs struggle with long-term dependencies due to vanishing gradients.

✅ LSTMs introduce memory cells and gates to manage long-term context effectively.

✅ They have broad applications in speech recognition, NLP, time series forecasting, and beyond.

In the next chapter, we'll explore another powerful alternative to LSTMs: Gated Recurrent Units (GRUs), which simplify LSTM's architecture while maintaining efficiency. 🚀

## 10.4. GRUs & Modern Alternatives to RNNs

Recurrent Neural Networks (RNNs) revolutionized deep learning for sequential data, but they come with challenges like vanishing gradients and training inefficiencies. While Long Short-Term Memory (LSTM) networks addressed these issues, they are computationally heavy due to their complex architecture. To simplify and improve efficiency, Gated Recurrent Units (GRUs) were introduced.

In this chapter, we'll explore GRUs, their advantages over LSTMs, and modern alternatives to RNNs, such as Transformers, which have surpassed traditional sequential models in many applications.

## 1. Gated Recurrent Units (GRUs)

GRUs were introduced by Kyunghyun Cho et al. (2014) as a simpler alternative to LSTMs. Like LSTMs, GRUs use gating mechanisms to control information flow but with a more compact architecture.

### 1.1. LSTM vs. GRU: Key Differences

| Feature | LSTM | GRU |
|---|---|---|
| Number of Gates | 3 (Forget, Input, Output) | 2 (Reset, Update) |
| Cell State | Separate cell state $C_t$ and hidden state $h_t$ | Single hidden state $h_t$ |
| Computational Complexity | Higher (more parameters) | Lower (faster training) |
| Performance on Small Datasets | Often better (richer control) | Performs similarly or better |

### 1.2. GRU Architecture

Unlike LSTMs, which have separate **cell state** ($C_t$) and **hidden state** ($h_t$), GRUs merge them into a single hidden state. The two key gates in a GRU are:

1. **Update Gate ($z_t$):** Controls how much of the past hidden state should be retained.

$$z_t = \sigma(W_z[h_{t-1}, x_t] + b_z)$$

- If $z_t \approx 1$, the past hidden state is mostly preserved.
- If $z_t \approx 0$, new information replaces the old state.

2. **Reset Gate ($r_t$):** Determines how much past information to forget.

$$r_t = \sigma(W_r[h_{t-1}, x_t] + b_r)$$

- If $r_t \approx 0$, the previous state is largely ignored.

The final **hidden state** $h_t$ is updated as:

$$h_t = z_t \cdot h_{t-1} + (1 - z_t) \cdot \tilde{h}_t$$

where $\tilde{h}_t$ is the candidate state:

$$\tilde{h}_t = \tanh(W_h[r_t \cdot h_{t-1}, x_t] + b_h)$$

## 1.3. Advantages of GRUs

✅ **Fewer parameters than LSTMs** → Faster training and inference.

✅ **Efficient for smaller datasets** → Works well when training data is limited.

✅ Retains long-term dependencies similar to LSTMs but with less complexity.

## 1.4. When to Use GRUs?

- When computational efficiency is critical.
- When working with smaller datasets.
- When a lighter architecture is preferred (e.g., embedded systems, mobile applications).

## 2. Modern Alternatives to RNNs

While GRUs and LSTMs improved sequential learning, they still struggle with long-range dependencies, parallelization, and scalability. This led to the rise of attention-based models and Transformers, which have now become the state-of-the-art for most NLP and sequential tasks.

## 2.1. The Rise of Attention Mechanisms

The Attention Mechanism, introduced in 2014, allows models to focus on relevant parts of input sequences rather than processing them sequentially. This paved the way for the Transformer model, which eliminates the need for recurrence altogether.

## 2.2. Transformers: The New Standard

Transformers, introduced by Vaswani et al. (2017) in the famous paper "Attention Is All You Need", completely replaced RNNs in many areas. Instead of processing sequences one step at a time, Transformers use self-attention to analyze entire sequences in parallel, making them faster and more effective.

**How Transformers Work:**

- **Self-Attention**: Computes dependencies between all words in a sequence simultaneously.
- **Positional Encoding**: Retains order information since Transformers do not have recurrence.
- **Multi-Head Attention**: Allows the model to attend to different parts of the sequence simultaneously.
- **Feedforward Layers**: Transform attention outputs into meaningful representations.

## 2.3. Why Transformers Outperform RNNs

| Feature | RNNs (LSTM/GRU) | Transformers |
| --- | --- | --- |
| Sequential Processing | Yes (one step at a time) | No (parallelized) |
| Long-Term Dependencies | Difficult due to vanishing gradients | Handled effectively with self-attention |
| Training Time | Slow | Faster (leverages GPUs efficiently) |
| Scalability | Limited for long sequences | Scales well with large data |

## 2.4. Notable Transformer-Based Models

✐ **BERT (Bidirectional Encoder Representations from Transformers)** – Revolutionized NLP with pre-training and fine-tuning.

✐ **GPT (Generative Pre-trained Transformer)** – Advanced text generation, used in ChatGPT.

✐ **T5 (Text-to-Text Transfer Transformer)** – Generalized NLP model for multiple tasks.

✐ **ViTs (Vision Transformers)** – Applied Transformers to image processing.

## 3. Implementing GRUs & Transformers in Python

### 3.1. Implementing a GRU Model with TensorFlow/Keras

```python
import tensorflow as tf
from tensorflow.keras.models import Sequential
from tensorflow.keras.layers import GRU, Dense

# Build GRU model
model = Sequential([
    GRU(50, activation='tanh', return_sequences=True, input_shape=(10, 1)),
    GRU(50, activation='tanh'),
    Dense(1)
])

# Compile and summarize model
model.compile(optimizer='adam', loss='mse')
model.summary()
```

### 3.2. Implementing a Transformer Encoder with PyTorch

```python
import torch
import torch.nn as nn

class TransformerEncoder(nn.Module):
    def __init__(self, input_dim, embed_dim, num_heads, ff_dim):
        super().__init__()
        self.attention = nn.MultiheadAttention(embed_dim, num_heads)
        self.feedforward = nn.Sequential(
            nn.Linear(embed_dim, ff_dim),
            nn.ReLU(),
            nn.Linear(ff_dim, embed_dim)
        )
```

```
    self.layer_norm = nn.LayerNorm(embed_dim)

  def forward(self, x):
    attn_output, _ = self.attention(x, x, x)
    x = self.layer_norm(x + attn_output)
    ff_output = self.feedforward(x)
    return self.layer_norm(x + ff_output)

# Example usage
encoder = TransformerEncoder(input_dim=128, embed_dim=64, num_heads=4,
ff_dim=256)
print(encoder)
```

While GRUs offer a simpler, faster alternative to LSTMs, Transformers have revolutionized sequence modeling, becoming the new standard for NLP and beyond.

**Key Takeaways**

✅ **GRUs** simplify LSTMs by reducing the number of gates, making them more computationally efficient.

✅ **LSTMs & GRUs** still have limitations, such as difficulty handling long-range dependencies.

✅ Transformers surpass **RNNs** by leveraging self-attention, making them faster and more scalable.

As deep learning continues evolving, models like Transformers and their variations (BERT, GPT, ViTs) are replacing RNNs in many fields. If you're working on NLP, time series forecasting, or even image processing, learning Transformers is now essential. 🚀

# 11. Transformers & Attention Mechanisms

Transformers have revolutionized the field of natural language processing (NLP) and deep learning by enabling models to process and generate sequences of data more efficiently than traditional RNNs. In this chapter, you'll dive into the Transformer architecture, understanding how it uses self-attention mechanisms to focus on relevant parts of input data, regardless of their position in a sequence. You'll learn how attention allows the model to weigh the importance of different words or elements in a sentence, which is crucial for tasks like translation, summarization, and question answering. Through detailed examples, you'll see how Transformers power advanced models like GPT, BERT, and T5, and gain hands-on experience implementing them for NLP applications. This chapter will equip you with the knowledge to work with cutting-edge deep learning architectures that are reshaping the AI landscape.

## 11.1. The Shift from RNNs to Transformers: Why It Matters

Deep learning has undergone a major shift in how we handle sequential data. For years, Recurrent Neural Networks (RNNs) and their variations—Long Short-Term Memory (LSTMs) and Gated Recurrent Units (GRUs)—were the gold standard for tasks like natural language processing (NLP), speech recognition, and time-series forecasting. However, these architectures suffered from long-range dependency issues, vanishing gradients, and sequential bottlenecks that made training slow and inefficient.

Then came Transformers—a revolutionary deep learning architecture introduced in the landmark paper "Attention Is All You Need" (Vaswani et al., 2017). Transformers solved many of the problems inherent in RNN-based models by eliminating recurrence and leveraging a mechanism called self-attention, which allowed them to process entire sequences in parallel. This fundamental shift has led to groundbreaking models like BERT, GPT, T5, and Vision Transformers (ViTs) that outperform RNNs in almost every sequential task.

This chapter explores why this transition from RNNs to Transformers matters, what makes Transformers superior, and how they have transformed the AI landscape.

### 1. Limitations of RNNs and Why They Were Replaced

Despite their effectiveness, RNNs have several key weaknesses that hinder performance, particularly when handling long sequences. Let's explore some of these limitations:

## 1.1. Sequential Processing Bottleneck

RNNs process input one step at a time, meaning that each computation depends on the previous step. This sequential nature introduces training inefficiencies because:

- It cannot leverage parallel computation efficiently.
- It slows down training, especially on long sequences.
- It limits scalability on large datasets.

In contrast, Transformers process the entire sequence in parallel, making them significantly faster and more scalable.

## 1.2. Vanishing & Exploding Gradient Problems

The core of an RNN is a loop where hidden states are passed from one timestep to the next. However, when training on long sequences, gradients can vanish (become too small to update weights) or explode (become excessively large, destabilizing training). While LSTMs and GRUs partially addressed this with gating mechanisms, they still struggle with very long-term dependencies.

Transformers overcome this by using self-attention, which allows them to capture dependencies between words regardless of distance.

## 1.3. Difficulty in Capturing Long-Range Dependencies

RNNs struggle to retain information over long distances. For example, in a long sentence, an RNN might forget the subject by the time it reaches the verb, making it harder to capture long-range dependencies.

Transformers solve this problem with attention mechanisms that directly link distant words or features, making them more effective at understanding context.

## 1.4. Challenges in Training

RNNs require backpropagation through time (BPTT), a variant of backpropagation that works sequentially. This makes training slow and computationally expensive.

Transformers use standard backpropagation, enabling faster training and the ability to scale to massive datasets, such as those used in models like GPT-4.

## 2. The Transformer Revolution: Why It Works Better

Transformers replaced recurrence with self-attention and positional encoding, allowing them to efficiently process sequences in parallel. Here's why they outperform RNNs:

### 2.1. Self-Attention: The Game-Changer

The self-attention mechanism is the heart of Transformers. Instead of processing words one by one, self-attention allows the model to compare each word to every other word in a sentence simultaneously. This enables:

- **Better long-range dependencies**: The model can directly connect related words, even if they are far apart.
- **Parallel computation**: All tokens in a sequence are processed simultaneously.
- **Improved context understanding**: The model attends to important words dynamically.

**Mathematically, self-attention is computed as:**

$$\text{Attention}(Q, K, V) = \text{softmax}\left(\frac{QK^T}{\sqrt{d_k}}\right) V$$

where:

- $Q$ (queries), $K$ (keys), and $V$ (values) are **word embeddings**.

- $d_k$ is the scaling factor.

- The **softmax function** ensures that attention scores sum to 1.

This mechanism allows Transformers to focus on relevant words without processing them sequentially.

### 2.2. Positional Encoding: Overcoming the Lack of Recurrence

Since Transformers don't process sequences step by step like RNNs, they need a way to encode word order. Positional encoding adds information about the position of each word in a sentence, enabling the model to maintain order while benefiting from parallelism.

## 2.3. Multi-Head Attention: Handling Multiple Contexts

Transformers use multi-head attention, meaning they apply multiple attention mechanisms in parallel. This allows them to focus on different aspects of a sentence simultaneously, capturing more nuanced relationships between words.

## 2.4. Scalability & Efficiency

Transformers are highly parallelizable, making them efficient on GPUs and TPUs. This has enabled the training of massive models like GPT-4, BERT, and T5, which wouldn't be feasible with RNN-based architectures.

## 3. The Impact of Transformers on AI

The shift from RNNs to Transformers has transformed several fields of AI:

## 3.1. Natural Language Processing (NLP)

✍ **BERT** (Bidirectional Encoder Representations from Transformers) revolutionized NLP by pre-training on massive datasets and fine-tuning for specific tasks. Unlike RNNs, BERT processes entire sentences bidirectionally, improving contextual understanding.

✍ **GPT** (Generative Pre-trained Transformer) models excel in text generation, chatbots, and creative writing. Unlike RNNs, they generate text based on deep contextual understanding.

## 3.2. Computer Vision

✍ **Vision Transformers** (ViTs) apply Transformer models to image recognition tasks, outperforming convolutional neural networks (CNNs) in certain domains.

## 3.3. Speech & Time-Series Analysis

✍ Transformers are being adapted for speech recognition, time-series forecasting, and bioinformatics, replacing RNNs in domains where sequential data is critical.

## 4. The Future: Are RNNs Obsolete?

With the rise of Transformers, are RNNs still relevant? The short answer is: It depends on the task.

✅ **RNNs** are still useful for small-scale tasks, where computational efficiency matters.
✅ **GRUs/LSTMs** may still be preferred for low-latency applications with limited resources.

❌ For large-scale NLP, speech, and vision tasks, Transformers have taken over.

As AI continues to evolve, Transformers will likely remain dominant, but research into hybrid architectures (e.g., Transformer-RNN hybrids) may further refine sequence modeling.

### 5. Conclusion: Why This Shift Matters

The transition from RNNs to Transformers is one of the most significant advancements in AI. By removing sequential dependencies and leveraging self-attention, Transformers have:

- Accelerated deep learning research by enabling parallel processing.
- Improved long-range dependencies in text, speech, and image tasks.
- Revolutionized NLP, vision, and beyond, powering state-of-the-art models.

Understanding this shift is crucial for AI practitioners, as modern AI applications increasingly rely on Transformer-based architectures. If you're building AI models today, learning Transformers and attention mechanisms is no longer optional—it's essential. 🚀

# 11.2. Understanding Attention Mechanisms

One of the most transformative breakthroughs in deep learning has been the attention mechanism. Originally introduced to improve sequence-to-sequence (Seq2Seq) models in machine translation, attention has since become the foundation of modern neural networks, enabling models like Transformers, BERT, and GPT to achieve state-of-the-art performance in natural language processing (NLP), computer vision, and more.

At its core, attention allows a model to focus on the most relevant parts of an input sequence while processing each element. Instead of treating all inputs equally, an attention mechanism dynamically assigns different importance (weights) to different elements, enabling more effective learning of long-range dependencies.

This chapter explores the fundamentals of attention, its different types, and how it powers modern AI architectures.

## 1. What is Attention?

Imagine reading a long article. As you read, you don't remember every single word but rather focus on the most relevant parts—key sentences, important names, or specific details. Similarly, in deep learning, attention helps models prioritize the most important inputs while ignoring irrelevant details.

In traditional recurrent neural networks (RNNs), each word in a sequence was processed sequentially, making it difficult to retain information from earlier words when predicting later words. Attention overcomes this by allowing the model to refer back to all previous words at every step, assigning different importance to each based on relevance.

Mathematically, attention is a mechanism that computes a weighted sum of input features, where the weights are dynamically learned based on the input itself.

## 2. Types of Attention Mechanisms

There are multiple types of attention mechanisms, each designed to address specific challenges in deep learning:

### 2.1. Additive vs. Multiplicative Attention

There are two primary ways to compute attention scores:

- **Additive Attention**: Uses a neural network to compute the attention weights. It is computationally more expensive but works well with small hidden dimensions.
- **Multiplicative (Dot-Product) Attention**: Computes attention using dot products between vectors, making it faster and more efficient for large models.

### 2.2. Soft vs. Hard Attention

- **Soft Attention**: Generates a weighted sum of all inputs, ensuring that all words contribute, but with different levels of importance.
- **Hard Attention**: Selects only one or a few key elements to focus on, making it non-differentiable and requiring reinforcement learning techniques.

### 2.3. Self-Attention vs. Cross-Attention

- **Self-Attention**: Computes attention within the same input sequence (e.g., in Transformers, every word attends to every other word).
- **Cross-Attention**: Computes attention between two different sequences (e.g., in sequence-to-sequence translation, the decoder attends to the encoder output).

### 3. The Self-Attention Mechanism: The Heart of Transformers

Self-attention is what enables Transformers to capture global dependencies without relying on recurrence. It works by comparing each word in a sequence with every other word, allowing the model to understand relationships and context efficiently.

### 3.1. Key Components of Self-Attention

Self-attention operates using three key components:

- **Query (Q):** Represents the current word we are focusing on.
- **Key (K):** Represents all words in the input.
- **Value (V):** Represents the corresponding word embeddings that will be weighted.

**The self-attention formula is:**

$$\text{Attention}(Q, K, V) = \text{softmax}\left(\frac{QK^T}{\sqrt{d_k}}\right) V$$

Where:

- $QK^T$ computes the similarity between the **query** and **keys**.

- $\sqrt{d_k}$ scales the values to prevent large gradients.

- The **softmax function** ensures the attention scores sum to 1.

### 3.2. Multi-Head Attention: The Power of Multiple Perspectives

Instead of computing attention once, Transformers use multiple attention heads to capture different types of relationships in data.

- Each attention head learns a different representation of the input.

- The results from all attention heads are combined, improving context understanding.

**The formula for multi-head attention is:**

$$\text{MultiHead}(Q, K, V) = \text{Concat}(\text{head}_1, \text{head}_2, ..., \text{head}_h)W^O$$

This allows the model to consider multiple perspectives at once, making it much more powerful than simple self-attention.

## 4. How Attention Powers Modern AI

Attention mechanisms are now a fundamental building block in state-of-the-art deep learning models:

### 4.1. Attention in Natural Language Processing (NLP)

- **Machine Translation**: Attention allows a model to focus on different parts of a sentence while translating.
- **Chatbots & Conversational AI**: GPT-4 and ChatGPT use attention to generate coherent responses.
- **Text Summarization**: Models like BERT and T5 use attention to identify key phrases.

### 4.2. Attention in Computer Vision

- **Vision Transformers (ViTs)** use attention instead of convolution to recognize patterns in images.
- **Image Captioning Models** use attention to describe important parts of an image while ignoring irrelevant details.

### 4.3. Attention in Speech & Time-Series Analysis

- **Speech Recognition**: Self-attention helps models transcribe spoken language accurately.
- **Financial Forecasting**: Attention-based models analyze past stock trends and predict future prices.

## 5. Conclusion: Why Attention Matters

The attention mechanism has revolutionized deep learning by making models faster, more accurate, and better at capturing relationships in data. It is the foundation of Transformers, which have surpassed traditional RNNs in almost every major AI application.

Understanding attention is crucial for any AI practitioner, as it continues to drive groundbreaking advancements in NLP, vision, and beyond. 🚀

# 11.3. The Transformer Model: Encoder-Decoder Architecture

The Transformer model has revolutionized deep learning by eliminating the need for recurrence while dramatically improving efficiency, scalability, and accuracy. Introduced in the landmark 2017 paper "Attention Is All You Need", the Transformer architecture has become the foundation of state-of-the-art AI models such as BERT, GPT, T5, and ViTs (Vision Transformers).

At the heart of the Transformer is the encoder-decoder architecture, which leverages self-attention and positional embeddings to process entire sequences in parallel. This chapter delves into how the Transformer model works, explaining its encoder, decoder, attention mechanisms, and training process in detail.

### 1. The Limitations of Previous Sequence Models

Before the Transformer, RNNs, LSTMs, and GRUs were the dominant models for handling sequential data, but they suffered from several key issues:

- **Sequential Processing**: RNNs process data one step at a time, making them slow and difficult to parallelize.
- **Long-Range Dependencies**: Despite LSTMs and GRUs improving memory retention, they still struggled with very long sequences.
- **Gradient Issues**: RNNs often suffered from the vanishing gradient problem, making training difficult for long sequences.

The Transformer overcomes these limitations by removing recurrence entirely and using self-attention to process sequences in parallel, dramatically improving training speed and performance.

### 2. The Encoder-Decoder Architecture

The Transformer follows an encoder-decoder structure, commonly used in machine translation and sequence-to-sequence tasks. Each component consists of multiple identical layers, each with its own self-attention mechanism and feedforward network.

## 2.1. The Encoder

The encoder is responsible for processing the input sequence and transforming it into a fixed-size representation. It consists of multiple identical layers, each containing:

- **Self-Attention Mechanism**: Enables each word in the input sequence to attend to all other words, capturing context effectively.
- **Feedforward Neural Network (FFN):** A fully connected network that further processes attention outputs.
- **Layer Normalization & Residual Connections**: Helps stabilize training and prevent gradient issues.

Each word in the input sequence is embedded into a vector and then passed through multiple layers of self-attention and feedforward transformations.

## 2.2. The Decoder

The decoder generates output sequences one token at a time, predicting the next word while considering previously generated words. Like the encoder, it consists of multiple layers, but with one key difference:

**Masked Self-Attention**: Prevents the decoder from seeing future words, ensuring predictions are generated in an autoregressive manner.

The decoder takes the encoded input representations from the encoder and combines them with previously generated words to produce the final output.

## 3. Self-Attention: The Core Mechanism

Self-attention allows the Transformer to focus on relevant parts of the input when processing each word, rather than relying on fixed-length context windows like RNNs.

## 3.1. How Self-Attention Works

Each input word is transformed into three key vectors:

- **Query (Q)** – Represents the current word.
- **Key (K)** – Represents all words in the input sequence.
- **Value (V)** – Contains contextual information about each word.

The attention scores are computed using:

$$\text{Attention}(Q, K, V) = \text{softmax}\left(\frac{QK^T}{\sqrt{d_k}}\right) V$$

This formula determines how much attention each word should pay to every other word in the sequence.

### 4. Multi-Head Attention: Enhancing Context Awareness

Instead of computing self-attention once, the Transformer uses multiple attention heads, each capturing different types of relationships within the data.

$$\text{MultiHead}(Q, K, V) = \text{Concat}(\text{head}_1, \text{head}_2, ..., \text{head}_h)W^O$$

Multi-head attention allows the model to consider different interpretations of the input simultaneously, making it more robust.

### 5. Positional Encoding: Handling Word Order

Unlike RNNs, which process inputs sequentially, the Transformer processes all words at once. However, this creates a problem—how does the model know the order of words?

To address this, positional encodings are added to input embeddings:

$$PE_{(pos, 2i)} = \sin(pos/10000^{2i/d})$$

$$PE_{(pos, 2i+1)} = \cos(pos/10000^{2i/d})$$

These encodings inject information about the position of words, allowing the model to understand order without recurrence.

## 6. The Feedforward Network (FFN)

Each encoder and decoder layer contains a fully connected feedforward network, which processes the self-attention outputs to introduce non-linearity and improve model expressiveness.

$$\text{FFN}(x) = \max(0, xW_1 + b_1)W_2 + b_2$$

This network ensures that information is further refined before being passed to the next layer.

## 7. Layer Normalization & Residual Connections

To improve training stability, each layer includes:

- **Residual Connections**: Helps prevent information loss and improves gradient flow.
- **Layer Normalization**: Stabilizes training by normalizing activations.

## Each sub-layer is wrapped as:

$$\text{LayerNorm}(x + \text{Sublayer}(x))$$

This ensures smooth information flow across the network.

## 8. Why Transformers Outperform RNNs

Compared to traditional sequence models, Transformers offer several advantages:

| Feature | RNN/LSTM | Transformer |
| --- | --- | --- |
| Parallelization | ✗ No | ✓ Yes |
| Long-Range Dependencies | ✗ Struggles | ✓ Captures efficiently |
| Training Speed | ⏳ Slow | ⚡ Fast |
| Gradient Issues | 〰 Vanishing gradients | ✓ No gradient problems |
| Context Understanding | ✗ Limited | ✓ Global |

These benefits have made the Transformer the dominant architecture in NLP and beyond.

## 9. Applications of Transformer Models

The Transformer architecture powers many advanced AI applications:

- **NLP**: GPT, BERT, T5, and ChatGPT use Transformers for language understanding.
- **Computer Vision**: Vision Transformers (ViTs) outperform CNNs in image recognition.
- **Speech Recognition**: Models like Whisper leverage Transformers for transcriptions.
- **Protein Folding**: AlphaFold uses Transformers for scientific breakthroughs.

## 10. Conclusion: The Future of AI with Transformers

The encoder-decoder Transformer architecture has redefined deep learning, enabling breakthroughs in NLP, vision, and multimodal AI. By eliminating recurrence, leveraging attention, and enabling parallel computation, it has become the gold standard for modern AI.

Understanding the Transformer is crucial for AI practitioners, as it continues to drive the next wave of AI innovation. 🚀

# 11.4. Implementing a Transformer Using PyTorch/TensorFlow

The Transformer model, introduced in "Attention Is All You Need", has revolutionized deep learning by replacing recurrence with self-attention and parallel processing. In this section, we will implement a mini-Transformer model using PyTorch.

This implementation follows the original encoder-decoder architecture and includes:

✓ Multi-head self-attention

✓ Positional encoding

✓ Feedforward networks

✓ Layer normalization

✓ Masked attention for autoregression

## 1. Installing Dependencies

Ensure you have PyTorch installed. If not, install it using:

*pip install torch torchvision torchtext*

## 2. Importing Required Libraries

```
import torch
import torch.nn as nn
import torch.optim as optim
import torch.nn.functional as F
import numpy as np
import math
```

## 3. Implementing Positional Encoding

Since Transformers lack recurrence, we use sinusoidal positional encoding to inject order information.

```
class PositionalEncoding(nn.Module):
    def __init__(self, d_model, max_len=5000):
        super(PositionalEncoding, self).__init__()

        # Create a matrix of shape (max_len, d_model)
        pos = torch.arange(max_len).unsqueeze(1)
        div_term = torch.exp(torch.arange(0, d_model, 2) * (-math.log(10000.0) /
d_model))

        pe = torch.zeros(max_len, d_model)
        pe[:, 0::2] = torch.sin(pos * div_term)
        pe[:, 1::2] = torch.cos(pos * div_term)

        pe = pe.unsqueeze(0)  # Add batch dimension
        self.register_buffer('pe', pe)

    def forward(self, x):
        return x + self.pe[:, :x.size(1)]
```

## 4. Implementing Multi-Head Self-Attention

Multi-head attention allows the model to focus on different parts of the sequence simultaneously.

```
class MultiHeadAttention(nn.Module):
    def __init__(self, d_model, num_heads):
        super(MultiHeadAttention, self).__init__()
        assert d_model % num_heads == 0  # Ensure heads divide evenly

        self.d_model = d_model
        self.num_heads = num_heads
        self.head_dim = d_model // num_heads  # Dimension per head

        self.qkv_linear = nn.Linear(d_model, d_model * 3)  # Queries, Keys, Values
        self.out_linear = nn.Linear(d_model, d_model)

        self.scale = torch.sqrt(torch.FloatTensor([self.head_dim])).to('cpu')

    def forward(self, x, mask=None):
        batch_size, seq_len, d_model = x.shape
        qkv = self.qkv_linear(x).reshape(batch_size, seq_len, 3, self.num_heads, self.head_dim)
        q, k, v = qkv.unbind(dim=2)  # Split into Q, K, V

        # Compute attention scores
        scores = torch.matmul(q, k.transpose(-2, -1)) / self.scale
        if mask is not None:
            scores = scores.masked_fill(mask == 0, -1e9)  # Mask padding tokens

        attn = torch.softmax(scores, dim=-1)
        output = torch.matmul(attn, v)

        # Reshape and pass through output linear layer
        output = output.permute(0, 2, 1, 3).reshape(batch_size, seq_len, d_model)
        return self.out_linear(output)
```

## 5. Feedforward Network (FFN)

Each Transformer layer contains a fully connected feedforward network with ReLU activation.

```
class FeedForward(nn.Module):
    def __init__(self, d_model, d_ff):
        super(FeedForward, self).__init__()
        self.fc1 = nn.Linear(d_model, d_ff)
        self.fc2 = nn.Linear(d_ff, d_model)
        self.relu = nn.ReLU()

    def forward(self, x):
        return self.fc2(self.relu(self.fc1(x)))
```

## 6. Transformer Encoder Layer

Each encoder layer consists of:

- Multi-head self-attention
- Feedforward network
- Layer normalization & residual connections

```
class TransformerEncoderLayer(nn.Module):
    def __init__(self, d_model, num_heads, d_ff, dropout=0.1):
        super(TransformerEncoderLayer, self).__init__()
        self.self_attn = MultiHeadAttention(d_model, num_heads)
        self.ffn = FeedForward(d_model, d_ff)

        self.norm1 = nn.LayerNorm(d_model)
        self.norm2 = nn.LayerNorm(d_model)
        self.dropout = nn.Dropout(dropout)

    def forward(self, x, mask=None):
        attn_output = self.self_attn(x, mask)
        x = self.norm1(x + self.dropout(attn_output))

        ffn_output = self.ffn(x)
        x = self.norm2(x + self.dropout(ffn_output))
        return x
```

## 7. Transformer Encoder

The full Transformer Encoder consists of multiple stacked layers.

```python
class TransformerEncoder(nn.Module):
    def __init__(self, num_layers, d_model, num_heads, d_ff, vocab_size, max_len=5000):
        super(TransformerEncoder, self).__init__()
        self.embedding = nn.Embedding(vocab_size, d_model)
        self.pos_encoding = PositionalEncoding(d_model, max_len)

        self.layers = nn.ModuleList([
            TransformerEncoderLayer(d_model, num_heads, d_ff) for _ in range(num_layers)
        ])

    def forward(self, x, mask=None):
        x = self.embedding(x)
        x = self.pos_encoding(x)

        for layer in self.layers:
            x = layer(x, mask)

        return x
```

## 8. Full Transformer Model

Now, let's define the full Transformer model, including both encoder and decoder.

```python
class Transformer(nn.Module):
    def __init__(self, num_layers, d_model, num_heads, d_ff, vocab_size, max_len=5000):
        super(Transformer, self).__init__()
        self.encoder = TransformerEncoder(num_layers, d_model, num_heads, d_ff, vocab_size, max_len)
        self.decoder = nn.Linear(d_model, vocab_size)  # Output layer for token prediction

    def forward(self, x, mask=None):
        enc_output = self.encoder(x, mask)
        return self.decoder(enc_output)
```

## 9. Training the Transformer Model

### Loss Function & Optimizer

```
model = Transformer(num_layers=6, d_model=512, num_heads=8, d_ff=2048,
vocab_size=10000)
optimizer = optim.Adam(model.parameters(), lr=1e-4)
criterion = nn.CrossEntropyLoss()
```

### Training Loop

```
def train_model(model, data_loader, epochs=10):
    model.train()
    for epoch in range(epochs):
        for batch in data_loader:
            optimizer.zero_grad()
            inputs, targets = batch
            outputs = model(inputs)

            loss = criterion(outputs.view(-1, outputs.size(-1)), targets.view(-1))
            loss.backward()
            optimizer.step()

        print(f"Epoch {epoch + 1}, Loss: {loss.item()}")
```

Congratulations! 🎉 You've implemented a mini-Transformer model using PyTorch. This model can be extended to language modeling (GPT), text classification (BERT), and even vision tasks (ViTs).

# 12. Autoencoders & Generative Models

Autoencoders and generative models open up exciting possibilities for unsupervised learning and data generation. In this chapter, you'll learn about autoencoders, a type of neural network used to compress and reconstruct data by learning an efficient representation of the input. You'll explore how they are used for tasks such as anomaly detection, image denoising, and dimensionality reduction. Moving beyond autoencoders, the chapter delves into Generative Models like Generative Adversarial Networks (GANs), which consist of two competing networks—a generator and a discriminator—that can generate realistic images, text, and even music. Through practical examples, you'll see how these models are transforming industries, from creating realistic synthetic images to advancing creative AI. This chapter provides a deep dive into the world of generative deep learning, equipping you to build your own creative AI models.

## 12.1. Introduction to Autoencoders & Dimensionality Reduction

Autoencoders are a class of artificial neural networks used to learn efficient representations of data, often for dimensionality reduction. Unlike traditional supervised learning models, autoencoders are trained in an unsupervised manner, meaning they learn to encode and reconstruct input data without explicit labels.

The main goal of an autoencoder is to compress the input data into a lower-dimensional representation (encoding) and then reconstruct it as accurately as possible. This makes autoencoders particularly useful for:

- **Dimensionality Reduction** (like PCA but more powerful)
- **Denoising Data** (removing noise from images or signals)
- **Anomaly Detection** (identifying outliers in data)
- **Feature Extraction** (finding essential features in large datasets)
- **Generative Modeling** (forming the foundation of Variational Autoencoders)

### 2. The Architecture of an Autoencoder

An autoencoder consists of two main components:

### 2.1. Encoder

- The encoder compresses the input data into a latent space representation (also called the bottleneck or latent vector).
- This part of the network learns to extract the most important features from the input.
- The dimensionality of the latent space is usually much smaller than the input.

## 2.2. Decoder

- The decoder takes the compressed representation and attempts to reconstruct the original input as closely as possible.
- If trained correctly, the decoder can reconstruct high-dimensional data with minimal loss.

## 2.3. Bottleneck Layer (Latent Space Representation)

- This is the most compressed part of the autoencoder.
- It acts as a feature extractor and can be used for dimensionality reduction or data generation.

The entire autoencoder is trained to minimize reconstruction error, which means that the model tries to produce an output that closely matches the input.

## 3. Mathematical Foundation of Autoencoders

Autoencoders can be described mathematically as follows:

Let X be the input data. The encoder function $E(\cdot)$ maps the input to a lower-dimensional latent space Z, and the decoder function $D(\cdot)$ reconstructs the input from Z.

$$Z = E(X)$$

$$X' = D(Z)$$

The goal of training an autoencoder is to minimize the reconstruction loss between the original input X and the reconstructed output X'. A common loss function used is Mean Squared Error (MSE):

$$Loss = ||X - X'||^2$$

where $||X - X'||^2$ measures the difference between the original and reconstructed data.

## 4. Autoencoders for Dimensionality Reduction

### 4.1. Why Dimensionality Reduction?

High-dimensional data can be computationally expensive and often contains redundant or irrelevant features. Reducing dimensionality helps in:

- Reducing computational costs
- Avoiding the curse of dimensionality
- Improving model generalization
- Better visualization of data

### 4.2. Autoencoders vs. PCA (Principal Component Analysis)

Both autoencoders and PCA are used for dimensionality reduction, but they have key differences:

| Feature | PCA | Autoencoder |
|---|---|---|
| Type | Linear | Non-linear |
| Representation | Projects onto principal components | Learns features via neural networks |
| Complexity | Simple, fast | More computationally expensive |
| Performance on complex data | Struggles with non-linearity | Handles non-linearity well |

PCA assumes a linear transformation, while autoencoders can capture non-linear relationships, making them more powerful for complex datasets.

## 5. Types of Autoencoders

There are different types of autoencoders designed for specific tasks:

### 5.1. Vanilla Autoencoder

- The simplest form of an autoencoder.

- Uses fully connected (dense) layers in both the encoder and decoder.

### 5.2. Denoising Autoencoder (DAE)

- Trained to remove noise from input data.
- The model is given a corrupted version of the input and learns to reconstruct the clean version.

### 5.3. Sparse Autoencoder

- Introduces sparsity constraints to force the network to learn meaningful features.
- Often used for feature selection.

### 5.4. Variational Autoencoder (VAE)

- A probabilistic version of autoencoders used for generative modeling.
- Instead of encoding data into a fixed vector, VAEs learn a probability distribution over the latent space.

## 6. Implementing an Autoencoder in Python (Using TensorFlow/Keras)

### 6.1. Import Dependencies

```
import tensorflow as tf
from tensorflow.keras.layers import Input, Dense
from tensorflow.keras.models import Model
import numpy as np
import matplotlib.pyplot as plt
```

### 6.2. Define Autoencoder Architecture

```
# Define encoder
input_dim = 784  # Example for MNIST dataset
encoding_dim = 32  # Compressing to 32 dimensions

input_layer = Input(shape=(input_dim,))
encoded = Dense(encoding_dim, activation='relu')(input_layer)

# Define decoder
decoded = Dense(input_dim, activation='sigmoid')(encoded)
```

```
# Define full autoencoder model
autoencoder = Model(input_layer, decoded)

# Define encoder model separately (for feature extraction)
encoder = Model(input_layer, encoded)

# Compile model
autoencoder.compile(optimizer='adam', loss='mse')
```

## 6.3. Train the Autoencoder

```
# Load dataset (Example: MNIST)
from tensorflow.keras.datasets import mnist

(x_train, _), (x_test, _) = mnist.load_data()
x_train = x_train.astype('float32') / 255.
x_test = x_test.astype('float32') / 255.
x_train = x_train.reshape((len(x_train), np.prod(x_train.shape[1:])))
x_test = x_test.reshape((len(x_test), np.prod(x_test.shape[1:])))

# Train autoencoder
autoencoder.fit(x_train, x_train, epochs=50, batch_size=256, shuffle=True,
validation_data=(x_test, x_test))
```

## 6.4. Visualize the Compressed Representation

```
encoded_imgs = encoder.predict(x_test)

plt.scatter(encoded_imgs[:, 0], encoded_imgs[:, 1], c='blue')
plt.xlabel("Feature 1")
plt.ylabel("Feature 2")
plt.title("Latent Space Representation")
plt.show()
```

## 7. Applications of Autoencoders

Autoencoders are widely used in various fields:

- **Dimensionality Reduction** - Compressing high-dimensional data for visualization and analysis.
- **Denoising Images** - Removing noise from corrupted images.
- **Anomaly Detection** - Identifying fraud in financial transactions.
- **Generative Modeling** - Used in GANs (Generative Adversarial Networks) and VAEs.
- **Data Compression** - Efficiently encoding data for storage and transmission.

Autoencoders are a powerful class of neural networks that learn efficient data representations without supervision. By compressing data into a lower-dimensional latent space, they help in dimensionality reduction, denoising, feature extraction, and anomaly detection. Unlike traditional methods like PCA, autoencoders can capture complex, non-linear structures in data, making them more effective for real-world applications.

# 12.2. Variational Autoencoders (VAEs) & Their Applications

Variational Autoencoders (VAEs) are a type of generative model that extends traditional autoencoders by learning a probabilistic distribution over the latent space. Unlike standard autoencoders that encode data into a fixed set of values, VAEs learn to represent data as probability distributions, allowing them to generate new data samples similar to the training data.

**This makes VAEs particularly useful for:**

- **Data Generation** (e.g., generating new images, text, or audio)
- **Anomaly Detection** (e.g., fraud detection, medical diagnosis)
- **Latent Space Interpolation** (e.g., morphing between two images smoothly)

**Unsupervised Representation Learning**

### 2. The Difference Between Autoencoders and VAEs

Traditional autoencoders encode input data into a latent space and then reconstruct it. However, this process lacks control over the structure of the latent space, which makes it difficult to generate new meaningful samples.

VAEs solve this by forcing the latent space to follow a known probability distribution (usually a Gaussian distribution). This ensures that generated samples are smooth and continuous, leading to more realistic and meaningful outputs.

| Feature | Standard Autoencoder | Variational Autoencoder (VAE) |
| --- | --- | --- |
| Latent Space Representation | Fixed values | Probabilistic (Gaussian) |
| Generative Capabilities | Limited | Strong |
| Continuity in Latent Space | Disorganized | Smooth |
| Applications | Feature extraction, dimensionality reduction | Data generation, anomaly detection |

## 3. The VAE Architecture

A Variational Autoencoder consists of three main components:

### 3.1. Encoder

- Maps input X to a latent space.
- Instead of producing a single latent vector, it outputs two vectors: mean ($\mu$) and variance ($\sigma^2$), representing a probability distribution.

$$Z \sim \mathcal{N}(\mu, \sigma^2)$$

### 3.2. Reparameterization Trick

To allow backpropagation through stochastic variables, VAEs use the reparameterization trick, where a random variable $\epsilon$ is sampled from a normal distribution:

$$Z = \mu + \sigma \cdot \epsilon, \quad \text{where} \quad \epsilon \sim \mathcal{N}(0, 1)$$

This ensures the model is differentiable and can be trained using gradient descent.

### 3.3. Decoder

- The decoder takes the latent variable Z and reconstructs the original input X'.
- It learns to map the latent distribution back to the original data space.

## 4. The VAE Loss Function

VAEs optimize a combined loss function that balances two objectives:

## Reconstruction Loss (Ensuring the output resembles the input)

- Measures how well the reconstructed data matches the original.
- Typically uses Mean Squared Error (MSE) or Binary Cross-Entropy (BCE).

$$L_{\mathrm{recon}} = ||X - X'||^2$$

## Kullback-Leibler (KL) Divergence (Ensuring a smooth latent space)

- Ensures the learned latent space follows a Gaussian distribution.
- Prevents overfitting by forcing the latent representation to be continuous and well-structured.

$$L_{\mathrm{KL}} = D_{KL}(q(Z|X)||p(Z))$$

The total loss function is:

$$L_{\mathrm{VAE}} = L_{\mathrm{recon}} + \beta L_{\mathrm{KL}}$$

where β is a weighting factor (in β-VAEs, adjusting this helps control the trade-off between compression and reconstruction quality).

## 5. Implementing a VAE in Python (Using TensorFlow/Keras)

### 5.1. Import Dependencies

```
import tensorflow as tf
from tensorflow.keras.layers import Input, Dense, Lambda
from tensorflow.keras.models import Model
from tensorflow.keras.losses import mse
import numpy as np
import matplotlib.pyplot as plt
```

### 5.2. Define the Encoder

```
latent_dim = 2  # Size of the latent space
input_dim = 784  # Example for MNIST dataset

# Input layer
inputs = Input(shape=(input_dim,))
h = Dense(256, activation='relu')(inputs)

# Mean and variance layers
z_mean = Dense(latent_dim)(h)
z_log_var = Dense(latent_dim)(h)

# Reparameterization trick
def sampling(args):
    z_mean, z_log_var = args
    epsilon =
tf.keras.backend.random_normal(shape=(tf.keras.backend.shape(z_mean)[0],
latent_dim))
    return z_mean + tf.keras.backend.exp(0.5 * z_log_var) * epsilon

z = Lambda(sampling)([z_mean, z_log_var])
```

## 5.3. Define the Decoder

```
decoder_h = Dense(256, activation='relu')
decoder_out = Dense(input_dim, activation='sigmoid')

h_decoded = decoder_h(z)
outputs = decoder_out(h_decoded)

# Define VAE model
vae = Model(inputs, outputs)
```

## 5.4. Define the Loss Function

```
reconstruction_loss = mse(inputs, outputs) * input_dim
kl_loss = -0.5 * tf.keras.backend.sum(1 + z_log_var - tf.keras.backend.square(z_mean)
- tf.keras.backend.exp(z_log_var), axis=-1)
vae_loss = tf.keras.backend.mean(reconstruction_loss + kl_loss)
```

```
vae.add_loss(vae_loss)
vae.compile(optimizer='adam')
```

## 5.5. Train the VAE

```
from tensorflow.keras.datasets import mnist

(x_train, _), (x_test, _) = mnist.load_data()
x_train = x_train.astype('float32') / 255.
x_test = x_test.astype('float32') / 255.
x_train = x_train.reshape((len(x_train), np.prod(x_train.shape[1:])))
x_test = x_test.reshape((len(x_test), np.prod(x_test.shape[1:])))

vae.fit(x_train, epochs=50, batch_size=256, validation_data=(x_test, None))
```

## 6. Applications of Variational Autoencoders

## 6.1. Generating New Data

- VAEs can generate new images, text, or audio samples similar to the training data.
- Example: Generating faces, handwritten digits, or synthetic speech.

## 6.2. Anomaly Detection

- Since VAEs learn the distribution of normal data, they can detect anomalous inputs that deviate from the learned distribution.
- Example: Fraud detection in financial transactions.

## 6.3. Data Denoising

- VAEs can reconstruct clean images from noisy inputs, similar to denoising autoencoders.
- **Example**: Restoring blurry or corrupted images.

## 6.4. Feature Learning & Latent Space Interpolation

- The smooth latent space allows VAEs to create interpolations between different data points.
- **Example**: Morphing between two different images.

Variational Autoencoders (VAEs) are a powerful extension of traditional autoencoders that introduce probabilistic modeling in the latent space. By enforcing a structured latent space, VAEs enable data generation, anomaly detection, and feature extraction in a way that is more robust than standard autoencoders.

With applications in image synthesis, text generation, medical diagnosis, and more, VAEs continue to be a critical tool in deep learning and AI research.

## 12.3. Generative Adversarial Networks (GANs): How They Work

Generative Adversarial Networks (GANs) are a class of deep learning models designed for generating new, realistic data that closely resembles a given dataset. Introduced by Ian Goodfellow et al. in 2014, GANs have revolutionized the field of artificial intelligence, enabling the generation of high-quality images, videos, music, and even synthetic human voices.

At their core, GANs consist of two neural networks working against each other in a game-theoretic setting:

- The Generator (G): Creates synthetic data samples.
- The Discriminator (D): Evaluates whether a given sample is real or fake.

Through adversarial training, the generator improves its ability to produce realistic samples, while the discriminator sharpens its ability to distinguish between real and fake data.

This chapter will dive into the inner workings of GANs, explain their training dynamics, and explore real-world applications.

### 2. The Architecture of a GAN

GANs consist of two deep learning models competing with each other:

### 2.1. The Generator Network (G)

- **Goal**: To generate realistic-looking synthetic data (images, text, audio, etc.).

- **Input**: A random noise vector z (sampled from a latent space, usually a Gaussian or uniform distribution).
- **Output**: A generated sample that attempts to mimic real data.
- **Structure**: Typically uses fully connected layers, convolutional layers (for image generation), and batch normalization.

$$G(z) \rightarrow \text{Fake Data}$$

## 2.2. The Discriminator Network (D)

- **Goal**: To determine whether an input sample is real (from the dataset) or fake (from the generator).
- **Input**: A sample (either real or fake).
- **Output**: A probability score (1 = real, 0 = fake).
- **Structure**: Usually a convolutional neural network (CNN) for image-based GANs.

$$D(x) \rightarrow \text{Probability that } x \text{ is real}$$

## 2.3. The Adversarial Game Between G and D

The generator tries to fool the discriminator, while the discriminator aims to correctly identify real vs. fake samples.

- Initially, the generator produces completely random outputs that are easily spotted by the discriminator.
- Over time, the generator improves by learning from the discriminator's feedback, making its outputs increasingly realistic.
- Training stops when the discriminator can no longer differentiate between real and generated data with high confidence.

## 3. The GAN Training Process

GANs are trained using a minimax game formulation, where the generator tries to minimize the discriminator's success rate, while the discriminator tries to maximize its classification accuracy.

## 3.1. The Loss Functions

## (A) Discriminator Loss

The discriminator's goal is to correctly classify real data (x) and generated data (G(z)). It tries to maximize the probability of assigning:

- 1 (**real**) to real samples.

- 0 (**fake**) to generated samples.

$$L_D = -\mathbb{E}[\log D(x)] - \mathbb{E}[\log(1 - D(G(z)))]$$

where:

- $D(x)$ is the probability of a real sample being real.

- $D(G(z))$ is the probability of a fake sample being real.

## (B) Generator Loss

The generator's goal is to fool the discriminator, meaning it wants the discriminator to classify fake samples as real. It tries to minimize:

$$L_G = -\mathbb{E}[\log D(G(z))]$$

In other words, the generator wants $D(G(z))$ **to be close to 1** so that its generated samples are indistinguishable from real ones.

## 3.2. Training Steps

**Train the discriminator:**

- Feed real samples x into D, update weights to classify correctly.
- Feed fake samples G(z) into D, update weights to classify correctly.

**Train the generator:**

- Generate fake samples G(z).
- Train G by updating weights based on how well D was fooled.
- Repeat until the generator produces highly realistic data.

# 4. Implementing a Simple GAN Using TensorFlow/Keras

## 4.1. Import Dependencies

```
import tensorflow as tf
from tensorflow.keras.layers import Dense, Flatten, Reshape, LeakyReLU
from tensorflow.keras.models import Sequential
import numpy as np
import matplotlib.pyplot as plt
```

## 4.2. Build the Generator

```
def build_generator():
    model = Sequential([
        Dense(128, activation='relu', input_shape=(100,)),
        Dense(256, activation='relu'),
        Dense(784, activation='sigmoid'),
        Reshape((28, 28))
    ])
    return model

generator = build_generator()
```

## 4.3. Build the Discriminator

```
def build_discriminator():
    model = Sequential([
        Flatten(input_shape=(28, 28)),
        Dense(256, activation=LeakyReLU(alpha=0.2)),
        Dense(128, activation=LeakyReLU(alpha=0.2)),
        Dense(1, activation='sigmoid')
    ])
    return model

discriminator = build_discriminator()
discriminator.compile(loss='binary_crossentropy', optimizer='adam',
metrics=['accuracy'])
```

## 4.4. Combine Both to Form GAN

```
discriminator.trainable = False
gan = Sequential([generator, discriminator])
gan.compile(loss='binary_crossentropy', optimizer='adam')
```

## 4.5. Train the GAN

```
(X_train, _), (_, _) = tf.keras.datasets.mnist.load_data()
X_train = X_train.astype('float32') / 255.0

batch_size = 64
epochs = 10000
latent_dim = 100

for epoch in range(epochs):
    # Train discriminator
    real_samples = X_train[np.random.randint(0, X_train.shape[0], batch_size)]
    noise = np.random.normal(0, 1, (batch_size, latent_dim))
    fake_samples = generator.predict(noise)

    d_loss_real = discriminator.train_on_batch(real_samples, np.ones((batch_size, 1)))
    d_loss_fake = discriminator.train_on_batch(fake_samples, np.zeros((batch_size, 1)))

    # Train generator
    noise = np.random.normal(0, 1, (batch_size, latent_dim))
    g_loss = gan.train_on_batch(noise, np.ones((batch_size, 1)))

    if epoch % 1000 == 0:
        print(f"Epoch {epoch} | D Loss: {d_loss_real[0] + d_loss_fake[0]} | G Loss:
{g_loss}")
```

## 5. Applications of GANs

## 5.1. Image Generation

- GANs are used for creating realistic human faces, landscapes, and artwork.
- Example: This Person Does Not Exist (website generating AI-generated human faces).

## 5.2. Style Transfer & Super-Resolution

- GANs power DeepDream, Prisma, and Super-Resolution GANs (SRGANs) for image enhancement.

### 5.3. Synthetic Data for Training AI Models

- GANs generate synthetic datasets to improve AI training, particularly for medical imaging, autonomous driving, and security applications.

### 5.4. Video & Animation Generation

- GANs help create deepfake videos, AI-powered animations, and text-to-image synthesis.

Generative Adversarial Networks (GANs) have redefined artificial intelligence by enabling high-quality synthetic data generation. Their ability to create hyper-realistic content has revolutionized fields such as art, gaming, medicine, and security.

# 12.4. Implementing a Simple GAN for Image Generation

Generative Adversarial Networks (GANs) have become a cornerstone of deep learning for generating realistic images. This chapter focuses on implementing a simple GAN from scratch using Python, TensorFlow/Keras, and MNIST (a dataset of handwritten digits).

**By the end of this chapter, you will:**

- Understand the architecture of a simple GAN.
- Implement the generator and discriminator models.
- Train the GAN to generate synthetic images.
- Evaluate and visualize the results.

### 2. GAN Architecture Overview

A GAN consists of two neural networks that compete in an adversarial manner:

### 2.1. Generator (G)

- **Goal**: Generate fake images from random noise.
- **Input**: A noise vector sampled from a normal distribution.
- **Output**: A synthetic image.

- **Training Objective**: Generate images that are indistinguishable from real images.

$$G(z) \rightarrow \text{Fake Image}$$

## 2.2. Discriminator (D)

- **Goal**: Classify whether an image is real or fake.
- **Input**: A real or fake image.
- **Output**: A probability score (1 = real, 0 = fake).
- **Training Objective**: Correctly classify real and generated images.

$$D(x) \rightarrow \text{Probability that } x \text{ is real}$$

## 2.3. Adversarial Training

- The discriminator is trained to classify real and fake images accurately.
- The generator is trained to fool the discriminator into classifying fake images as real.
- Over multiple iterations, both networks improve, leading to high-quality synthetic images.

## 3. Implementing a Simple GAN Using TensorFlow/Keras

### 3.1. Import Dependencies

*import tensorflow as tf*
*from tensorflow.keras.layers import Dense, Flatten, Reshape, LeakyReLU*
*from tensorflow.keras.models import Sequential*
*import numpy as np*
*import matplotlib.pyplot as plt*

### 3.2. Define the Generator Model

The generator takes a random noise vector and transforms it into a structured image using fully connected layers.

*def build_generator():*
  *model = Sequential([*

```
    Dense(128, activation='relu', input_shape=(100,)),  # Input: 100-dimensional noise
    Dense(256, activation='relu'),
    Dense(784, activation='sigmoid'),  # Output: Flattened 28x28 image
    Reshape((28, 28))  # Reshape into 28x28 pixels
])
return model


generator = build_generator()
```

### 3.3. Define the Discriminator Model

The discriminator is a binary classifier that determines whether an image is real or fake.

```
def build_discriminator():
    model = Sequential([
        Flatten(input_shape=(28, 28)),  # Convert 2D image to 1D vector
        Dense(256, activation=LeakyReLU(alpha=0.2)),  # LeakyReLU prevents vanishing
gradients
        Dense(128, activation=LeakyReLU(alpha=0.2)),
        Dense(1, activation='sigmoid')  # Output probability (real or fake)
    ])
    return model


discriminator = build_discriminator()
discriminator.compile(loss='binary_crossentropy', optimizer='adam',
metrics=['accuracy'])
```

### 3.4. Build the GAN by Combining G and D

Now, we connect the generator and discriminator to form a GAN.

The discriminator is frozen during GAN training (so it does not learn too quickly).

```
discriminator.trainable = False  # Freeze discriminator during GAN training


gan = Sequential([generator, discriminator])
gan.compile(loss='binary_crossentropy', optimizer='adam')
```

### 4. Training the GAN

## 4.1. Load and Preprocess the Dataset

We will use the MNIST dataset, which contains 28x28 grayscale images of handwritten digits.

```
(X_train, _), (_, _) = tf.keras.datasets.mnist.load_data()
X_train = X_train.astype('float32') / 255.0  # Normalize pixel values between 0 and 1
```

## 4.2. Define the Training Loop

The training process involves the following steps:

- Train the discriminator on both real and fake images.
- Train the generator to improve fake image quality.
- Repeat for multiple epochs to improve performance.

```
batch_size = 64
epochs = 10000
latent_dim = 100


for epoch in range(epochs):
    # Train discriminator
    real_samples = X_train[np.random.randint(0, X_train.shape[0], batch_size)]  #
Sample real images
    noise = np.random.normal(0, 1, (batch_size, latent_dim))  # Generate noise
    fake_samples = generator.predict(noise)  # Generate fake images

    d_loss_real = discriminator.train_on_batch(real_samples, np.ones((batch_size, 1)))  #
Train on real
    d_loss_fake = discriminator.train_on_batch(fake_samples, np.zeros((batch_size, 1)))
# Train on fake

    # Train generator
    noise = np.random.normal(0, 1, (batch_size, latent_dim))
    g_loss = gan.train_on_batch(noise, np.ones((batch_size, 1)))  # The generator tries
to fool the discriminator

    # Print progress every 1000 epochs
    if epoch % 1000 == 0:
```

```
    print(f"Epoch {epoch} | D Loss: {d_loss_real[0] + d_loss_fake[0]} | G Loss:
{g_loss}")
```

## 5. Visualizing Generated Images

Once training is complete, we can generate and visualize new images.

```
def generate_images(generator, num_images=5):
    noise = np.random.normal(0, 1, (num_images, 100))
    generated_images = generator.predict(noise)

    plt.figure(figsize=(10, 2))
    for i in range(num_images):
        plt.subplot(1, num_images, i + 1)
        plt.imshow(generated_images[i], cmap='gray')
        plt.axis('off')
    plt.show()

generate_images(generator)
```

## 6. Key Challenges in Training GANs

GANs are notoriously difficult to train due to:

- **Mode Collapse**: The generator may produce a limited variety of samples instead of diverse ones.
- **Vanishing Gradient**: The generator stops learning when the discriminator becomes too powerful.
- **Training Instability**: Small changes in hyperparameters can drastically affect results.

### 6.1. Solutions to Common GAN Problems

- Use Batch Normalization to stabilize training.
- Use LeakyReLU instead of standard ReLU to avoid dead neurons.
- Use Wasserstein Loss (WGAN) instead of binary cross-entropy to improve stability.
- Train the discriminator more frequently than the generator.

## 7. Real-World Applications of GANs

GANs are widely used in:

- **Art & Creativity**: AI-generated paintings and music (e.g., DeepArt).
- **Medical Imaging**: Enhancing low-resolution images.
- **Super-Resolution**: Increasing image quality (e.g., SRGAN).
- **Deepfakes**: Generating realistic human faces (e.g., This Person Does Not Exist).
- **Text-to-Image Models**: Creating images from text descriptions (e.g., DALL·E).

In this chapter, we implemented a simple GAN for image generation using TensorFlow/Keras. We built both the generator and discriminator, trained them in an adversarial fashion, and visualized the results.

# 13. Hyperparameter Tuning & Model Selection

In this chapter, you'll learn how to fine-tune the performance of your neural networks by selecting the right hyperparameters and choosing the best model for your task. Hyperparameters, such as learning rates, batch sizes, and the number of layers, can significantly impact a model's accuracy and efficiency. You'll explore techniques like grid search, random search, and Bayesian optimization for systematically finding the optimal values. The chapter also covers strategies for model selection, helping you evaluate and compare different architectures and configurations to ensure you choose the best model for your data. By the end of this chapter, you'll have the skills to maximize the performance of your neural networks and ensure that your models are not only accurate but also robust and efficient in real-world applications.

## 13.1. Understanding Hyperparameters: Learning Rate, Batch Size, & More

Hyperparameters are the tunable configurations that define how a neural network learns. Unlike model parameters (such as weights and biases, which the network learns during training), hyperparameters must be set manually before training begins. Choosing the right hyperparameters significantly affects a model's performance, training stability, and generalization ability.

**This chapter will cover:**

- The importance of hyperparameter tuning.
- Key hyperparameters like learning rate, batch size, epochs, weight initialization, and dropout rate.
- Best practices for choosing optimal hyperparameters.

### 2. What Are Hyperparameters?

Hyperparameters control various aspects of a neural network, including:

- **Training efficiency** (how fast and effectively a model learns).
- **Generalization** (how well a model performs on unseen data).
- **Stability** (preventing issues like vanishing gradients and overfitting).

## 2.1. Types of Hyperparameters

Hyperparameters can be broadly categorized into three groups:

### Optimization-related hyperparameters:

- Learning rate
- Batch size
- Number of epochs
- Optimizer type

### Regularization-related hyperparameters:

- Dropout rate
- Weight decay (L1/L2 regularization)
- Early stopping criteria

### Model architecture-related hyperparameters:

- Number of hidden layers
- Number of neurons per layer
- Activation functions

In this section, we'll focus on three crucial hyperparameters: learning rate, batch size, and number of epochs.

## 3. Learning Rate ($\alpha$)

### 3.1. What is Learning Rate?

The learning rate ($\alpha$) determines the step size in which the model updates its weights during training.

- A high learning rate updates weights quickly but may overshoot the optimal solution.
- A low learning rate converges slowly and may get stuck in local minima.

### 3.2. Effect of Learning Rate on Training

| Learning Rate | Effect on Training |
|---|---|
| Too High ($\alpha > 0.1$) | The model may oscillate or diverge. |
| Too Low ($\alpha < 0.0001$) | The model learns very slowly or stops improving. |
| Optimal ($\alpha \approx 0.001 - 0.01$) | Balanced speed and stability. |

## 3.3. Finding the Right Learning Rate

- Use a learning rate scheduler (e.g., exponential decay, cosine annealing).
- Start with 0.01 or 0.001 and adjust based on performance.
- Use learning rate warm-up to gradually increase $\alpha$ during the initial epochs.

## 3.4. Adaptive Learning Rate Optimizers

Instead of manually setting a fixed learning rate, optimizers like Adam, RMSprop, and AdaGrad adjust it dynamically.

## 4. Batch Size

## 4.1. What is Batch Size?

Batch size determines the number of training samples processed before the model updates its weights.

| Batch Size | Characteristics |
|---|---|
| Small (e.g., 16, 32) | More updates per epoch, better generalization, but slower training. |
| Large (e.g., 128, 256, 512) | Faster training, but higher memory usage and risk of overfitting. |

## 4.2. Choosing the Right Batch Size

- **Small batches (16-64):** Good for noisy data and small datasets.
- **Large batches (128-512):** Faster training but requires more GPU memory.
- A common rule is to start with batch size = 32 or 64 and adjust based on performance.

## 4.3. Mini-Batch Gradient Descent

- **Batch Gradient Descent** (Full dataset per update): Stable but slow.

- **Stochastic Gradient Descent** (SGD, single sample per update): Faster but noisy.
- **Mini-Batch Gradient Descent** (Common approach, batch size 32-256): Balances speed and stability.

## 5. Number of Epochs

### 5.1. What is an Epoch?

An epoch is one full pass through the training dataset. More epochs help the model learn better, but too many can lead to overfitting.

### 5.2. How to Choose the Right Number of Epochs

| Scenario | Recommended Epochs |
|---|---|
| Small dataset (few thousand samples) | 50 - 200 |
| Large dataset (millions of samples) | 10 - 50 |
| Fine-tuning pre-trained models | 5 - 20 |

### 5.3. Early Stopping for Optimal Epochs

Instead of setting a fixed number of epochs, early stopping monitors validation loss and stops training when performance stops improving.

*from tensorflow.keras.callbacks import EarlyStopping*

*early_stop = EarlyStopping(monitor='val_loss', patience=5, restore_best_weights=True)*

## 6. Finding the Best Hyperparameters

### 6.1. Hyperparameter Tuning Techniques

Manually tuning hyperparameters is inefficient, so we use automated methods:

### Grid Search

- Trains models with different combinations of hyperparameters.
- Computationally expensive but guarantees the best results.

*from sklearn.model_selection import GridSearchCV*

**Random Search**

- Selects random hyperparameter values from a given range.
- Faster than grid search but less exhaustive.

*from scipy.stats import uniform*

**Bayesian Optimization**

Uses probabilistic models to find the best hyperparameters.

*from skopt import gp_minimize*

**Hyperparameter Tuning with Optuna**

*import optuna*

```
def objective(trial):
    learning_rate = trial.suggest_loguniform('learning_rate', 1e-5, 1e-2)
    batch_size = trial.suggest_categorical('batch_size', [16, 32, 64, 128])
    return train_model(learning_rate, batch_size)

study = optuna.create_study(direction='minimize')
study.optimize(objective, n_trials=50)
```

## 7. Summary & Best Practices

### 7.1. Key Takeaways

- **Learning rate (α):** Small α improves stability; large α speeds up learning but may cause divergence.
- **Batch size**: Small batches generalize better; large batches train faster.
- **Number of epochs**: Use early stopping to prevent overfitting.

### 7.2. Best Practices for Hyperparameter Tuning

✅ Start with default values (learning rate = 0.001, batch size = 32, epochs = 50).

✅ Use learning rate schedulers for better convergence.

✓ Monitor validation loss to detect overfitting early.

✓ Use automated tuning methods like Grid Search, Random Search, or Bayesian Optimization.

By mastering hyperparameter tuning, you can significantly improve model accuracy, speed up training, and reduce overfitting, leading to better deep learning models. 🚀

# 13.2. Grid Search vs. Random Search vs. Bayesian Optimization

Hyperparameter tuning is one of the most critical steps in building an effective deep learning model. Selecting the right hyperparameters—such as learning rate, batch size, dropout rate, and number of hidden layers—can significantly impact a model's accuracy, training speed, and generalization performance.

However, manually choosing hyperparameters is impractical, especially for complex models with many tunable parameters. To address this challenge, automated hyperparameter tuning techniques are widely used. The three most popular approaches are:

- **Grid Search**: Exhaustively searches a predefined set of hyperparameter values.
- **Random Search**: Samples hyperparameters randomly from a given range.
- **Bayesian Optimization**: Uses probabilistic models to find the best hyperparameters more efficiently.

In this chapter, we'll compare these methods, discuss their pros and cons, and guide you on when to use each approach.

## 2. Grid Search: Exhaustive Search for Optimal Parameters

### 2.1. What is Grid Search?

Grid Search systematically evaluates all possible combinations of hyperparameters within a given search space. It trains and evaluates a model for each combination and selects the best-performing set.

### 2.2. How Grid Search Works

- Define a set of hyperparameter values to search through.
- Train the model for each combination of parameters.
- Evaluate the model's performance.
- Select the best-performing combination.

## 2.3. Example of Grid Search in Python (Using Scikit-Learn)

```
from sklearn.model_selection import GridSearchCV
from sklearn.ensemble import RandomForestClassifier

# Define hyperparameters
param_grid = {
    'n_estimators': [50, 100, 200],
    'max_depth': [None, 10, 20, 30],
    'min_samples_split': [2, 5, 10]
}

# Initialize model
model = RandomForestClassifier()

# Perform Grid Search
grid_search = GridSearchCV(model, param_grid, cv=3, scoring='accuracy')
grid_search.fit(X_train, y_train)

# Print best parameters
print("Best Parameters:", grid_search.best_params_)
```

## 2.4. Pros & Cons of Grid Search

✓ Advantages:

- Guarantees finding the best-performing parameter combination.
- Easy to implement.
- Works well for small search spaces.

✗ Disadvantages:

- Computationally expensive for large hyperparameter spaces.

- Redundant evaluations (some hyperparameter settings may have little impact).

## 2.5. When to Use Grid Search

- When you have a small number of hyperparameters to tune.
- When computational resources are not a limitation.
- When you need guaranteed best results within a predefined range.

## 3. Random Search: A Faster Alternative

## 3.1. What is Random Search?

Instead of exhaustively testing all parameter combinations, Random Search selects hyperparameter values randomly from a defined range. This allows it to explore a wider variety of values while reducing computation time.

## 3.2. How Random Search Works

- Define the range for each hyperparameter.
- Randomly select a subset of hyperparameter combinations.
- Train and evaluate the model for each combination.
- Select the best-performing set.

## 3.3. Example of Random Search in Python (Using Scikit-Learn)

```
from sklearn.model_selection import RandomizedSearchCV
from scipy.stats import randint
from sklearn.ensemble import RandomForestClassifier

# Define hyperparameters
param_dist = {
    'n_estimators': randint(50, 200),
    'max_depth': [None, 10, 20, 30],
    'min_samples_split': randint(2, 10)
}

# Initialize model
model = RandomForestClassifier()

# Perform Random Search
```

```
random_search = RandomizedSearchCV(model, param_distributions=param_dist,
n_iter=10, cv=3, scoring='accuracy', random_state=42)
random_search.fit(X_train, y_train)

# Print best parameters
print("Best Parameters:", random_search.best_params_)
```

### 3.4. Pros & Cons of Random Search

✅ Advantages:

- Faster than Grid Search.
- More efficient in high-dimensional spaces.
- More diverse hyperparameter selection.

❌ Disadvantages:

- Does not guarantee finding the absolute best combination.
- Can miss good parameter values if not enough samples are tested.

### 3.5. When to Use Random Search

- When dealing with a large number of hyperparameters.
- When computation time is a concern.
- When you want a quick but effective tuning approach.

### 4. Bayesian Optimization: Smarter Search

### 4.1. What is Bayesian Optimization?

Bayesian Optimization is an intelligent search algorithm that uses a probabilistic model (usually a Gaussian Process) to estimate the most promising hyperparameters and explore them efficiently. Unlike Grid and Random Search, which blindly test values, Bayesian Optimization learns from previous evaluations to make better choices.

### 4.2. How Bayesian Optimization Works

- Select initial hyperparameter values randomly.
- Train and evaluate the model.

- Use a probabilistic model to predict promising hyperparameter values.
- Update predictions based on previous results.
- Continue searching until an optimal set is found.

## 4.3. Example of Bayesian Optimization in Python (Using Optuna)

```python
import optuna

def objective(trial):
    n_estimators = trial.suggest_int('n_estimators', 50, 200)
    max_depth = trial.suggest_categorical('max_depth', [None, 10, 20, 30])
    min_samples_split = trial.suggest_int('min_samples_split', 2, 10)

    model = RandomForestClassifier(n_estimators=n_estimators,
max_depth=max_depth, min_samples_split=min_samples_split)
    model.fit(X_train, y_train)

    return model.score(X_val, y_val)  # Return accuracy

study = optuna.create_study(direction="maximize")
study.optimize(objective, n_trials=20)

print("Best Parameters:", study.best_params)
```

## 4.4. Pros & Cons of Bayesian Optimization

✔ Advantages:

- Finds optimal hyperparameters faster.
- More efficient than Grid and Random Search.
- Adapts intelligently based on previous results.

✖ Disadvantages:

- More complex to implement.
- Computational overhead for updating probabilistic models.

## 4.5. When to Use Bayesian Optimization

- When you need the best performance with fewer evaluations.
- When computational resources are limited.
- When hyperparameter space is very large and complex.

## 5. Comparing the Three Approaches

| Method | Speed | Best for | Guarantees Best Parameters? | Suitable for Deep Learning? |
|---|---|---|---|---|
| Grid Search | Slow | Small search spaces | ☑ Yes | ✕ No (too computationally expensive) |
| Random Search | Fast | Large search spaces | ✕ No | ☑ Yes (fast and efficient) |
| Bayesian Optimization | Very Fast | Large & complex search spaces | ☑ Yes (most efficient) | ☑ Yes (best choice for deep learning) |

Hyperparameter tuning plays a crucial role in achieving better accuracy, stability, and generalization for machine learning and deep learning models.

- Use Grid Search if the search space is small and computational resources are not an issue.
- Use Random Search if the search space is large and you want a quick solution.
- Use Bayesian Optimization when dealing with complex models and limited computational power.

By choosing the right tuning method, you can significantly enhance your model's performance while minimizing computational costs. 🚀

# 13.3. Using Tools Like Optuna & Hyperopt for Tuning

Hyperparameter tuning is essential for optimizing deep learning models. Choosing the right combination of hyperparameters, such as learning rate, batch size, dropout rate, and number of layers, can significantly impact model performance. However, manually tuning these parameters is time-consuming and inefficient.

To address this challenge, automated hyperparameter optimization tools have become popular, with Optuna and Hyperopt leading the way. These tools offer smarter, faster, and more efficient ways to find the best hyperparameter combinations.

In this chapter, we'll explore how Optuna and Hyperopt work, compare their features, and demonstrate how to use them to tune neural networks efficiently.

## 2. What is Optuna?

### 2.1. Overview

Optuna is an open-source hyperparameter optimization framework that uses advanced search techniques like Tree-structured Parzen Estimators (TPE) and Bayesian Optimization to efficiently find optimal hyperparameter settings.

### 2.2. Key Features of Optuna

- **Automated Search**: Optuna intelligently selects promising hyperparameter values.
- **Pruning Mechanism**: It stops unpromising trials early to save time.
- **Flexible Search Space**: Supports different types of hyperparameters (discrete, continuous, categorical).
- **Parallel Execution**: Can run multiple trials in parallel to speed up optimization.

### 2.3. Implementing Hyperparameter Tuning with Optuna

Let's optimize a simple neural network using Optuna.

### Step 1: Install Optuna

*pip install optuna*

### Step 2: Define the Objective Function

The objective function trains a neural network and returns the validation accuracy.

*import optuna*
*import tensorflow as tf*
*from tensorflow import keras*

*# Define objective function for tuning*
*def objective(trial):*
    *# Define hyperparameters*
    *learning_rate = trial.suggest_loguniform('learning_rate', 1e-4, 1e-1)*

```python
    num_units = trial.suggest_int('num_units', 32, 256)
    dropout_rate = trial.suggest_uniform('dropout_rate', 0.1, 0.5)

    # Build the model
    model = keras.Sequential([
        keras.layers.Dense(num_units, activation='relu'),
        keras.layers.Dropout(dropout_rate),
        keras.layers.Dense(10, activation='softmax')
    ])

    model.compile(optimizer=keras.optimizers.Adam(learning_rate=learning_rate),
            loss='sparse_categorical_crossentropy',
            metrics=['accuracy'])

    # Train the model
    (X_train, y_train), (X_val, y_val) = keras.datasets.mnist.load_data()
    X_train, X_val = X_train / 255.0, X_val / 255.0
    model.fit(X_train, y_train, epochs=5, batch_size=32, verbose=0,
validation_data=(X_val, y_val))

    # Evaluate model
    loss, accuracy = model.evaluate(X_val, y_val, verbose=0)
    return accuracy  # Optuna will maximize this value

# Run the optimization
study = optuna.create_study(direction="maximize")  # We want to maximize accuracy
study.optimize(objective, n_trials=20)

# Print best parameters
print("Best hyperparameters:", study.best_params)
```

## 2.4. Benefits of Optuna

✅ Smarter search using Bayesian optimization.

✅ Fast training with trial pruning.

✅ Scales well with large search spaces.

## 2.5. When to Use Optuna

- When search space is large and manual tuning is impractical.
- When training deep neural networks where hyperparameters significantly impact performance.
- When you need efficient tuning with fewer iterations.

## 3. What is Hyperopt?

### 3.1. Overview

Hyperopt is another powerful Bayesian optimization framework for hyperparameter tuning. It supports various search algorithms like TPE, random search, and simulated annealing.

### 3.2. Key Features of Hyperopt

- Tree-structured Parzen Estimator (TPE) optimization for smarter searches.
- Supports different search spaces (discrete, continuous, categorical).
- Parallel execution for faster optimization.
- Compatible with TensorFlow, PyTorch, and Scikit-Learn.

### 3.3. Implementing Hyperparameter Tuning with Hyperopt

### Step 1: Install Hyperopt

*pip install hyperopt*

### Step 2: Define the Search Space & Objective Function

```
from hyperopt import fmin, tpe, hp, Trials
import tensorflow as tf
from tensorflow import keras

# Define search space
search_space = {
    'learning_rate': hp.loguniform('learning_rate', -4, -1),  # 10^-4 to 10^-1
    'num_units': hp.choice('num_units', [32, 64, 128, 256]),
    'dropout_rate': hp.uniform('dropout_rate', 0.1, 0.5)
}

# Define objective function
```

```python
def objective(params):
    model = keras.Sequential([
        keras.layers.Dense(params['num_units'], activation='relu'),
        keras.layers.Dropout(params['dropout_rate']),
        keras.layers.Dense(10, activation='softmax')
    ])


    model.compile(optimizer=keras.optimizers.Adam(learning_rate=params['learning_rate']),
                  loss='sparse_categorical_crossentropy',
                  metrics=['accuracy'])

    (X_train, y_train), (X_val, y_val) = keras.datasets.mnist.load_data()
    X_train, X_val = X_train / 255.0, X_val / 255.0
    model.fit(X_train, y_train, epochs=5, batch_size=32, verbose=0,
validation_data=(X_val, y_val))

    loss, accuracy = model.evaluate(X_val, y_val, verbose=0)
    return -accuracy  # Hyperopt minimizes the objective function, so we negate accuracy

# Run Hyperopt optimization
trials = Trials()
best_params = fmin(fn=objective, space=search_space, algo=tpe.suggest,
max_evals=20, trials=trials)

print("Best Hyperparameters:", best_params)
```

### 3.4. Benefits of Hyperopt

✅ Flexible search space definition.

✅ Efficient with large parameter sets.

✅ Good for both deep learning and traditional ML models.

### 3.5. When to Use Hyperopt

- When you need a flexible and scalable tuning framework.
- When you prefer Pythonic syntax for search space definition.
- When you need support for distributed optimization.

## 4. Optuna vs. Hyperopt: Which One Should You Use?

| Feature | Optuna | Hyperopt |
|---|---|---|
| Search Algorithm | TPE, Bayesian | TPE, Simulated Annealing, Random |
| Trial Pruning | ☑ Yes | ✕ No |
| Parallel Execution | ☑ Yes | ☑ Yes |
| Search Space Flexibility | ☑ Yes | ☑ Yes |
| Ease of Use | ☑ Simple | ◉ Slightly Complex |
| Best for | Deep Learning | Both ML & Deep Learning |

### 4.1. When to Use Optuna

- When you need intelligent pruning for faster results.
- When working on deep learning models with large search spaces.
- When using TensorFlow or PyTorch.

### 4.2. When to Use Hyperopt

- When working with both machine learning & deep learning models.
- When needing custom search algorithms beyond Bayesian optimization.
- When using distributed tuning over multiple machines.

Hyperparameter tuning is essential for maximizing model performance, and tools like Optuna and Hyperopt provide powerful ways to automate the process.

- Optuna is great for deep learning models, thanks to its trial pruning and Bayesian optimization.
- Hyperopt is flexible and scalable, making it a solid choice for both ML and DL applications.

By integrating these tools into your workflow, you can optimize hyperparameters more efficiently, reduce computational costs, and achieve higher accuracy with fewer trials. 🚀

# 13.4. Transfer Learning & Fine-Tuning Pretrained Models

Training deep learning models from scratch requires vast amounts of data and computational power. However, transfer learning provides a powerful alternative by leveraging pre-trained models that have already learned useful patterns from large datasets. Instead of starting from zero, we can fine-tune these models for specific tasks with much less data and computation.

In this chapter, we will explore the fundamentals of transfer learning, how to use popular pre-trained models such as ResNet, VGG, and BERT, and the process of fine-tuning them for custom applications.

## 2. What is Transfer Learning?

### 2.1. Definition

Transfer learning is a machine learning technique where a model trained on one task is reused for a different but related task. Instead of training a model from scratch, we use a pre-trained model and adapt it to our needs.

### 2.2. How Transfer Learning Works

- **Pre-training Phase**: A model is trained on a massive dataset (e.g., ImageNet for images, GPT/BERT for text).
- **Feature Extraction**: The pre-trained model extracts useful patterns and representations.
- **Fine-Tuning**: The last few layers of the model are re-trained on a new, smaller dataset specific to the target task.

### 2.3. Benefits of Transfer Learning

✓ **Faster training**: Reduces training time since the model already learned useful features.

✓ **Better performance**: Improves accuracy with smaller datasets.

✓ **Less data required**: Can achieve good results even with limited labeled data.

✓ **Reduces computational cost**: Uses fewer resources compared to training from scratch.

## 3. Types of Transfer Learning

### 3.1. Feature Extraction

- The pre-trained model is used as a fixed feature extractor.
- The lower layers remain frozen, and only the final classifier layers are retrained.
- Works well when the new dataset is small and similar to the original dataset.

## 3.2. Fine-Tuning

- Some or all of the pre-trained layers are unfrozen and retrained.
- Allows the model to adjust weights for the new dataset.
- Works best when the new dataset is large and different from the original dataset.

## 4. Popular Pretrained Models

## 4.1. Computer Vision Models (CNNs)

✦ **VGG16/VGG19** – Simple but large models trained on ImageNet.

✦ **ResNet (Residual Networks)** – Deep networks with skip connections to prevent vanishing gradients.

✦ **InceptionNet** – Uses multiple convolution filters for better feature extraction.

✦ **EfficientNet** – More computationally efficient than ResNet and VGG.

## 4.2. Natural Language Processing (NLP) Models

✦ **BERT** (Bidirectional Encoder Representations from Transformers) – A state-of-the-art transformer-based model for text processing.

✦ **GPT** (Generative Pretrained Transformer) – Used for text generation and NLP tasks.

✦ **T5** (Text-to-Text Transfer Transformer) – Converts all NLP problems into a text-generation task.

## 5. Implementing Transfer Learning in Computer Vision

## 5.1. Using a Pretrained Model for Image Classification

Let's use TensorFlow to implement transfer learning with ResNet50 for an image classification task.

## Step 1: Install Dependencies

*pip install tensorflow keras*

## Step 2: Load the Pretrained Model

```
import tensorflow as tf
from tensorflow import keras
from tensorflow.keras.applications import ResNet50
from tensorflow.keras.layers import Dense, Flatten
from tensorflow.keras.models import Model

# Load pre-trained ResNet50 model without top layers
base_model = ResNet50(weights='imagenet', include_top=False, input_shape=(224,
224, 3))

# Freeze the base model layers to use as a feature extractor
base_model.trainable = False

# Add custom layers
x = Flatten()(base_model.output)
x = Dense(256, activation='relu')(x)
x = Dense(10, activation='softmax')(x)  # 10 classes for classification

# Define new model
model = Model(inputs=base_model.input, outputs=x)

# Compile the model
model.compile(optimizer='adam', loss='categorical_crossentropy', metrics=['accuracy'])

# Print model summary
model.summary()
```

## Step 3: Train the Model

```
# Load dataset (example: CIFAR-10)
(X_train, y_train), (X_test, y_test) = keras.datasets.cifar10.load_data()
X_train, X_test = X_train / 255.0, X_test / 255.0  # Normalize data

# Train only the custom layers
model.fit(X_train, y_train, epochs=5, batch_size=32, validation_data=(X_test, y_test))
```

## 6. Fine-Tuning a Pretrained Model

Fine-tuning allows adjusting the weights of some pre-trained layers instead of keeping them frozen.

### Step 1: Unfreeze the Top Layers

```
# Unfreeze the top 10 layers for fine-tuning
for layer in base_model.layers[-10:]:
    layer.trainable = True
```

### Step 2: Recompile and Train Again

```
# Recompile model with a lower learning rate
model.compile(optimizer=keras.optimizers.Adam(learning_rate=1e-5),
        loss='categorical_crossentropy', metrics=['accuracy'])
```

```
# Continue training
model.fit(X_train, y_train, epochs=10, batch_size=32, validation_data=(X_test, y_test))
```

Fine-tuning helps the model adapt to the new dataset without forgetting the previously learned features.

## 7. Transfer Learning for NLP: Fine-Tuning BERT

We can fine-tune BERT for text classification using Hugging Face's Transformers library.

### 7.1. Install Transformers Library

```
pip install transformers datasets torch
```

### 7.2. Load Pretrained BERT Model

```
from transformers import BertTokenizer, BertForSequenceClassification
import torch
```

```
# Load pre-trained BERT tokenizer and model
tokenizer = BertTokenizer.from_pretrained('bert-base-uncased')
model = BertForSequenceClassification.from_pretrained('bert-base-uncased',
num_labels=2)
```

### 7.3. Tokenize & Fine-Tune on a Custom Dataset

```
from transformers import Trainer, TrainingArguments
from datasets import load_dataset

# Load dataset (example: IMDB reviews)
dataset = load_dataset("imdb")
train_texts, train_labels = dataset['train']['text'], dataset['train']['label']

# Tokenize the dataset
train_encodings = tokenizer(train_texts, truncation=True, padding=True,
max_length=512)

# Convert to PyTorch tensors
train_inputs = torch.tensor(train_encodings['input_ids'])
train_labels = torch.tensor(train_labels)

# Define training arguments
training_args = TrainingArguments(output_dir="./results", num_train_epochs=3)

trainer = Trainer(model=model, args=training_args, train_dataset=train_inputs,
eval_dataset=train_labels)
trainer.train()
```

Fine-tuning adapts BERT to specific NLP tasks like sentiment analysis, text classification, or question answering.

Transfer learning and fine-tuning are game-changers in deep learning. Instead of training models from scratch, we leverage powerful pre-trained models and adapt them for new tasks.

**Key Takeaways**

✓ Feature extraction is useful for small datasets.

✓ Fine-tuning is best for large, domain-specific datasets.

✓ Pretrained models like ResNet, VGG, and BERT can drastically improve performance.

✓ Tools like TensorFlow, PyTorch, and Hugging Face Transformers make transfer learning easy.

By using transfer learning, we can achieve state-of-the-art results with minimal data and computation! 🚀

# 14. Neural Networks in Production

Building a neural network is only half the battle—deploying it in production is where the real challenge begins. In this chapter, you'll learn how to take your trained models and integrate them into real-world applications. You'll explore the process of model deployment, including creating APIs, using frameworks like TensorFlow Serving and Flask, and working with cloud platforms like AWS, Google Cloud, and Azure to scale your models. The chapter also covers model monitoring to ensure your deployed networks perform well over time, and versioning to manage updates and changes. Additionally, you'll learn about optimizing neural networks for efficiency and latency to ensure they run seamlessly in production environments. With this knowledge, you'll be equipped to move from model creation to successful deployment, ensuring your AI solutions are reliable, scalable, and ready for the real world.

# 14.1. Preparing a Model for Deployment

Training a neural network is just the beginning; deploying it into a production environment is where it creates real-world value. Before deployment, a model must be optimized, packaged, and integrated into an application. This chapter explores the essential steps for preparing a machine learning model for deployment, including model optimization, serialization, versioning, and security considerations.

### 2. Key Steps in Model Deployment

To ensure a smooth transition from development to production, the following steps are necessary:

- **Model Optimization** – Reducing model size and improving inference speed.
- **Serialization & Saving** – Converting the model into a deployable format.
- **Version Control** – Managing updates and ensuring reproducibility.
- **Packaging & Serving** – Deploying the model as a service or embedding it in an application.
- **Security & Monitoring** – Protecting against adversarial attacks and monitoring performance.

### 3. Model Optimization for Deployment

### 3.1. Quantization

Quantization reduces the precision of model parameters (e.g., converting floating-point numbers to integers) to decrease model size and improve inference speed.

- **Post-training quantization** – Applied after training to reduce computational requirements.
- **Quantization-aware training** – Models are trained with quantization in mind to maintain accuracy.

**Example in TensorFlow**

```
import tensorflow as tf

# Load a trained model
model = tf.keras.models.load_model("my_model.h5")

# Convert the model to a quantized TFLite format
converter = tf.lite.TFLiteConverter.from_keras_model(model)
converter.optimizations = [tf.lite.Optimize.DEFAULT]
tflite_model = converter.convert()

# Save the quantized model
with open("model.tflite", "wb") as f:
    f.write(tflite_model)
```

## 3.2. Pruning

Pruning removes unnecessary weights from the network, reducing memory usage and improving speed.

- **Unstructured pruning** – Removes individual neurons.
- **Structured pruning** – Removes entire layers or filters.

**Example Using TensorFlow Model Optimization**

```
import tensorflow_model_optimization as tfmot

# Apply pruning
pruned_model = tfmot.sparsity.keras.prune_low_magnitude(model)
```

# 4. Saving and Serializing the Model

## 4.1. Saving Models in Different Formats

- **HDF5 (.h5)** – Used in TensorFlow and Keras.
- **ONNX (.onnx)** – Used for cross-framework compatibility.
- **TensorFlow Lite (.tflite)** – Used for mobile and edge devices.
- **TorchScript (.pt)** – Used for PyTorch model deployment.

## Saving a Model in ONNX Format

```
import torch
import torchvision.models as models
import onnx

# Load a PyTorch model
model = models.resnet18(pretrained=True)

# Convert to ONNX
dummy_input = torch.randn(1, 3, 224, 224)
torch.onnx.export(model, dummy_input, "resnet18.onnx")
```

# 5. Model Versioning and Management

## 5.1. Why Model Versioning Matters

- Tracks changes in model architecture and hyperparameters.
- Enables rollback to previous models in case of failure.
- Ensures reproducibility across different environments.

## 5.2. Model Registry Tools

- MLflow Model Registry
- TensorFlow Model Garden
- Amazon SageMaker Model Registry

## Registering a Model in MLflow

```
import mlflow
mlflow.set_tracking_uri("http://localhost:5000")
```

```python
with mlflow.start_run():
    mlflow.sklearn.log_model(model, "my_model")
```

## 6. Deploying the Model as an API

### 6.1. Using Flask to Serve a Model

```python
from flask import Flask, request, jsonify
import tensorflow as tf
import numpy as np

app = Flask(__name__)

# Load model
model = tf.keras.models.load_model("my_model.h5")

@app.route('/predict', methods=['POST'])
def predict():
    data = request.get_json()
    prediction = model.predict(np.array([data["input"]]))
    return jsonify({"prediction": prediction.tolist()})

if __name__ == '__main__':
    app.run(port=5000)
```

### 6.2. Deploying with FastAPI for High Performance

```python
from fastapi import FastAPI
import tensorflow as tf

app = FastAPI()
model = tf.keras.models.load_model("my_model.h5")

@app.post("/predict/")
async def predict(data: dict):
    prediction = model.predict([data["input"]])
    return {"prediction": prediction.tolist()}
```

## 7. Security Considerations for Deployment

### 7.1. Preventing Adversarial Attacks

Attackers can manipulate inputs to mislead machine learning models. Techniques to mitigate this include:

- **Adversarial training** – Training the model with adversarial examples.
- **Input validation** – Filtering out suspicious inputs.

### 7.2. Securing APIs

- Use authentication (OAuth, API keys, JWTs).
- Limit request rates to prevent abuse.
- Encrypt model communications with HTTPS.

### 8. Monitoring & Updating Models in Production

### 8.1. Model Drift Detection

A model's performance may degrade over time due to changes in data distribution. Monitoring tools like Prometheus, Grafana, or MLflow help detect drift.

### 8.2. Automating Model Updates

- **CI/CD Pipelines** – Automate retraining and redeployment.
- **Shadow Deployment** – Deploy new models alongside the current model for testing.
- **A/B Testing** – Compare different models before full deployment.

Deploying a machine learning model requires careful preparation, from optimization and serialization to security and monitoring. By following best practices, we can ensure that our models perform efficiently, securely, and reliably in real-world applications.

# 14.2. Model Optimization: Quantization & Pruning

Deploying deep learning models in real-world applications requires optimizing them for efficiency. While high-performing models like deep neural networks (DNNs) can be powerful, they often demand significant computational resources, making them impractical for edge devices, mobile applications, and real-time inference.

To overcome these challenges, quantization and pruning are two widely used optimization techniques that reduce model size and computational complexity while maintaining accuracy. This chapter explores these techniques, their benefits, implementation strategies, and practical examples using TensorFlow and PyTorch.

## 2. What is Model Quantization?

### 2.1. Understanding Quantization

Quantization reduces the numerical precision of model parameters and activations, decreasing the model's size and improving inference speed, especially on specialized hardware like TPUs, FPGAs, and mobile processors.

Deep learning models typically use 32-bit floating-point (FP32) arithmetic, but quantization allows them to run with:

- 16-bit floating-point (FP16)
- 8-bit integers (INT8)
- 4-bit or lower precision

### 2.2. Benefits of Quantization

✅ **Reduces memory footprint** – Lower precision numbers require less storage.
✅ **Speeds up inference** – Integer operations are faster than floating-point operations.
✅ **Enables edge deployment** – Runs efficiently on mobile and IoT devices.

### 2.3. Types of Quantization

### 2.3.1. Post-Training Quantization (PTQ)

Applied after training to convert weights and activations to lower precision.

- **Pros**: Simple and effective.
- **Cons**: Can lead to slight accuracy degradation.

### 2.3.2. Quantization-Aware Training (QAT)

The model is trained with quantization in mind, allowing it to adjust weights for better accuracy.

- **Pros**: Higher accuracy than PTQ.
- **Cons**: Requires retraining and more computation.

### 2.3.3. Dynamic vs. Static Quantization

- **Dynamic Quantization**: Converts weights to lower precision while keeping activations in higher precision.
- **Static Quantization**: Precomputes and quantizes both weights and activations, resulting in faster execution.

## 3. Implementing Quantization

### 3.1. Quantization in TensorFlow

**Post-Training Quantization in TensorFlow Lite**

```
import tensorflow as tf

# Load pre-trained model
model = tf.keras.models.load_model("model.h5")

# Convert the model to a quantized TensorFlow Lite format
converter = tf.lite.TFLiteConverter.from_keras_model(model)
converter.optimizations = [tf.lite.Optimize.DEFAULT]
tflite_quantized_model = converter.convert()

# Save the quantized model
with open("model_quantized.tflite", "wb") as f:
    f.write(tflite_quantized_model)
```

**Quantization-Aware Training in TensorFlow**

```
import tensorflow_model_optimization as tfmot

# Apply quantization-aware training
quantize_model = tfmot.quantization.keras.quantize_model(model)

# Compile and train the quantized model
```

```
quantize_model.compile(optimizer="adam", loss="sparse_categorical_crossentropy",
metrics=["accuracy"])
quantize_model.fit(train_data, train_labels, epochs=5)
```

## 3.2. Quantization in PyTorch

### Dynamic Quantization in PyTorch

```
import torch
import torch.quantization

# Load a pre-trained model
model = torch.load("model.pth")
model.eval()

# Apply dynamic quantization
quantized_model = torch.quantization.quantize_dynamic(model, {torch.nn.Linear},
dtype=torch.qint8)

# Save the quantized model
torch.save(quantized_model, "model_quantized.pth")
```

### Quantization-Aware Training in PyTorch

```
import torch.quantization

# Prepare model for quantization-aware training
model.qconfig = torch.quantization.get_default_qat_qconfig("fbgemm")
torch.quantization.prepare_qat(model, inplace=True)

# Train the quantized model
model.train()
for epoch in range(5):
    train(model, train_loader, criterion, optimizer)

# Convert to a fully quantized model
torch.quantization.convert(model, inplace=True)
```

## 4. What is Model Pruning?
```
```

## 4.1. Understanding Pruning

Pruning removes unnecessary connections (weights) in a neural network to reduce its size and computational cost.

Deep learning models often have millions or billions of parameters, many of which contribute little to overall accuracy. By pruning unimportant weights, models can achieve:

✓ **Smaller model size** – Less memory consumption.
✓ **Faster inference** – Fewer computations per forward pass.
✓ **Energy efficiency** – Useful for mobile and embedded devices.

## 4.2. Types of Pruning

### 4.2.1. Unstructured Pruning

- Removes individual weights without affecting layer structure.
- Commonly used in sparse networks.

### 4.2.2. Structured Pruning

- Removes entire neurons, filters, or layers.
- More hardware-friendly and efficient.

### 4.2.3. Magnitude-Based Pruning

- Removes weights with the smallest magnitudes (least impactful).

### 4.2.4. Variational Pruning

- Uses Bayesian techniques to prune weights with minimal accuracy loss.

## 5. Implementing Pruning

## 5.1. Pruning in TensorFlow

```
import tensorflow_model_optimization as tfmot

# Apply pruning to a model
pruning_params = {
```

```
"pruning_schedule": tfmot.sparsity.keras.PolynomialDecay(initial_sparsity=0.3,
                                                         final_sparsity=0.8,
                                                         begin_step=2000,
                                                         end_step=10000)
}

pruned_model = tfmot.sparsity.keras.prune_low_magnitude(model, **pruning_params)

# Compile and train the pruned model
pruned_model.compile(optimizer="adam", loss="sparse_categorical_crossentropy",
metrics=["accuracy"])
pruned_model.fit(train_data, train_labels, epochs=5)
```

## 5.2. Pruning in PyTorch

```
import torch.nn.utils.prune as prune

# Prune 50% of the weights in a linear layer
prune.l1_unstructured(model.fc, name="weight", amount=0.5)

# Remove pruning reparameterization (optional)
prune.remove(model.fc, "weight")
```

## 6. Combining Quantization & Pruning

For maximum efficiency, quantization and pruning can be applied together:

- Prune the model to reduce unnecessary connections.
- Apply quantization to optimize the remaining weights.

### TensorFlow Example (Pruning + Quantization)

```
# Apply pruning first
pruned_model = tfmot.sparsity.keras.prune_low_magnitude(model)

# Convert pruned model to TensorFlow Lite with quantization
converter = tf.lite.TFLiteConverter.from_keras_model(pruned_model)
converter.optimizations = [tf.lite.Optimize.DEFAULT]
quantized_pruned_model = converter.convert()
```

```
with open("pruned_quantized_model.tflite", "wb") as f:
    f.write(quantized_pruned_model)
```

Model optimization is essential for deploying deep learning models in production environments, especially on resource-limited devices. Quantization reduces numerical precision to improve efficiency, while pruning removes unnecessary parameters to make models lighter.

# 14.3. Deploying Models with TensorFlow Serving & ONNX

Deploying deep learning models efficiently is a critical step in transforming research and development into real-world applications. After training a model, it must be served in a scalable, efficient, and accessible manner. Two of the most widely used approaches for model deployment are:

- **TensorFlow Serving (TFS):** A powerful, production-ready system specifically designed for serving TensorFlow models.
- **Open Neural Network Exchange (ONNX):** An open-source framework that allows models trained in different deep learning libraries (TensorFlow, PyTorch, etc.) to be deployed across various platforms.

This chapter explores how to deploy deep learning models using TensorFlow Serving and ONNX, covering their advantages, setup, and real-world use cases.

## 2. Why Deploy Models?

Deep learning models are typically trained offline on GPUs or TPUs, but to be useful, they must be:

✓ **Accessible** – Available via APIs for web or mobile applications.

✓ **Scalable** – Capable of handling multiple concurrent requests.

✓ **Efficient** – Optimized for latency and throughput.

✓ **Portable** – Deployable across different hardware and software environments.

Both TensorFlow Serving and ONNX aim to meet these goals by enabling smooth model deployment.

## 3. Deploying Models with TensorFlow Serving (TFS)

### 3.1. What is TensorFlow Serving?

TensorFlow Serving is a specialized framework designed to deploy, manage, and serve TensorFlow models in production. It provides:

- **Efficient inference** – Optimized for latency and throughput.
- **Dynamic model updates** – Load new models without restarting the server.
- **Scalability** – Handles multiple requests efficiently.

### 3.2. Installing TensorFlow Serving

TensorFlow Serving can be installed via Docker (recommended) or directly on a machine.

### Install via Docker (Recommended)

```
docker pull tensorflow/serving
```

### Install on Ubuntu (Without Docker)

```
echo "deb [arch=amd64] http://storage.googleapis.com/tensorflow-serving-apt stable main" | sudo tee /etc/apt/sources.list.d/tensorflow-serving.list
curl https://storage.googleapis.com/tensorflow-serving-apt/tensorflow-serving.release.pub.gpg | sudo apt-key add -
sudo apt update
sudo apt install tensorflow-model-server
```

### 3.3. Saving a Model for Serving

TensorFlow Serving requires models in the SavedModel format.

```
import tensorflow as tf

# Create and save a simple model
model = tf.keras.Sequential([
    tf.keras.layers.Dense(64, activation='relu', input_shape=(10,)),
    tf.keras.layers.Dense(1, activation='sigmoid')
])

model.compile(optimizer='adam', loss='binary_crossentropy')
```

*model.save("saved_model/my_model")*

This will create a directory saved_model/my_model containing the model's weights, structure, and metadata.

### 3.4. Running TensorFlow Serving

**Start the TensorFlow Serving server and load the model:**

*docker run -p 8501:8501 --name=tf_serving \*
  *--mount type=bind,source=$(pwd)/saved_model/my_model,target=/models/my_model*
*\*
  *-e MODEL_NAME=my_model -t tensorflow/serving*

**Once the server is running, the model is accessible via a REST API at:**

*http://localhost:8501/v1/models/my_model:predict*

### 3.5. Making Predictions via REST API

**Use Python to send a request:**

*import requests*
*import numpy as np*

*url = "http://localhost:8501/v1/models/my_model:predict"*

*data = {"instances": [[0.1, 0.2, 0.3, 0.4, 0.5, 0.6, 0.7, 0.8, 0.9, 1.0]]}*
*response = requests.post(url, json=data)*

*print(response.json())*

### 4. Deploying Models with ONNX

### 4.1. What is ONNX?

ONNX (Open Neural Network Exchange) is an open standard format that allows models trained in one framework (e.g., TensorFlow, PyTorch) to be used in another.

ONNX supports deployment on:

✅ **Cloud & Edge Devices** (AWS Inferentia, Azure ML, Google Coral)

✅ **Cross-Framework Compatibility** (PyTorch → TensorFlow, etc.)

✅ **Optimized Inference Engines** (ONNX Runtime, TensorRT)

## 4.2. Converting a TensorFlow Model to ONNX

**First, install the ONNX converter for TensorFlow:**

*pip install tf2onnx*

**Convert a TensorFlow model to ONNX:**

```
import tf2onnx
import tensorflow as tf

model = tf.keras.models.load_model("saved_model/my_model")

onnx_model, _ = tf2onnx.convert.from_keras(model, output_path="model.onnx")
```

## 4.3. Converting a PyTorch Model to ONNX

```
import torch
import torch.onnx

# Sample PyTorch model
class SimpleNN(torch.nn.Module):
    def __init__(self):
        super(SimpleNN, self).__init__()
        self.fc = torch.nn.Linear(10, 1)

    def forward(self, x):
        return torch.sigmoid(self.fc(x))

# Create and export model
model = SimpleNN()
dummy_input = torch.randn(1, 10)
torch.onnx.export(model, dummy_input, "model.onnx")
```

## 4.4. Running ONNX Inference with ONNX Runtime

ONNX models can be deployed using ONNX Runtime for optimized inference:

**Install ONNX Runtime:**

*pip install onnxruntime*

**Load and run inference:**

```
import onnxruntime as ort
import numpy as np

# Load the ONNX model
session = ort.InferenceSession("model.onnx")

# Prepare input data
input_data = np.random.randn(1, 10).astype(np.float32)
inputs = {session.get_inputs()[0].name: input_data}

# Run inference
outputs = session.run(None, inputs)
print(outputs)
```

## 5. Comparing TensorFlow Serving & ONNX

| Feature | TensorFlow Serving (TFS) | ONNX |
|---|---|---|
| Framework Support | TensorFlow only | Multi-framework (PyTorch, TensorFlow, etc.) |
| Ease of Use | Simple for TF models | Requires conversion for different frameworks |
| Performance | Optimized for TF models | Optimized for multiple backends |
| Cross-Platform | Limited | Supports cloud, mobile, edge devices |
| Hardware Acceleration | TPU, GPU | TensorRT, DirectML, OpenVINO |

Choosing between TensorFlow Serving and ONNX depends on your deployment needs:

◆ Use TensorFlow Serving if you're deploying a TensorFlow model and need seamless production scaling.

◆ Use ONNX if you need cross-framework compatibility, hardware flexibility, or optimizations for different platforms.

# 14.4. Monitoring & Maintaining AI Models in Production

Deploying an AI model is only the beginning of its lifecycle. Once in production, models must be monitored, evaluated, and maintained to ensure optimal performance. Over time, models can degrade due to issues like data drift, concept drift, and hardware limitations. Without proper monitoring, AI models can become ineffective, leading to poor decisions and business losses.

This chapter covers key strategies for monitoring and maintaining AI models, including:

- Performance monitoring metrics
- Detecting and handling model drift
- Automated retraining pipelines
- Model versioning and rollback strategies

By implementing these best practices, organizations can ensure that their AI models remain robust, reliable, and efficient in real-world applications.

### 2. Why AI Model Monitoring is Crucial

AI models work with real-world data, which can change over time. Effective monitoring helps detect and resolve issues before they affect users. Some key challenges include:

#### ✓ Data Drift

- The statistical properties of input data change over time, causing the model to perform poorly.
- **Example**: A financial fraud detection model trained on past data may struggle if new fraud patterns emerge.

#### ✓ Concept Drift

- The relationship between inputs and outputs changes, making previous patterns obsolete.

- **Example**: A recommendation system trained on user behavior may become ineffective if customer preferences shift.

## ✅ Performance Degradation

- Models may slow down due to increasing computational demands or outdated optimizations.

## ✅ Scalability Issues

- Increased user demand can lead to inference bottlenecks, requiring optimization.
- To address these challenges, AI models must be actively monitored and updated.

## 3. Key Metrics for AI Model Monitoring

AI model monitoring involves tracking performance, data quality, and resource usage. Key metrics include:

### 3.1. Model Performance Metrics

- **Accuracy, Precision, Recall, F1-Score** (for classification models)
- **Mean Squared Error** (MSE), Root Mean Squared Error (RMSE) (for regression models)
- **Inference Latency** – Measures how fast the model makes predictions.

### 3.2. Data Quality Metrics

- **Feature Drift** – Changes in input feature distributions.
- **Missing Values** – Unexpected null values in production data.
- **Anomalous Inputs** – Inputs outside expected ranges.

### 3.3. Infrastructure Metrics

- **CPU/GPU Utilization** – Detects hardware resource overload.
- **Memory Usage** – Prevents memory leaks and crashes.
- **Throughput** – Ensures models can handle increasing requests.

Monitoring these metrics helps detect problems early, ensuring model reliability.

## 4. Tools for AI Model Monitoring

Several tools are available for monitoring AI models in production:

| Tool | Use Case |
|------|----------|
| Prometheus | Monitoring infrastructure and metrics collection. |
| Grafana | Visualizing model and infrastructure performance. |
| MLflow | Tracking experiments, model performance, and versioning. |
| Evidently AI | Detecting data and concept drift in production models. |
| Seldon Core | Deploying and monitoring machine learning models at scale. |
| TensorFlow Model Analysis | Evaluating TensorFlow models in production. |

These tools provide dashboards, alerts, and insights to keep models running efficiently.

## 5. Detecting and Handling Model Drift

### 5.1. Identifying Model Drift

Drift detection methods include:

- **Statistical Tests**: KS-Test, Chi-Square Test (to compare data distributions).
- **Embedding Distance Measures**: Cosine similarity, Euclidean distance (for NLP and image models).
- **Performance Decay**: Comparing real-time accuracy against historical benchmarks.

### 5.2. Strategies to Handle Drift

If drift is detected, solutions include:

- **Retrain with Fresh Data** – Update the model using the latest data.
- **Transfer Learning** – Fine-tune the model instead of full retraining.
- **Adaptive Models** – Use models that dynamically adjust weights.
- **Fallback to Previous Versions** – Roll back to a stable model version.

By continuously monitoring for drift, AI systems remain effective over time.

## 6. Automating Model Retraining

Manual retraining can be time-consuming. Instead, automated retraining pipelines improve efficiency.

### 6.1. Steps in Automated Model Retraining

- **Monitor Performance** – Check accuracy, precision, recall, and drift.
- **Trigger Retraining** – If performance degrades, start retraining.
- **Evaluate New Model** – Compare it with the existing model.
- **Deploy New Model** – If performance improves, update the model.

### 6.2. Tools for Automated Retraining

- **Kubeflow Pipelines** – Automates end-to-end machine learning workflows.
- **Apache Airflow** – Schedules and manages retraining tasks.
- **Amazon SageMaker Pipelines** – Automates model retraining in AWS.

By automating retraining, organizations ensure AI models stay accurate without manual intervention.

### 7. Model Versioning & Rollback Strategies

Deploying new models can introduce bugs or unexpected behavior. Versioning ensures that older models can be restored if needed.

### 7.1. Model Versioning Strategies

- **Semantic Versioning** (e.g., v1.0, v1.1, v2.0) – Helps track major/minor updates.
- **Time-Based Versioning** (e.g., model_2024_02_07) – Useful for tracking model updates over time.

### 7.2. Rollback Strategies

- **Shadow Deployment** – Run the new model alongside the old model before full deployment.
- **Canary Release** – Deploy the new model to a small percentage of users before scaling.
- **A/B Testing** – Compare new vs. old models to measure improvements.

These strategies help avoid disruptions and maintain AI model stability.

### 8. Case Study: AI Model Monitoring in Real-World Applications

Use Case: Fraud Detection System

A bank deploys a fraud detection AI model to flag suspicious transactions. Over time, customers change their spending habits, leading to increased false positives.

#### ✅ Step 1: Monitor Performance Metrics

The false positive rate increases, indicating model drift.

#### ✅ Step 2: Detect Concept Drift

New fraud patterns emerge, requiring updated data.

#### ✅ Step 3: Automate Model Retraining

The system retrains the model with fresh transaction data.

#### ✅ Step 4: Deploy New Model with A/B Testing

The new model is tested against the old version before full deployment.

By continuously monitoring and updating the model, the bank ensures accurate fraud detection.

AI models are not static—they must be monitored, retrained, and optimized to remain effective. Key takeaways:

◆ Monitor model performance, data quality, and infrastructure usage.
◆ Detect data and concept drift early to prevent performance degradation.
◆ Use automated retraining pipelines to keep models up-to-date.
◆ Implement model versioning and rollback strategies for safe deployment.

By following these best practices, organizations can maintain AI models that deliver reliable, accurate, and scalable results in production. 🚀

# 15. Ethics & Challenges in Deep Learning

As neural networks and deep learning continue to reshape industries and society, it's crucial to consider the ethical implications and challenges that arise. In this chapter, you'll explore the ethical issues associated with AI, such as bias in training data, transparency, and accountability in model decisions. You'll learn how bias can perpetuate inequality and how to mitigate its impact through careful data curation and model evaluation. The chapter also addresses the challenges of interpretability, helping you understand the importance of making complex models more understandable and accessible to non-experts. Additionally, you'll delve into the environmental impact of training large models and the need for sustainable AI practices. By the end of this chapter, you'll be prepared to approach deep learning projects with a strong sense of responsibility, ensuring your AI systems are ethical, fair, and beneficial to society.

## 15.1. Bias in Neural Networks & Fairness in AI

Artificial intelligence (AI) and neural networks are transforming industries, from healthcare to finance, but they also introduce ethical challenges—one of the most critical being bias. Bias in AI can lead to unfair treatment, reinforcing existing social inequalities and discrimination. For example, facial recognition models have been found to misidentify people from certain racial groups at higher rates than others. Loan approval models may favor certain demographics over others, leading to unfair financial decisions.

**This chapter explores:**

- What bias in neural networks means
- How biases arise in AI systems
- Methods to detect and mitigate bias
- The role of fairness in AI ethics

By understanding and addressing bias, AI developers can build fair, inclusive, and responsible machine learning models that benefit society.

### 2. What is Bias in AI?

Bias in AI occurs when a machine learning model systematically favors or disadvantages certain groups due to imbalances in training data, flawed algorithms, or subjective human decisions. Bias can manifest in various ways, such as:

- **Selection Bias** – When the training data is not representative of the entire population.
- **Historical Bias** – When past societal inequalities are embedded into AI models.
- **Measurement Bias** – When incorrect or incomplete labels distort the model's learning process.
- **Algorithmic Bias** – When the structure of an AI model unintentionally favors certain outcomes.

To create fair AI systems, developers must actively detect and mitigate bias at all stages of model development.

## 3. How Bias Arises in Neural Networks

### 3.1. Data Collection & Representation Bias

The foundation of any AI model is data. If the training data lacks diversity, the model will struggle to make fair predictions.

- **Example**: If a hiring AI model is trained mostly on male applicants, it may learn to prefer male candidates over females.
- **Solution**: Ensure diverse, well-balanced datasets that accurately represent different demographics.

### 3.2. Labeling & Annotation Bias

If human annotators introduce subjective opinions or cultural biases while labeling data, the model inherits these biases.

- **Example**: A sentiment analysis model trained on social media comments may misinterpret certain cultural expressions as negative.
- **Solution**: Use diverse annotators and define strict labeling guidelines to reduce subjectivity.

### 3.3. Model Architecture & Training Bias

Neural networks can amplify biases due to:

**Imbalanced class distribution** – If certain groups are underrepresented, the model performs poorly on them.

**Overfitting on dominant groups** – If a model mostly sees data from one demographic, it generalizes poorly for others.

**Example**: A healthcare AI trained on patients from wealthy areas may not work well for patients from underprivileged communities.

**Solution**: Use balanced loss functions and re-weight training data to ensure fair learning.

### 3.4. Bias in Model Evaluation & Deployment

Even if a model is trained fairly, biases can emerge in real-world deployment. If AI is tested only in controlled environments, real-world edge cases may expose biases.

- **Example**: A self-driving car AI trained in urban settings may struggle in rural environments.
- **Solution**: Monitor real-world performance and continuously update models based on feedback.

### 4. Detecting Bias in Neural Networks

To ensure fairness, AI developers must measure and audit bias using statistical and algorithmic techniques.

### 4.1. Statistical Fairness Metrics

Bias can be measured using fairness metrics like:

| Metric | Definition | Use Case |
|---|---|---|
| Demographic Parity | Ensures equal predictions across groups. | Hiring, Loan approvals |
| Equal Opportunity | Ensures equal true positive rates across groups. | Healthcare AI, Crime risk models |
| Disparate Impact | Measures disproportionate impact on different groups. | Credit scoring, Insurance AI |
| Calibration | Ensures the model's confidence levels are fair across demographics. | Facial recognition, Sentiment analysis |

### 4.2. Bias Detection Tools

Several open-source tools can help detect AI bias:

- **AI Fairness 360 (IBM)** – Evaluates bias and provides mitigation techniques.
- **Fairlearn (Microsoft)** – Analyzes model fairness and improves decision-making.
- **Google's What-If Tool** – Visualizes fairness metrics and model biases.

By integrating these tools, AI teams can proactively identify and mitigate bias.

## 5. Mitigating Bias in Neural Networks

Once bias is detected, various techniques can reduce or eliminate its impact on AI models.

### 5.1. Data Preprocessing Techniques

- **Rebalancing Training Data** – Increase underrepresented samples using data augmentation.
- **Synthetic Data Generation** – Use GANs (Generative Adversarial Networks) to create diverse training samples.
- **Re-weighting Training Data** – Assign higher importance to minority class data points.

### 5.2. Algorithmic Bias Mitigation

- **Fair Loss Functions** – Modify loss functions to penalize biased predictions.
- **Adversarial Debiasing** – Train AI to minimize differences between demographic groups.
- **Differential Privacy** – Ensures AI models do not memorize biased patterns from specific individuals.

### 5.3. Post-Training Fairness Adjustments

- **Reject Option Classification** – If predictions are unfair, defer decisions to human review.
- **Bias Correction Layers** – Modify model outputs to reduce unfair disparities.
- **Regular Audits & Model Updates** – Continuously refine models as societal norms evolve.

By applying these strategies, AI models can reduce bias and promote fairness across different user groups.

## 6. Ethical Considerations & Fair AI Practices

- Beyond technical solutions, AI developers and organizations must prioritize ethical AI development.

### 6.1. Transparency & Explainability

Users must understand how AI makes decisions.

- **Solution**: Use Explainable AI (XAI) techniques like SHAP and LIME to make AI more interpretable.

### 6.2. Inclusive AI Development

Diverse teams create more inclusive AI models.

- **Solution**: Ensure diverse representation among AI developers, data scientists, and decision-makers.

### 6.3. AI Governance & Regulations

Government policies are emerging to enforce AI fairness.

- **Example**: The EU AI Act regulates high-risk AI applications.
- **Solution**: Follow ethical AI guidelines to comply with legal standards.

## 7. Case Study: Bias in AI and Its Real-World Impact

**Case Study**: Racial Bias in Facial Recognition

In 2018, a study by MIT & Stanford found that facial recognition models misclassified darker-skinned individuals at a higher error rate than lighter-skinned individuals.

The reason? Training data was skewed towards lighter-skinned faces.

**Solution**: Expanding datasets to include diverse demographics significantly improved accuracy.

This example highlights why fairness must be a core focus in AI model development.

**8. Conclusion: Towards Ethical AI Development**

Bias in AI is an urgent problem that must be addressed through responsible design, evaluation, and deployment practices. Key takeaways:

✓ Bias arises from data, algorithms, and human decisions.

✓ Fairness metrics and bias detection tools help identify AI discrimination.

✓ Techniques like rebalancing data, adversarial debiasing, and fairness-aware algorithms can mitigate bias.

✓ AI ethics must prioritize transparency, inclusivity, and accountability.

As AI continues to shape our world, ensuring fairness is not just a technical challenge, but a moral responsibility. By integrating ethical considerations into AI development, we can build trustworthy, inclusive, and unbiased AI systems that serve all of humanity. 🚀

# 15.2. Explainability & Interpretability in Deep Learning

As deep learning models become more complex, their decision-making processes become increasingly difficult to understand. Unlike traditional machine learning models, where one can interpret the impact of each variable, deep neural networks operate as "black boxes" with millions of parameters. This lack of transparency raises concerns in critical applications such as healthcare, finance, and autonomous systems.

**Why does explainability matter?**

- **Trust & Accountability** – Users must trust AI decisions, especially in high-stakes domains.
- **Debugging & Model Improvement** – Understanding how models make predictions helps refine them.
- **Regulatory Compliance** – Many industries require AI models to be interpretable to meet ethical and legal standards.
- **Bias Detection** – Explainability can help uncover hidden biases and ensure fairness.

This chapter explores the difference between explainability and interpretability, methods to achieve them, and tools for making deep learning models more transparent.

## 2. Explainability vs. Interpretability: Understanding the Difference

Though often used interchangeably, explainability and interpretability have distinct meanings in AI:

| Concept | Definition | Example |
|---|---|---|
| Interpretability | The extent to which a model's decisions can be understood by humans. | A linear regression model is interpretable because each feature directly contributes to the output. |
| Explainability | The ability to explain how a model arrived at a particular prediction, often using external tools. | Deep learning models require explanation techniques like SHAP or LIME. |

## 3. Why Deep Learning Models Lack Interpretability

### 3.1. Complexity of Neural Networks

Neural networks have multiple layers, interconnected neurons, and millions of parameters, making it difficult to trace how they arrive at a decision.

### 3.2. Non-Linearity & Feature Interactions

Unlike linear models where the effect of each feature is clear, deep learning models create high-dimensional feature representations, making direct interpretation difficult.

### 3.3. Lack of Explicit Rules

Traditional models rely on clear rules, whereas neural networks learn complex patterns that are difficult to articulate in human terms.

### 3.4. Overfitting & Spurious Correlations

Deep learning models can pick up irrelevant correlations in training data, leading to misleading or unexpected results.

These challenges highlight the need for post-hoc explainability techniques to demystify neural network decisions.

## 4. Techniques for Explainability & Interpretability in Deep Learning

### 4.1. Model-Specific vs. Model-Agnostic Methods

Interpretability methods can be categorized as:

| Method Type | Description | Example |
| --- | --- | --- |
| Model-Specific | Designed for particular architectures (e.g., CNNs, RNNs). | Feature visualization in CNNs. |
| Model-Agnostic | Applicable to any black-box model. | SHAP, LIME, Integrated Gradients. |

### 4.2. Feature Importance Methods

Feature importance techniques highlight which inputs have the most impact on predictions.

### SHAP (Shapley Additive Explanations)

- Based on game theory, assigns a contribution value to each feature.
- Provides global (overall model) and local (specific prediction) explanations.
- Works well for tabular data, NLP, and image models.

### LIME (Local Interpretable Model-Agnostic Explanations)

- Approximates deep learning models with simpler interpretable models (e.g., linear regression).
- Creates perturbed versions of the input and analyzes their impact on predictions.
- Useful for image, text, and tabular data.

### Feature Ablation

- Involves removing one feature at a time to see how predictions change.
- Common in vision and NLP models.

### 4.3. Visualization Techniques for Neural Networks

### 4.3.1. Feature Visualization in CNNs

- **Activation Maps (Grad-CAM)** – Highlights important regions of an image that influenced the model's decision.
- **Saliency Maps** – Identifies which pixels contribute most to a classification.
- **Filter Visualization** – Shows what each convolutional filter detects, helping interpret feature extraction.

### 4.3.2. Explaining RNNs & NLP Models

- **Attention Mechanisms** – Helps visualize which words contribute most to predictions in NLP models.
- **LIME & SHAP for Text** – Explainable AI techniques adapted for text-based deep learning models.

### 4.4. Explainability in Transformer Models

Transformers like GPT-4 and BERT have billions of parameters, making them difficult to interpret.

- **Attention Score Analysis** – Examines attention weights to understand which words impact predictions.
- **Layer-Wise Relevance Propagation (LRP)** – Tracks how input changes propagate through layers.
- **SHAP & LIME Adaptations** – Explain individual token contributions.

Explainability tools like Hugging Face's transformers library offer built-in methods to analyze model predictions.

### 5. Tools for Explainability in Deep Learning

Several open-source tools help researchers and developers improve model interpretability:

| Tool | Description | Use Case |
|---|---|---|
| SHAP | Provides feature importance scores based on game theory. | Model-agnostic explanations. |
| LIME | Creates local interpretable models to approximate predictions. | NLP, images, tabular data. |
| Grad-CAM | Visualizes CNN decision regions. | Image classification. |
| Captum (PyTorch) | Collection of explainability techniques. | Works with PyTorch-based models. |
| What-If Tool (Google) | Analyzes AI fairness and interpretability. | Debugging biased models. |

These tools are crucial for ensuring that AI models align with ethical and regulatory guidelines.

## 6. Challenges in Achieving Explainability

### 6.1. Trade-Off Between Accuracy & Interpretability

- Simpler models (e.g., logistic regression) are more interpretable but less accurate.
- Complex models (e.g., deep neural networks) are more accurate but less explainable.

### 6.2. Explainability vs. Security

- Making AI fully interpretable could expose vulnerabilities that allow adversarial attacks.

### 6.3. Human-Centered Explanations

- Not all users understand technical explanations.
- AI explanations should be tailored for different audiences (e.g., data scientists vs. business leaders).

## 7. Case Study: Explainability in Healthcare AI

- Imagine an AI model diagnosing lung diseases from X-ray images. If a doctor does not understand why the AI suggests a certain diagnosis, they may distrust the model.

**Solution:**

- Grad-CAM can highlight the affected lung areas the AI focused on.
- SHAP values can explain feature importance, such as lesion size or opacity levels.

By providing human-interpretable explanations, AI can gain medical professionals' trust and improve adoption in critical applications.

### 8. Conclusion: The Future of Explainable AI

Deep learning explainability is an evolving field, with research improving our ability to interpret and trust AI systems. Key takeaways:

✅ Explainability and interpretability are essential for AI adoption in sensitive domains.

✅ Techniques like SHAP, LIME, Grad-CAM, and attention analysis help demystify neural networks.

✅ Open-source tools provide practical ways to make AI models more transparent.

✅ Balancing accuracy, security, and interpretability remains a key challenge.

As AI regulations strengthen worldwide, explainability will become a necessity rather than an option. Future advancements in neurosymbolic AI, causal reasoning, and self-explaining models will push AI towards greater transparency and trustworthiness. 🚀

# 15.3. The Energy Cost of Large Neural Networks

Deep learning has revolutionized industries ranging from healthcare to finance, enabling groundbreaking innovations in natural language processing (NLP), computer vision, and autonomous systems. However, beneath this progress lies a pressing concern—the energy consumption of large-scale neural networks.

Training and running AI models, especially deep neural networks (DNNs) and transformer-based architectures, require immense computational power. With models like GPT-4, BERT, and DALL·E consuming millions of kilowatt-hours during training, AI's environmental footprint is becoming increasingly significant.

**This chapter explores:**

✓ Why neural networks require massive energy resources

✓ How energy consumption scales with model size

✓ The environmental impact of AI computing

✓ Strategies to reduce the energy footprint of AI

As the AI industry continues its rapid expansion, balancing innovation with sustainability is crucial.

## 2. Why Neural Networks Consume So Much Energy

### 2.1. The Computational Complexity of Deep Learning

Training a deep learning model involves millions to billions of parameters, requiring intensive matrix multiplications and gradient calculations. The complexity increases as models grow larger:

**Small Neural Networks (Shallow MLPs, Small CNNs)**

- Trained on CPUs or small-scale GPUs.
- Low computational demand.
- Suitable for low-power devices.

**Large-Scale Transformers (GPT, BERT, T5, Vision Transformers)**

- Require thousands of GPUs/TPUs.
- Billions of parameters processed in parallel.
- Weeks of training, consuming vast amounts of energy.

### 2.2. Training vs. Inference: Where Energy is Spent

AI systems have two major energy-intensive phases:

| Phase | Description | Energy Impact |
|---|---|---|
| Training | Learning from vast datasets, adjusting millions of weights over multiple iterations. | **Extremely high** (weeks/months on powerful GPUs). |
| Inference | Using trained models for predictions in real-world applications. | **Lower but still significant**, especially for large-scale deployments. |

While training consumes more energy, inference at scale (like billions of daily searches in AI-powered assistants) accumulates a massive carbon footprint over time.

## 3. Measuring AI's Environmental Impact

### 3.1. CO$_2$ Emissions of AI Models

A 2019 study by the University of Massachusetts Amherst estimated that training a large NLP model (Transformer-based) emits:

🔥 **284,000 kg of CO$_2$** — equivalent to five lifetime emissions of an average car.

**Other AI models' estimated emissions:**

| Model | CO$_2$ Emissions (kg) | Equivalent (Car Lifetime Emissions) |
|---|---|---|
| BERT (Large NLP Model) | 650 | 1 Month |
| GPT-3 | 550,000 | 100+ Years |
| GPT-4 (Estimated) | 1,000,000+ | 200+ Years |

### 3.2. Energy Use in Data Centers

AI models rely on data centers—massive server farms requiring:

- Cooling systems to prevent overheating.
- Continuous power supply for GPUs and TPUs.
- Backup energy to maintain uptime.

Global data centers contribute 1% of the world's total electricity consumption, a figure expected to rise as AI adoption grows.

### 3.3. Geographic Energy Variability

AI's carbon footprint depends on where models are trained:

- Coal-powered regions (e.g., China, India) → Higher emissions
- Renewable-powered regions (e.g., Norway, Iceland) → Lower emissions

Shifting AI workloads to regions using clean energy sources can significantly reduce environmental impact.

## 4. Strategies to Reduce AI's Energy Footprint

### 4.1. Efficient Model Architectures

Not all AI models need to be massive. Optimizing architectures can reduce energy consumption without sacrificing performance.

✅ **Distillation** – Using a smaller model trained on a larger model's knowledge. Example: DistilBERT (40% smaller than BERT, same accuracy).
✅ **Sparse Models** – Only activate relevant neurons, reducing computational load.
✅ **Low-bit Precision Computing** – Reducing calculations from 32-bit floating point to 8-bit improves efficiency.

### 4.2. Green AI: Prioritizing Energy Efficiency

Green AI emphasizes training models with less energy consumption while maintaining high performance.

- **Meta's Open Pretrained Transformers (OPT-175B)** – Aimed at reducing energy consumption compared to GPT-3.
- **Google's Pathways AI** – Designed to train multiple tasks in a single model, reducing redundant training cycles.

### 4.3. Hardware & Chip Innovations

Companies are designing specialized chips to improve AI energy efficiency:

| Technology | Impact |
| --- | --- |
| Tensor Processing Units (TPUs) | Google's AI chips, optimized for deep learning workloads. Reduce power usage compared to GPUs. |
| Graphcore Intelligence Processing Unit (IPU) | Designed specifically for AI, reducing redundant calculations. |
| Neuromorphic Computing | Mimics human brain efficiency, lowering power consumption. |

New-generation AI chips could cut energy costs by 10x while maintaining high accuracy.

### 4.4. Renewable Energy-Powered AI

AI companies are shifting toward carbon-neutral data centers:

- **Google AI** → Uses 100% renewable energy for training models.

- **Microsoft Azure AI** → Committed to becoming carbon negative by 2030.

- **Amazon Web Services (AWS)** → Investing in solar and wind energy for AI operations.

By powering AI with renewables, companies can significantly reduce the environmental impact of large-scale models.

### 5. Case Study: OpenAI's Energy-Efficient Training for GPT-4

OpenAI, the creator of GPT-4, faced massive energy challenges when training its trillion-parameter model. To minimize impact, they:

✅ Used optimized data batching to reduce redundant calculations.

✅ Trained in carbon-neutral data centers in partnership with Microsoft.

✅ Experimented with low-power tensor operations to reduce unnecessary computations.

While large AI models are energy-intensive, companies can adopt smarter, greener training approaches to reduce their footprint.

### 6. The Future: Sustainable AI Development

AI's energy consumption will continue growing exponentially unless we prioritize sustainability. Key trends shaping the future:

◆ **Smaller, efficient models** – Moving away from giant models like GPT-4 to specialized, energy-efficient models.

◆ **Hybrid AI computing** – Combining cloud-based AI with on-device AI processing to minimize energy use.

◆ **AI for energy optimization** – Using AI itself to optimize power grids, reduce waste, and improve efficiency.

By focusing on efficiency, sustainability, and innovation, we can ensure AI remains an advancement, not an environmental burden.

### 7. Conclusion: The Balance Between AI Growth & Sustainability

As AI models grow in size and complexity, their energy demands continue to rise. The challenge lies in balancing AI innovation with environmental responsibility.

### 💡 Key Takeaways

✓ Deep learning models consume vast energy, requiring sustainable AI practices.

✓ Data centers contribute significantly to AI's carbon footprint.

✓ Optimized architectures, efficient chips, and renewable energy can reduce AI's impact.

✓ Companies must adopt "Green AI" approaches for responsible AI development.

The future of AI must be both powerful and sustainable. By prioritizing energy-efficient AI, we can build a smarter, eco-friendly digital world. 🌍💡

# 15.4. The Future of Deep Learning: Trends & Open Challenges

Deep learning has transformed artificial intelligence (AI), powering advancements in natural language processing (NLP), computer vision, robotics, and autonomous systems. From generative AI models like GPT-4 and DALL·E to real-time medical diagnosis and self-driving cars, neural networks continue to push technological boundaries.

However, as deep learning scales to trillion-parameter models, critical challenges emerge:

✓ **Compute and energy efficiency** – Can we reduce the cost of training massive AI models?

✓ **Explainability and trust** – How do we make AI more interpretable and unbiased?

✓ **Generalization and adaptability** – Can AI become more flexible and robust to novel situations?

✓ **Ethical and regulatory concerns** – How do we ensure AI development aligns with human values?

This chapter explores emerging trends in deep learning and major open challenges shaping its future.

## 2. Emerging Trends in Deep Learning

### 2.1. Smaller, More Efficient AI Models

Recent breakthroughs show that bigger is not always better. While models like GPT-4 and Google's Gemini are massive, there is a shift toward lightweight and efficient AI architectures that deliver high performance with fewer resources.

◆ **Model Distillation** – Training smaller AI models to mimic larger ones, reducing computational needs.

◆ **Sparse Networks** – Activating only necessary neurons, reducing redundant calculations.

◆ **Quantization & Pruning** – Lowering precision in computations and eliminating unnecessary parameters to speed up inference.

✓ **Example**: DistilBERT achieves 95% of BERT's accuracy with 40% fewer parameters, making it faster and more efficient.

### 2.2. Multimodal AI: The Rise of Generalist Models

Traditional AI models specialize in one type of data (text, images, audio). The next wave of AI models is multimodal, meaning they can understand and generate multiple types of data simultaneously.

✓ Examples:

- **OpenAI's GPT-4V** → Understands both text and images.
- **Google's Gemini AI** → Processes text, images, videos, and audio together.

Multimodal AI will revolutionize fields like robotics, autonomous systems, and human-computer interaction.

## 2.3. AI Agents & Autonomous Learning

Today's deep learning models require human-curated datasets and constant fine-tuning. The future of AI is self-learning models that can adapt, reason, and improve autonomously.

🚀 **Key Advancements:**

✓ **Reinforcement Learning with Human Feedback (RLHF)** – Used in ChatGPT to improve responses based on user feedback.
✓ **Neural-Symbolic AI** – Combining deep learning with logical reasoning for better decision-making.
✓ AI agents that actively explore environments and learn through interaction.

## 2.4. Edge AI & On-Device Processing

Cloud-based AI is powerful but expensive. The next leap in AI is moving neural networks to edge devices like smartphones, IoT sensors, and embedded systems.

◆ **Benefits of Edge AI:**

✓ Faster inference (low latency)

✓ Reduced reliance on cloud servers

✓ Increased privacy (data stays on the device)

✓ **Example**: Apple's Neural Engine enables on-device AI processing for features like Face ID and Siri without sending data to the cloud.

## 3. Open Challenges in Deep Learning

## 3.1. The Need for Explainable & Trustworthy AI

Modern neural networks operate as black boxes, making decisions that even their creators struggle to interpret. The lack of transparency raises concerns in healthcare, finance, and autonomous systems where trust is critical.

## ☐ Challenges:

- How do we explain why a neural network made a decision?
- Can AI justify its predictions in a human-understandable way?
- How do we detect and prevent biases in AI models?

## 🚀 Ongoing Solutions:

✓☐ **SHAP (Shapley Additive Explanations)** – Breaks down AI decisions into understandable components.

✓☐ **Counterfactual AI** – Asking "what-if" questions to understand model behavior.

### 3.2. AI Bias & Fairness Issues

AI models trained on biased datasets inherit and amplify biases, leading to unfair outcomes. This is a critical issue in hiring algorithms, facial recognition, and credit scoring systems.

## 🔎 Real-World Examples:

- **Amazon's AI hiring tool (2018)** – Showed bias against female candidates due to historical hiring data.
- **Facial recognition software** – More error-prone for people of color, leading to wrongful arrests.

## ✅ Possible Solutions:

- Diverse and balanced training datasets.
- Bias-detection tools integrated into AI pipelines.
- Transparent AI decision-making processes.

### 3.3. AI's Carbon Footprint & Energy Demand

As discussed in 15.3, deep learning models consume massive amounts of energy. The challenge is to balance AI advancements with sustainability.

## ◆ How to Reduce AI's Carbon Footprint?

✅ Training models in renewable-energy-powered data centers.

✅ Developing energy-efficient architectures (e.g., TinyML, sparsity-based models).

✅ Using transfer learning instead of retraining models from scratch.

### 3.4. AI's Struggle with Generalization

Today's AI models excel at narrow, specific tasks but struggle with generalizing to new scenarios. Humans can learn from a few examples, while deep learning models require millions.

## 🚀 Key Research Areas to Solve This:

✓ **Few-shot and zero-shot learning** – Training models to generalize with minimal examples.
✓ **Self-supervised learning** – Reducing dependency on labeled data.
✓ **Causal AI** – Teaching AI to understand cause-and-effect relationships, not just patterns.

### 3.5. Ethical & Regulatory Challenges in AI

As AI becomes more powerful, concerns over privacy, misinformation, and security increase. Governments and organizations are actively working on AI regulation to ensure responsible development.

## ✅ Key Developments in AI Governance:

- **The EU AI Act** → The world's first comprehensive AI regulation.

- **The US AI Bill of Rights** → A framework for responsible AI development.

- **China's AI Regulation Policies** → Stricter guidelines on AI-powered services.

## ☐ Unanswered Questions:

- How do we regulate AI without stifling innovation?
- Who is responsible when AI makes harmful or biased decisions?
- How do we ensure AI aligns with human values as it becomes more autonomous?

## 4. The Future of Deep Learning: Where Do We Go from Here?

### ☿ Predictions for the Next Decade:

✓ AI will become more efficient – Smaller, optimized models will reduce computational waste.

✓ AI will learn like humans – Fewer examples, better generalization.

✓ Explainability will improve – Transparent AI will become a standard requirement.

✓ Multimodal AI will dominate – Unified models will handle text, images, and audio seamlessly.

✓ Edge AI will power real-world applications – AI will shift from the cloud to everyday devices.

✓ Regulations will shape AI's future – Ethical AI development will be a global priority.

## 5. Conclusion: Balancing Progress & Responsibility

Deep learning's future is full of possibilities, but it also presents complex challenges. While AI models continue to grow in power, we must:

✓ Make AI more interpretable and fair.
✓ Reduce its environmental footprint.
✓ Ensure it generalizes well beyond training data.
✓ Develop ethical guidelines to prevent misuse.

The road ahead requires collaboration between researchers, policymakers, and industry leaders. With responsible innovation, deep learning will remain one of the most transformative technologies of our time. 🚀

Neural networks are at the heart of modern artificial intelligence, powering everything from self-driving cars to voice assistants. **Neural Networks Demystified: A Deep Learning Guide** takes you on a structured journey through the foundations, implementation, and real-world applications of deep learning, breaking down complex concepts into clear, actionable steps.

Starting with the mathematical and biological foundations of neural networks, this book explores how simple perceptrons evolved into powerful multilayer architectures. You'll learn how neural networks process information, how they are trained using backpropagation, and how to optimize them for efficiency. By implementing a neural network from scratch, you'll gain an intuitive understanding of its inner workings before diving into deep learning frameworks like TensorFlow and PyTorch.

From Convolutional Neural Networks (CNNs) for image recognition to Transformers for natural language processing, this guide introduces cutting-edge architectures shaping the future of AI. You'll also explore hyperparameter tuning, model deployment, and ethical considerations in deep learning.

Whether you're a beginner taking your first steps in AI or an experienced professional looking to deepen your knowledge, this book provides the tools and insights you need to master neural networks. By the time you turn the last page, you'll be equipped to build, train, and deploy deep learning models with confidence.

*Neural networks are no longer a mystery—this book is your key to unlocking their power.*
🚀

*Dear Reader,*

Thank you for embarking on this journey with me through **Neural Networks Demystified: A Deep Learning Guide**. Writing this book has been a deeply fulfilling experience, and knowing that it has reached you—someone eager to learn and explore the world of deep learning—fills me with immense gratitude.

AI and neural networks have the power to shape the future, but their true potential is unlocked by curious minds like yours. Whether this book has helped you take your first steps in deep learning or deepen your existing knowledge, I sincerely hope it has been a valuable resource in your AI journey.

I am incredibly grateful for your time, trust, and enthusiasm. Your passion for learning is what drives me to continue sharing knowledge and making AI accessible to all. If this book has inspired or helped you, I'd love to hear your thoughts. Your feedback, insights, and experiences mean the world to me.

Thank you for being part of this learning adventure. Keep exploring, keep building, and most importantly—never stop learning.

With appreciation,

*Gilbert Gutiérrez*